A VICTORIAN'S INHERITANCE

BY COUNSELLOR + GENEALOGIST = GENEATHERAPIST

HELEN PARKER-DRABBLE

Published by Animi Press 2021

**Animi
Press**

Copyright © Helen Parker-Drabble 2021

ISBN: 978-1-9162466-1-4 Paperback
ISBN: 978-1-9162466-2-1 Hardback
ISBN: 978-1-9162466-3-8 Large print

Cover design by MiblArt
Interior design by MiblArt

Visit www.helenparkerdrabble.com to find articles, an interview with the author and more.

This book has been deposited with the British Library in accordance with
The Legal Deposit Libraries Act 2003.

Helen Parker-Drabble is a proud author member of the Alliance of Independent
Authors. ALLi is an ethical non-profit membership organisation for those who want
to control their intellectual property and publish independently. ALLi provides trusted
advice, supportive guidance, and a range of resources, within a welcoming and
dynamic community of independent authors and advisors.

If you would like to know more about the Alliance of Independent Authors,
please follow my affiliate link: https://allianceindependentauthors.org/?affid=7961
or visit www.allianceindependentauthors.org/.

'As soon as we die, we enter into fiction... once we cannot speak for ourselves, it is up to others to interpret us.'

— **Dame Hilary Mantel**
Author of personal memoirs, short stories, and historical fiction, double Man Booker prize-winner and Reith Lecturer 2017.

Contents

Chapter 4 An Alcoholic in the Family 83

Chapter 5 School and Education 107

Chapter 6 Traditional Games and Pastimes 131

Chapter 7 Thorney Village Life 151

Notes to the reader

This book is offered as a source of information and reference, primarily for family historians. It cannot be a replacement for professional guidance or help.

It follows British spelling (e.g. colour, neighbour).

The author had the benefit of a history consultant, Dr George Regkoukos, who oversaw this project. You can find out more about George at the end of the book.

The author accepts that the context of our ancestors' time is unknowable. The author is not qualified to diagnose psychiatric conditions and acknowledges that retrospective diagnosis is impossible. However, the author believes that introducing psychological theory, neuroscience, and epigenetics may offer a valuable lens through which we can deepen our understanding of our family and ourselves.

While the author has sought to provide historic and current scientific insight as a lens through which we can consider our ancestors this may feel an anachronism. However, such inclusions are integral to her work. See 'About the Author' for more about Helen's mission.

The family tree which closes many of the chapters include only those named in that chapter. (The URLs take you to a larger version on the website.)

The time formats are as they appear in the original sources.

Providing endnotes in an uninterrupted serial sequence was a conscious choice.

To help the narrative flow, the author has avoided the use of modal verbs wherever possible.

According to Walter's niece Mary, Walter called his parents 'Ma' and 'Pa'.

Currency

Prior to decimalisation in 1971, Britain used a system of pounds, shillings, and pence. (£sd or 'l', 's' and 'd'. LSD stands for the Latin words libra, solidus and denarius. There were 12 pence in a shilling and 20 shillings in a pound. The pound came in the form of a paper bill, called a note, or a gold coin, called a sovereign.

Money was divided into pounds (£, or l in some documents) shillings (s, or /-) and pennies (d). Thus, four pounds, eight shillings and fourpence would be written as £4/8/4d or £4-8-4d.

20 shillings in £1 – a shilling was often called a 'bob', so 'ten bob' was 10/-

12 pennies in 1 shilling

240 pennies in £1

For more information, please visit the resource page at www.helenparkerdrabble.com.

Walter's journey continues

in *A Victorian Migrates* and *A Victorian's Legacy*

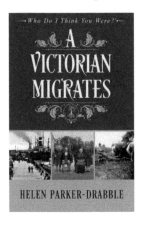
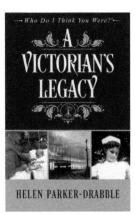

If you would like exclusive content sent to your inbox, visit the website www.helenparkerdrabble.com and click the 'Exclusive Content' button. (You can opt out at any time.) You will get:

1. An occasional update, images, or exclusive appetisers from the series *Who Do I Think You Were?*®

2. I will tell you when books from the series *Who Do I Think You Were?*® are released.

3. I will email occasional free resources for family historians.

4. I will enter you into any free giveaways I run to win a personalised colour hardback edition from the series *Who Do I Think You Were?*®

Thank you for your interest. It means a lot to me.

Take care,

Helen

Dedication

To my family, past, present, and future,

especially my mum,

Doreen Drabble née Parker,

1938–2002.

She was to have been part

of this journey.

Foreword

By
Dorothy Halfhide, Curator, Thorney Museum, The Thorney Society
& Margaret Fletcher, The Thorney Society

Thorney is an old village. Set in an expansive area of level fenlands, it grew around a seventh-century religious community. For hundreds of years it was part of the Russell family estates.

A *Summer Fair* in the *Tank Yard*
The Bedford Hall in the Tank Yard was converted in 1981 from a Victorian centre where the estate craftsmen worked. Photograph supplied with the kind permission of John Clark, Chris Lane and the Thorney Society.

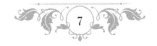

In the nineteenth century, the 7th Duke of Bedford installed an innovative water, drainage and sewage system powered by steam. He housed the heart of the system in the Tank Yard. Today, the Yard and the Bedford Hall are the focal point of our 2,500 strong community, whose history is recorded and preserved in Thorney's accredited museum.[1]

Helen was first introduced to the people of Thorney in The Tank Yard. She visited while following in the footsteps of her grandfather Walter, a proud Thorneyite. His adventure also started from the Tank Yard. Her meticulously crafted account of *A Victorian's Inheritance* provides unique insights into social history, village life, psychology, and the connections that bind them.

We chose Walter Parker's story to form a part of the Museum's 'Thorney Profiles', a Heritage Lottery-funded project which aims to link individuals associated with the village and broader historical or geographical themes. Walter is an example of such an individual whose life was shaped in Thorney and then by his emigration to Canada. Thanks to Helen's efforts, we know a great deal more about him and the Victorian village. Her innovative research is detailed and has already been well received. The Thorney Society, our museum and our visitors have been interested to learn about Walter, his family, and the village, and we thank Helen for her profound understanding of our local heritage.

We wish the author and her book a positive reception and hope it encourages other family history enthusiasts to create and share their family stories.

Preface

Why did Walter Parker refuse to doff his cap to the Duke of Bedford's estate manager? This was uncharacteristic behaviour for the quiet and shy lad, given that the man was one the most powerful men in Thorney.[2] Walter's disrespect put at risk his future, his pa's job, and the house in which they lived. Losing one's home could have grave consequences: according to the Vagrancy Act of 1824, anyone found to be sleeping in a public place or trying to beg could be arrested and sentenced to one month of hard labour.[3] Vagrants presenting themselves at the workhouse door were entirely at the mercy of the porter who decided whether they should be allowed a bed for the night in the casual ward.[4]

I was a child when my mother first told me the story of my grandfather's refusal to doff his cap. I imagined the manager in his carriage on his way to church. I visualised Walter and the other villagers waiting outside the entrance to the Abbey for their 'better' to enter and assume his seat. In my mind's eye, women and girls bobbed as the men and boys took off their hats and caps. All except Walter, who stood resolute with his hands buried in his pockets. According to the story my mother told me it was a lack of respect for the Duke's man that had stayed Walter's hand over a century ago. As a result, he had to leave the village to safeguard his family's future.

Walter fascinated me. I wanted him to share his life with me, to illuminate a time of profound social and political

change, when a working-class Englishman could become a landowner in Canada. But in the face of my naïve compulsion to connect with him, Walter remained mostly inaccessible. As an 11-year-old, I was delighted when he came to live with my family in 1974. At last, I would hear the longed-for stories of his Victorian childhood and his adventures as a bachelor homesteader on the Canadian Prairies. Yet no matter how hard I searched for a key to unlock his silence, the door to his past remained firmly shut. I desperately wanted to attach, to feel close to him, but his emotional distance defeated me. My mum gently explained Granddad was a Victorian fossil, that his decades on an isolated homestead had interrupted his growth.

A year later, Granddad died. I was furious. He had told me he would live to be a hundred and get a telegram from the Queen. I avoided the room in which he had died, packed away the heartache and buried my anger. Life moved on. The feelings and my unresolved questions lived beneath the day-to-day. Then in therapy (which I undertook as part of my counselling training) I unpacked that distressing time. I came to believe, alongside my desire, I had absorbed my mum's unmet, painful need to connect with her father.

In the summer of 2013, I unexpectedly found myself near Thorney. Imagine my delight to find that the house in the Tank Yard where Walter had grown up was now the Thorney Museum. Incredibly, the volunteer steward, Jeremy Culpin, overheard my interest in the Parker family. He asked if I wanted an introduction to a lady whose mother was a Parker. It had never occurred to me I could meet people who knew my granddad. My Cousin Phyllis Mary Skells née Woods, known as Mary, was Walter's niece and lived in nearby Peterborough. She was born in 1918 and had grown up in the village. At our first meeting, I discovered the cap incident was significant enough to be passed down our two estranged branches of the family. In Mary's version, Walter was with friends outside their school when the Duke's man passed by on his way to the station. She added a new and dark twist to the family tale by telling me that Walter had not doffed his cap because of the man's 'evil ways with young girls'. According to Mary, although this was apparently well known in the village, it was not openly acknowledged. Apparently, the villagers would not let Walter forget his audacious disrespect for the man. His principled stance would both liberate Walter from a closed agricultural village in the Fens and trap him in a Victorian mindset on the virgin prairies of Canada.

The joy of finding living family encouraged me to seek more. I sent a letter for publication to the *Fenland Citizen* in March 2014 asking for 'information about the Parkers of Upwell'. Days later, I was thrilled to receive an email from Cousin Sue Oldroyd, née Parker. Sue's grandfather Joel was Walter's first cousin. Cousin Mary did not know of her Parker cousins who stayed in Upwell. Interestingly, when I re-joined the branches by introducing Cousin Sue and Cousin Mary, they discovered they shared a love of figures, and had both worked for the council in various financial capacities. They also lived near each other, in Cambridgeshire, and had mutual acquaintances. Given where each lived and the people they knew, it surprised both of them, despite the generation gap, that they had not met and discovered that they were related. Mary, her youngest sister 'Rene, our Cousin Sue, and I had a few delightful years swapping stories.

During these meetings, the yearning for a deeper understanding of Granddad rocketed back to the surface. What had made this man? I set out to discover the answers to the questions which had burned in me through the decades. I pored over records in the Cambridgeshire Archives and spent days lost in study at the Peterborough Library. I visited museums and binge-read about Victorian life, including medicine, education, health, and addiction. I noticed that Sigmund Freud, (the father of psychoanalysis and the psychodynamic approach to psychology), was a contemporary of Walter's mother.

Re-reading Freud reminded me of my work and experience as a counsellor. I turned again to psychological theories of human development, identity and social behaviour and extended my understanding of neuroscience and neuropsychology, the crossover between science and psychology. Neuropsychology led me to epigenetics, the study of nature (our genes) and nurture (our environment). Epigenetics seeks to explain how our environment and life experiences trigger on-off mechanisms in our genes which can affect us, and our descendants, physically and psychologically.

I conceived of a project-kaleidoscope, which would bring together my passion for family history, advocacy for better mental health, and evidence-based psychology. Before our birth, we are influenced by our ancestors and the mental, emotional, and behavioural patterns of the family around us. This phenomenon is known as psychological inheritance. I pondered all I had discovered about Walter and his family and considered them through the lens of modern psychological theory.[5] I examined the family tree with the idea that 'our children will inherit what we have not made conscious' in mind.[6] A psychological inheritance unravelled, revealing intergenerational anxiety, trauma, loss, and depression familiar to so many families. I had discovered my voice and the overarching theme of my work.

Understanding our psychological inheritance can illuminate our ancestors, but it can also give us the language to consider our thoughts, beliefs, and behaviour. It can add to the narrative we construct to make sense of ourselves and our family. The good news for my grandfather Walter and his siblings is good news for all of us: our psychological inheritance need not define how we lead our lives. We can become more aware, live positively in our communities, thrive, and pass on a different legacy. Family historians cannot know their ancestors' psychological inheritance. But using historical and current theories, we can examine the records and speculate in an informed way.

We are all complicated, multi-dimensional, multi-layered products of our environment, relationships, experiences, and genes. No one is without scars, though few show physically. So too, do we have strengths, flaws, and vulnerabilities. James Hollis, a Jungian analyst, believes we are all governed by the haunting of ancestral and parental influences and that we are shaped by inner voices, dreams, impulses, untold stories, complexes, synchronicities, and mysteries which move through us and history. He sums it up by writing, 'What we resist, persists'.[7]

Reading about another's life can help us see from a fresh perspective, time, or place to our own. Elements of other people's lives can throw our own choices into light relief or suggest a new direction; they can add to our understanding of who we are. Let me tell you about Walter's life, his family, and the English village where he grew up. As you get to know him and what may have affected his development, consider your ancestors. What might their psychological inheritance be? *A Victorian's Inheritance* could help you answer some crucial questions about those who came before you.

Take care,

Helen

Helen Parker-Drabble
October 2020

CHAPTER 1

Family

Our family and the people around us are crucial to our development. In 1902, Charles Horton Cooley, an American sociologist, outlined the concept of the looking-glass self.[8] He believed that our view of ourselves depends on how others reflect their perception of us. Might some families impose their view when they label individuals as 'the clever one', 'the pretty one', or 'the black sheep'? Our family, peers, culture, media, even our employers can hold persuasive mirrors up to us, feeding into the story we tell ourselves about who we were, are, and will become. Psychologists believe the early attachments we form with our parents and the people close to us are crucial to the way we develop.[9] They often shape how our future relationships unfold, our resilience and how we manage adversity. Neuroscience has explained how our unique experiences, our diet, and even our geographical location help construct the architecture of our brain. Genealogically, the experiences of our grandparents and parents influence our development. Cultural and family values can be transmitted through our families of origin, which have their roots in past generations. Also, because our psychological and biological characteristics are profoundly affected by the contexts in which we grow up, what happens to grandparents reverberates through the ages to affect their descendants. So, to understand Walter's psychological inheritance, we must first consider his parents and grandparents and their likely legacies.

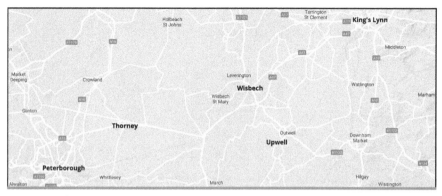

Map showing Peterborough, Upwell, Thorney, Wisbech, & Kings Lynn.
Map data ©2020 Google United Kingdom.

Walter's paternal Grandparents – Stephen Parker Snr and Frances née Moulton

Walter's paternal grandfather, Stephen Snr, was born in Upwell, on the Cambridgeshire/Norfolk border in 1816. It was called the Year Without a Summer (caused by the 1815 eruption of Mount Tambora in Indonesia).[10] Appalling weather ruined crops all over Europe, including locally.

> *The weather, which had given such cheering promise of continuing favourable for the already commenced operations of Harvest, has unhappily undergone a stormy and tempestuous change—Not a day has been uninterruptedly fine for nearly this week past.— On Saturday, the rain was without intermission, accompanied chilling wind, which increased during the night, to a perfect hurricane the effects, we lament to learn, have been general, in laying the fine crops of corn as completely flat as if they had been rolled*

down.—On Wednesday last, had a heavy fall of rain, attended at intervals with thunder and hail:— some of the hail stones were of a large size; so cold was the general state of the atmosphere, that they continued for some time after to cover the ground and the roofs with Wintry garb."

The crop failures led to food shortages and the low wages of the agricultural labourers could not meet the higher prices demanded for basic foods. In nearby Littleport and Ely riots broke out.[12] The Parker family was likely among the recipients of poor relief distributed on Monday 23d [sic] December 1816: 'A well-fed ox and 7 fat sheep [were provided] to the labouring poor of Upwell, amounting to near 500 families'.[13]

When Walter's pa, Stephen Jnr, arrived in 1856, his mother marked the birth register with an 'X' in place of her signature. This was not unusual; in 1837, only two-thirds of all men and just over half of all women could sign their name upon marriage.[14] Stephen Snr and Frances married at twenty-seven and twenty-six years of age in 1843, six years after Queen Victoria ascended to her uncle's throne. According to social historian Professor Emma Griffin of the University of East Anglia, there was an aspiration among the working class that upon marriage, a new household would be set up. Then as now 'couples needed to pool their resources and ingenuity to make that happen'.[15] The first child often followed a year after the wedding. Studies of parish registers suggest that by the early nineteenth century men married at an average age of twenty-five and women at twenty-three.[16] The delay in marriage meant that births could be limited, reducing the income needed to keep a family healthy. Stephen Parker Snr continued to work on the land after his marriage. It was an occupation leading to food poverty, which may have given Walter's descendants an advantage.

Broad Drove, Upwell, 2014.
From the author's collection.

House in Plawfield, 2014.
From the author's collection.

The Avon Longitudinal Study of Parents and Children showed that when a paternal grandfather experienced hunger before his teenage growth spurt, his grandsons enjoyed an increased lifespan by as much as thirty years.[17]

Walter's paternal grandparents moved several times over the years, with census returns showing the Parker family living at Back Drove, Broad Drove, Plawfield, and Green Road. These changes in address may reflect their improved circumstances as the family moved closer to the centre of the sizeable village, with Green Road being the closest and running parallel to the main road. In the 1881 census, Stephen Snr is recorded as being a 'farmer of 6 acres', probably supported by his adult children Stephen and James. In the absence of a universal state pension, it was not unusual for children to support their parents financially. Even if the parent received parish relief, it was customary to recoup as much of this as possible from adult working children. Those children who refused to contribute were hauled before petty sessional courts.

Frances and Stephen outlived two of their eight children, who died at eleven and sixteen years of age.

The use of opium – Addiction in the family?

In 1891, Walter's grandfather, Stephen Snr, was seventy-five and still working as a farm labourer. It would be reasonable to suppose that he had arthritis. Long hours in the fields, exposed to wet conditions and bitter temperatures, along with dietary deficiencies may have contributed to poor health. A pharmacist who practised in the area in the early 1900s defined 'the three scourges of the Fens' as 'ague, poverty and rheumatism'.[18] Ague was a crippling illness similar to malaria.[19] To manage his pain and to support his wife, Stephen Snr probably self-medicated by taking opium.[20] This widely accepted national practice included the buying of opium pills or opium-based products such as Godfrey's Cordial, also known as laudanum. What was curious was how many local people swallowed opium and the quantity they consumed. In an issue of the *British Medical Journal* of 1867, Dr Hawkins of King's Lynn stated that Lincolnshire and Norfolk consumed more than half the opiates imported into the country.[21] 'There was not a labourer's house... without its penny stick or pill of opium, and not a child that did not have it in some form.'[22]

Opium is addictive. As dependency grows, an increasing amount is needed to manage pain or satisfy the craving. If Walter's grandfather could not afford the shop-bought drug, Frances could harvest white poppies, as had been done in the Fens for hundreds of years.[23] Poppy-head tea was a typical drink at 'docky time', so-called because the labourers pay was docked while they ate

Victorian agricultural labourers at 'docky' time.

and drank.[24] Mothers and wives used shop-bought preparations of opium to treat arthritis, toothache, earache and colic, and to help with teething.[25] Despite their often innocuous-sounding names, these sinister preparations contained between one and four grains of opiate per ounce.[26] We can hope Frances did not resort to dosing Walter's pa and his siblings while she worked in the fields.

According to the *Norfolk Chronicle and Norwich Gazette*:

> *There can be no doubt of the prevalence of the use of opium and other opiates, amongst the poor. They must not [be] judged too harshly for this. Obliged to devote many hours to labour, and unable [to] procure [a] servant for their children, they endeavoured to send them to sleep, in order that their time may not be occupied in nursing them, but in other more profitable pursuits.[27]*

What the report does not say is that opium can switch off the instinct to breathe.[28] Another side-effect was to take away the infant's appetite, and many died of starvation rather than poisoning.[29] Significant regulation was not introduced until the 1908 Pharmacy Act.[30]

The consumption of opium may have had a profound effect on later generations, for 'addiction to depressants can cause

maladaptation of memory and reward circuits in the brain', underpinned by DNA and regulated by long-lasting changes in gene expression.[31] (Conceivably, such changes were reflected in Walter's ma's physiological inheritance and could influence her legacy.) Might the effects of 'medications' like these have led to the mistrust of medicine? Indeed, it was a prevailing attitude of Walter's (and his niece's) generation to 'work off' pain and ill health, rather than medicate.

Walter's maternal grandparents – James Bates and Ann née Rands

Walter's maternal grandfather, James Bates, was born in West Walton, Norfolk. Walter's grandmother, Ann Snr, came from Alconbury-cum-Weston, Huntingdonshire, thirty-eight miles from where her husband-to-be was born. Upon marriage, James was twenty-three and Ann twenty-four. According to the 1841 census, the year before their wedding, both were working as servants on different farms. The couple would have nine children: four would die aged five or younger, another upon reaching adulthood. Walter's ma was their second daughter named Ann.

Professor Griffin wrote that the people who worked the land were among those least able to establish their own home at a young age. Although this sometimes led to newlyweds living with one set of parents, others who married before they could support a family described themselves as living in 'inescapable grinding poverty'.[32] Like most agricultural workers, the Bates family were at times reliant on parish relief for part of the year. Often this meant going hungry, suffering from malnutrition, and spending time in the workhouse. To encourage people to support themselves, the conditions were less than the poorest working labourer could achieve, so inmates and those receiving relief could still be close to starvation.[33] Walter's maternal grandfather, James, could not escape crushing poverty.

What effect might this lifestyle have had on Walter's mother, Ann, and her descendants? A landmark epidemiological study that investigated the impact of famine on pregnant Dutch women during the Hunger Winter of 1944/1945 may offer some possibilities. Researchers found epigenetic differences regarding disease risk among individuals who were exposed to famine early in their mother's pregnancy when compared with their unexposed, same-sex siblings. The suggestion is that 'early-life environmental conditions can cause epigenetic changes in humans that persist throughout life' leading to increased risk of schizophrenia, coronary heart disease, obesity, and Type 2 diabetes.[34] Nor are effects limited to the female line. Epidemiologist Dr Marjolein Veenendaal and her team found that the offspring of fathers exposed to famine prenatally weighed more and had a higher body-mass index than offspring of unexposed fathers. This effect remained after an adjustment for birth weight, paternal weight, and body mass index.[35]

After the death of James's first wife Ann in 1860, he married Martha, a woman nineteen years his junior. Records show that James, Martha, and their daughters were admitted to the Union Workhouse at Huntingdon at harvest-time, on 30 August 1873, and again on 10 September. Further admissions show a family in crisis. James was presumably too ill, disabled, a dysfunctional addict or unable to find work.[36] He died in the workhouse in March 1875, aged fifty-six, ten years before his grandson Walter's birth. For a while, James's widow, Martha, found a way of sustaining herself and her daughters, but they were again admitted to the institution on 9 February 1876. Martha died less than eight weeks later, at the age of thirty-four. Ann's half-sisters were just eight and six years old.

Walter's parents –
Stephen Parker Jnr and Ann née Bates

Walter's Pa – Stephen Parker Jnr

We know a little about Stephen Jnr's early life from the census records. In 1861 he was living with his parents, and older siblings James, Jane, Jacob, Isaac, and Mary. Baby Susannah completed the family. Stephen Snr supported the family by farming three acres in Plaw Field, Broad Drove. Walter would not meet his uncle Jacob, a house servant and groom, who drowned in June 1861 aged only sixteen. Eleven years later, in 1872, Stephen's sister Susannah died painfully from 'inflammation of the bowel', at eleven years old.[37]

Stephen Parker Jnr (1856–1937), c1907.
From the author's collection.

Of the surviving siblings, we know little, but Stephen Jnr – Walter's father – was working as an agricultural labourer in 1871. Although land work had been declining for decades, Stephen Jnr would probably have worked from age seven or eight removing stones from the fields, looking after animals, picking fruit or as a human scarecrow chasing off the birds intent on eating precious young seedlings.[38]

We often think of the Victorian period as one of poor health and nutrition. However, there is compelling evidence to the contrary.

> *In the U.K. life expectancy at age 5 was as good or better than exists today, and the incidence of degenerative disease was 10 per cent of ours. They had little access to alcohol and tobacco; and due to their correspondingly high intake of fruits, whole grains, oily fish and vegetables, they consumed levels of micronutrients and phytonutrients at ten times the levels considered normal today.*[39]

The ability to write one's name improved over time. According to figures from the Registrar General, between 1871 and 1891 the ability of men to sign the register rose from 80 per cent to 94 per cent, and for women, it rose from 73 per cent to 93 per cent.[40]

Walter's Ma – Ann Bates

Ann Catherine Bates was born in the small village of Alconbury-Weston in Huntingdonshire. The 1861 census tells us that five-year-old Ann was living on the 'North Side of the Brook' with her widowed father, James, who worked as a labourer, having been a ratcatcher. Ann's mother had died a slow death the year before, aged only forty-two, from phthisis, more commonly known as consumption or pulmonary tuberculosis.

How might the loss of her mother have affected four-year-old Ann? The physiological and psychological effects of overwhelming emotional experiences, such as those which stem from natural

disasters, abuse, rape, losing a parent or child or violence have been studied in-depth, and the effects on a person's life-long health are sobering.[41]

Modern research shows the death of a parent can lead to social withdrawal, anxiety, and social problems, as well as lower self-esteem and that a quarter of children develop serious psychological issues following a parent's death.[42] It seems a forlorn hope that Ann's environment was more protective than in recent times. To manage life at home, it was inevitable

Ann Bates née Parker.
(1856-1938), c1907.
From the author's collection.

widower James had to rely heavily on his surviving older children: eighteen-year-old Mary, fourteen-year-old James, and twelve-year-old William. The 1861 census record shows that James's brother Criss lodged with them. Given the family lived, intermittently, in extreme poverty, it would not be unusual for a paying lodger, family or not, to sleep in the marital bed with the head of the household.[43]

I would like to think her older sister Mary mothered Ann, but by the time Ann was seven, Mary was twenty, married, and living in Upwell. Did Ann's ability to form close emotional attachments diminish after each of her losses? Although her granddaughter, Cousin Mary, told me she did not doubt her grandmother's love, she was not a grandparent who hugged her grandchildren. Nor could Cousin Mary recall a single time when

Cousin Mary in Ilfracombe.
Cousin Mary (Phyllis Mary Skells née Woods) Walter's niece, Stephen & Ann Parker's grandaughter.

Ann had laughed or even smiled. She remembered her, sadly, as a habitually black-clothed, unhappy alcoholic who was 'difficult to get along with'. (Cousin Mary said Ann's dependence on whisky was referred to in the family as her 'condition'.)

Ann's traumas may have affected the expression or suppression of specific genes, influencing not only her lifelong health and well-being, but succeeding generations, who did not know of them. Epigenetics offers a way to explain the connection between nature and nurture, or as biologist Nessa Carey puts it, 'how the environment talks to us and alters us, sometimes forever'. The process of epigenetics changes the chemical elements surrounding and attaching to our genetic material that, in turn, changes the way genes are activated or silenced without altering the genes themselves.[44] Although we should view it with caution, epigenetics promises exciting new data related to mental health conditions that are 'bound to touch all of us at some point in the not-too-distant future'.[45]

David Moore is a psychobiologist and Professor of Psychology at Pitzer College and Claremont Graduate University. His work underlines that genes behave differently in different contexts. They don't single-handedly dictate our talents, diseases, and preferences; 'what we do matters, and that the environments we occupy profoundly influence how we end up'.[46] In their study of mice, researchers from the University of Zurich and ETH Zurich discovered 'Not only trauma but also the reversal of trauma is inherited'.[47] The late Bruce McEwen, neuroendocrinologist and stress expert at Bruce Rockefeller University in New York pointed out that interventions cannot reverse developmental events but rather produce compensatory mechanisms. He concludes reactivating the plasticity of the brain through 'physical activity, social support, behavio[u]ral therapies including mindfulness and meditation and finding meaning and purpose' have a powerful impact on our resilience and well-being.[48] So perhaps in following her sister Mary May to Upwell in 1871, Ann could begin to counteract her earlier experiences. At fifteen, Ann was an independent maid-of-all-work for John Hawkins, a sixty-three-year-old farmer who lived steps away from her sister in Small Lode, Upwell, close to St Peter's Church. Ann reported to a housekeeper, aged forty-two. A seventeen-year-old male servant was the last of the live-in help. As a maid, Ann was not in a position to help her half-siblings or her father and stepmother stay out of the Union Workhouse at Huntingdon. Both Ann's father and stepmother died destitute before Ann married.

Marriage was more of a practical affair than a romantic one. A working-class couple needed to work hard as a team to bring in enough of an income, raise children and manage household

The interior of St Peter's Church, Upwell, 2018.

Stephen Parker and Ann née Bates married on Thursday, 23 December 1880 at St Peter's Church, Upwell. From the author's collection.

affairs. Although a partner could be found in the personal ads of some publications, it is plausible that Walter's parents were introduced by Ann's sister in their parish church after Ann had taken up the domestic post in Upwell.[49] Stephen and Ann's courtship could have taken place in public: at church socials, or while still in their Sunday best, on the two-mile walk from Upwell to Outwell and back, to 'see and be seen'.[50] We do not know when they decided to marry, but choosing a spouse was a serious matter. Despite the 1858 Divorce Act, there were limited options for ending a marriage. Stephen and Ann were joined in holy matrimony at St Peter's in Upwell on Thursday 23 December 1880. They were twenty-four and twenty-three years old respectively — the same ages at which Ann's parents had married. For Stephen, the timing perhaps reflected his confidence, for 'He had succeeded in opening up a tolerable trade as a carpenter and builder'.[51] For Ann, their vows may have represented a much-needed sense of security after the death of her parents, brothers, and sisters. By the time she married, only four of her nine full siblings were alive.

The 1881 census shows Walter's pa and ma living in King's Lynn as lodgers of Ann's older brother William (a tailor), his wife, Mary Ann, and their four children. Another lodger, a mason, also lived in the terraced house of Dilke Street. Skilled workers could afford these small homes which had two cramped rooms upstairs and two down. They were known as a 'through house' because they did not back on to another dwelling.[52] Stephen worked as a carpenter and builder. I hope with Stephen at her side Ann had faith that she would have a longer and more comfortable life than her mother had known.

It would appear Stephen first became a father at the age of twenty-six, after he and Ann had settled back in Upwell.

Their first-born, Lily Ann, tragically died while still a toddler. The same year, Stephen lost his mother, Frances, aged sixty-five. Stephen and Ann's second child, Ethel Mary, was born in 1884. Walter arrived a year later, and in 1886 Stephen and Ann had their third daughter and named her Lily Bates. Their last child, Lucy Maud, came into the world in 1889. The 1891 census shows Stephen, Ann, their four children, and a lodger (another carpenter) were living a few doors away from the Old Duke's Head on the 'High Road', Upwell. Walter's pa had left the land. He was earning more as a bricklayer.

Like all parents, Stephen and Ann were expected to raise their children to be useful members of the community. Psychologist and psychoanalyst Erik Erikson maintained that children's personality develops logically through eight psychosocial developmental stages from infancy to adulthood.[53] During the first stage, from birth to about eighteen months, infants develop a sense of attachment to their caregivers and begin to trust people. We do not know how emotionally available Ann was to her children in these formative years. Stephen worked till dusk, so during the shorter days of the year he could spend more time at home. An extended family surrounded Walter and his siblings which reminds me of the old African proverb, 'It takes a whole village to raise a child'.[54]

Elworthy Row, Upwell 2019.
Photograph by Amanda Carter.
According to a notebook owned by Walter's daughter Doreen, the Parker family lived in one of these terraced houses before moving to Thorney.

If Ann had mental health problems, her husband's family and stable community might have helped Walter and his siblings to develop a sense of trust.

According to Erikson, the second psychosocial stage, which occurs in the toddler years, covers autonomy versus shame and guilt. Walter became more independent as he learnt to control his body, including his bladder and bowel. Washing an infant's nappies in Victorian Britain was hard work and time-consuming so, I imagine Ann was compelled to toilet train as soon as her children were sufficiently developed. At this milestone self-esteem is boosted, leading to the beginnings of willpower and self-control. When Walter reached the third stage, at ages three to five, he had started imitating his parents. Rural working-class children inevitably learnt useful skills from an early age. It seems probable that Stephen encouraged Walter to take the initiative. To meet his community's expectations and those of his parents, Walter became competent in foraging, weeding, sweeping the grate and laying a fire. Outside his home, Walter explored and found a sense of purpose. In theory, should children not find a goal, Erikson suggested they could disappoint their parents, resulting in feelings of guilt.[35] Walter and his male peers emulated their fathers. They therefore looked forward to their graduation into long trousers.

Although the second half of the nineteenth century saw some people use education as a route out of land work and the poverty associated with it, social mobility was still restricted. Stephen Parker and his brother James had the personality and drive to seek opportunities and build assets. I wonder if they believed they were building a world where progress would march ever-forward, with each year better than the last.

Family tree

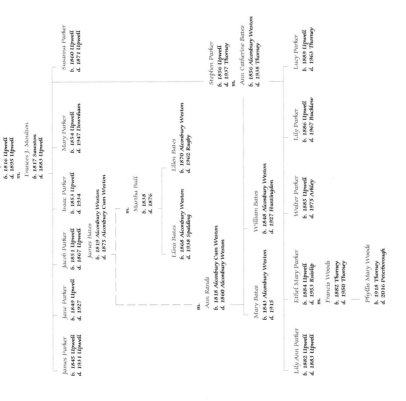

Stephen Parker
b. 1816 Upwell
d. 1895 Upwell
m.
Frances J. Moulton
b. 1817 Sawston
d. 1883 Upwell

James Parker
b. 1845 Upwell
d. 1931 Upwell

Jane Parker
b. 1849 Upwell
d. 1927

Jacob Parker
b. 1851 Upwell
d. 1867 Upwell

Isaac Parker
b. 1853 Upwell
d. 1934

Mary Parker
b. 1854 Upwell
d. 1947 Downham

Susanna Parker
b. 1860 Upwell
d. 1871 Upwell

James Bates
b. 1819 Alconbury Weston
d. 1875 Alconbury Cum Weston

m.

Martha Bull
b. 1838
d. 1876

Eliza Bates
b. 1868 Alconbury Weston
d. 1938 Spalding

Ellen Bates
b. 1870 Alconbury Weston
d. 1962 Rugby

William Bates
b. 1848 Alconbury Weston
d. 1927 Huntingdon

Stephen Parker
b. 1856 Upwell
d. 1937 Thorney
m.

Ann Catherine Bates
b. 1856 Alconbury Weston
d. 1938 Thorney

Ann Rands
b. 1818 Alconbury Cum Weston
d. 1860 Alconbury Weston
m.

Mary Bates
b. 1843 Alconbury Weston
d. 1915

Ethel Mary Parker
b. 1884 Upwell
d. 1953 Ruislip
m.

Walter Parker
b. 1885 Upwell
d. 1975 Arkley

Lily Parker
b. 1886 Upwell
d. 1967 Bucklow

Lucy Parker
b. 1889 Upwell
d. 1963 Thorney

Francis Woods
b. 1882 Thorney
d. 1950 Thorney

Phyllis Mary Woods
b. 1918 Thorney
d. 2016 Peterborough

Lily Ann Parker
b. 1882 Upwell
d. 1883 Upwell

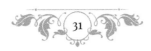

CHAPTER 2

Upwell

Upwell (from the old English word 'upp' meaning up and 'well' meaning spring)[56] is an ancient place. Many Georgian and Victorian houses line the two long, parallel highroads, which are split by a narrow river. On the west side of the river was Cambridgeshire, on the east side, the county of Norfolk. This pattern of building is not surprising given that the Roman emperor Hadrian set in motion the draining of the land and took advantage of Upwell's inland port. The waterways leading to and from Upwell have been used for trade (mainly fruits and vegetables). They also acted as a conduit for armies, such as those garrisoning at Hadrian's Wall.[57] During medieval times seagoing ships capable of sailing to Iceland, Norway and all over the Baltic Sea were based in Upwell.[58] In the 1880s some of the houses that back onto the canal or face the River Nene had a private jetty for boats or barges.

In Upwell, Walter saw men, women and children working in agriculture. He likely watched coal being transported by the modern tram to the Outwell depot, where the loads were transferred to the waiting barges for distribution through the Fens.[59] The trams trundled between Wisbech and Upwell carrying people, fruit and vegetables. As a six-year-old, had Walter looked forward to a dangerous local childhood rite of passage; jumping on and off the moving tram without being caught by the guard?[60] If so, it was not

St Peter's Church, Upwell
© Copyright Evelyn Simak
and licensed for reuse under
creativecommons.org/licenses/by-sa/2.0.
Walter was baptised at this font 17 May 1885.

A traditional christening dress
for boys and girls.
In the keeping of
Cousin Sue Oldroyd née Parker. 2018
image from the author's collection.

to be, for Walter's pa, Stephen, had an exciting new job and was to move the family to a parish owned by the Duke of Bedford.[61]

Research tell us that a parent's way of caring has a profound effect on a baby's psychological and physical growth.[62] Walter's mother, Ann, may not have been aware of the importance of her interactions with her children. Nor could she have known that an infant's caretakers directly influence a baby's brain development, it's mental health, even its resilience to adversity.[63] In humans and primates, a mother's sensitive recognition of a baby's needs helps kick-start the neural system and activate (or silence) genes regulating stress levels. For example, contact with adults regulates a baby's oxytocin levels and alpha waves.[64] Epigeneticists build on these findings to argue that psychological inheritance during the formative years is as critical as physiological inheritance.

St Peter's, Upwell, 2017.
From the author's collection.

Roof Demon, St Peter's Church, Upwell by Lynne Jayne Jenkins, 2018.

Roof angel & demon, St Peter's Church, Upwell by Lynne Jayne Jenkins, 2018.

Angel St Peter's Church, Upwell by Lynne Jayne Jenkins, 2018.

Upwell, looking towards St Peter's Church.

Lower Town Street, Upwell.
Postcard from the author's collection.

Town Street, Upwell.
Postcard from the author's collection.

New Bridge, Upwell.
Postcard from the author's collection.

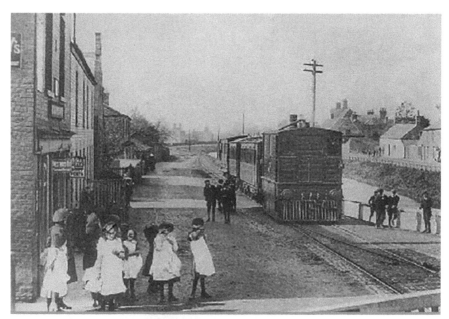

Boyces Bridge, The Wisbech & Upwell Tramway.
Postcard from the author's collection.

Steam Tram, Upwell.
This steam tram was a J70 0-6-0, originally the GER Class 53.
Postcard from the author's collection.

Local author Reverend W. Awdry based Toby on the Upwell tram. (According to https://www.lner.info/) Toby the Tram at Bitton Station on the Avon Valley Railway during a Thomas the Tank Engine day. Toby the Tram by Felixcatuk.
In the public domain.

STEAM TRAM, UPWELL STATION.

Upwell Station c1900.
In the public domain. According to https://www.lner.info/ local author, etc

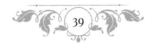

The Wisbech & Upwell Tramway, Elm Road, Wisbech.
From the author's collection.

Wisbech & Upwell Tramway, Elm High Road, Wisbech.
From the author's collection.

There is no way of knowing the physiological effect of the earliest interactions between Walter and his mother, but we can plausibly discuss their psychological effects. To do this, we need to explore his childhood.

A perilous birth – 18 April 1885

Walter was the third child born to Stephen and Ann. Preparing for Walter's birth, Ann understood that childbirth could kill her. At this time, one in twenty mothers died in or after delivery from infection or haemorrhage.[65] Ann would have certainly worried about herself, but there was the added danger to the baby. It would be natural for her to fear Walter would not survive. Around 1885, in surrounding Norfolk, approximately one baby out of every eight died.[66] Should Ann need inpatient care; their nearest hospital was in Wisbech, five miles from home.

Given Ann's rural location and class, her midwife was likely a woman.[67] Women of the extended family and her network of acquaintances could be called upon to help Ann. Her mother had died, but her sister Mary May lived locally. Mary understood Ann's anxiety as she and her husband had lost all four of their infants.[68] If Mary had felt unable to be with Ann, another labour companion could have been Ann's sister-in-law Jane Britten. Jane was a close neighbour to both women. She had testified at the inquest investigating the death of Mary's daughter Florence in 1881. On that occasion, the jury returned the verdict 'Died by the visitation of God'.[69] Ann's other local sister-in-law, Mary Utteridge, may not have been able to help. There is a newspaper report of Mary's husband Henry doing hard labour in 1877 for deserting his wife and family.[70] Walter's pa, Stephen, was likely working nearby. Infant mortality rates in Norfolk around 1881 were also high.[71] Ann's first-born, Lily Ann, had passed away as an infant, as had Ann's older sister Catharine who died at thirteen months.

Ann knew children were at risk. Ann's oldest brother, Davis, had died of meningitis aged five; Ann's namesake was just three years old when she passed of a fever; and Alfred, the youngest in the family, was taken by tabes mesenterica, a form of tuberculosis. A significant reduction in infant deaths was not achieved in the Fens until around 1910.[72] Ann could not have known that breastfeeding was Walter's best chance of surviving infancy.[73] But she was encouraged to feed her children naturally by contemporary guides, such as the *Cassell's Household Guide*

Lily Ann Parker, memorial card, 1883.
The memorial card of Lily Ann Parker, most likely given to the family by the undertaker. It reads: Sacred to the Memory of Lily Ann. The Beloved Daughter of Stephen and Ann Parker who died October 24th 1883. Aged 1 year and 7 months. Interred at Upwell Church, October 27th.

of 1877. Its author declared that 'the most suitable food for infants is that of Nature's own providing — mother's milk'.[74] The fact that we cannot know whether Ann, as a working-class mother, breast-fed or not, is itself thought-provoking. Dr Arthur Newsholme, a leading Victorian health expert, estimated that between 62 and 84 per cent of English working-class mothers breastfed.[75] This percentage may seem low to us, but can be explained by restrictions placed upon working mothers on the one hand and, aggressive marketing of formula milk on the other. By 1883, twenty-seven brands of formula milk, predominantly from cows, were available to the public.[76]

Another critical indicator of infant mortality was the health of the mother.[77] Stephen and Ann's first child, Lily Ann died from tubercular meningitis in 1883. With so little in the way of treatment, Ann and Stephen were helpless to relieve their little girl's suffering. Charles West, founder of the Hospital for Sick Children in Great Ormond Street (the first children's hospital in Great Britain) published his observations of this harrowing illness in 1848. His description finishes by stating:

> *The recurrence of convulsions usually hastens the end, but sometimes many days will pass, during which death is hourly expected, and earnestly prayed for, to put an end to the patient's sufferings.*[78]

Ann was five months pregnant with Walter's sister Ethel when Lily Ann died. With new life growing inside her and a family to feed and care for, it is unlikely Ann had the chance to grieve for Lily Ann. Only weeks after Walter's birth, his second Cousin Mary Parker, who lived close by, died of measles and diphtheria at the age of five. Tragically, all three of Mary Parker's siblings also died before their parents.

There is a common belief that our ancestors were less affected by loss, disaster, or trauma than we are. However, Hilary Marland, Professor of History, at the Centre for the History of Medicine at the University of Warwick, makes a convincing case that poverty contributed to and exacerbated mental suffering in women in Victorian Britain.[79] That the poor were somehow immune to the loss of their loved ones is also soundly contested by Julie-Marie Strange, Professor of Modern British History at Durham University. Strange demonstrates in her book about death, grief and poverty that poverty increased rather than deadened the anguish of the poor.[80] It would, therefore, be understandable if Ann emotionally distanced herself from Walter and his siblings to cope with her loss.

A working-class mother's responsibilities

After the death of her daughter, it is reasonable to suppose Ann took 'prevention is better than cure' seriously, so she probably dosed her children with castor oil. This is one of the oldest medicines known. It was an unpleasant tonic that was

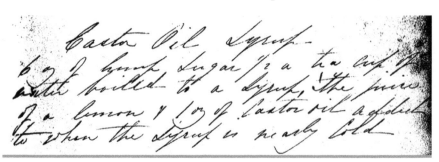

Castor oil syrup recipe.
This recipe for castor oil syrup came from a family recipe book which belonged to Mrs Charles Aaron Allot, née Mary Hopkinson. She started recording recipes in this notebook in 1860. Mary married James Parker in 1906. The book is in the keeping of Cousin Sue Oldroyd née Parker, great-granddaughter of James Parker.

believed to promote wound healing, relieve pain, treat acne, fight infection, and keep the scalp and hair healthy. It has been proven to induce labour and cure constipation.[81] Should castor oil fail, Ann would have prepared another age-old cure for regular bowel movements using Epsom salts, magnesium sulphate, lemon and sugar dissolved in boiling water.[82] For conjunctivitis,

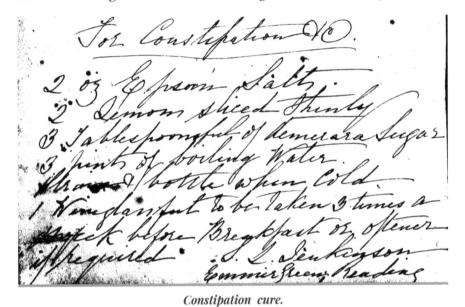

Constipation cure.

she turned to a homemade recipe made up from filtered snow water and one drop of white vitriol (zinc sulphate).[83] If Walter

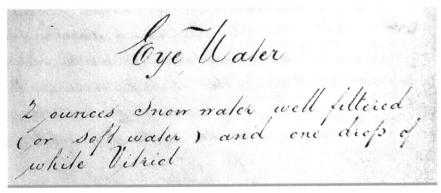

Eye water recipe.

had a cough, Ann could mix honey and treacle with the bitter laudanum.[84]

Cough recipe.

Vinegar too was a part of the housewife's arsenal. It was used in the home to clean wounds and treat infection.[85] For sprains, sore throats, and rheumatism, a local newspaper suggested:

Vinegar Recipe.

Take half a pint of turpentine and one egg, put them into a large bottle, cork it, and shake it till it becomes a thick cream, then add gradually one pint of vinegar: bottle for use. This mixture will keep for years and is improved by the addition of a small lump of camphor.[86]

According to a Parker family recipe book for his colds, Walter could be given either a hot 'Whisky Cordial' or sweetened blackcurrant vinegar.[87] Strong spirits may seem an odd treatment, but alcohol was a valued part of the home medicine kit and was often prescribed by doctors. Research 'supports the folklore that

Whisky cordial recipe.
Photograph by Debanjali Biswas.

Black Currant Vinegar

Stew the currants in the oven with a little water then strain through a flannel bag to every pint of juice add one pint of vinegar 1½ lb of loaf sugar. Put into a jar in the oven until the sugar is dissolved and the liquor quite hot when cold bottle it for use

For colds &c.

Blackcurrant vinegar recipe.

Elder Flower Wine

To every 6 gallons of water put 18 lbs lump sugar boil it ½ an hour, when it is milk warm add to it ¼ of Peck of Elder flowers picked from the stalks, the juice & peel of 6 lemons 6 lbs of raisins and 5 spoonsful of yeast. Stir it frequently for 3 or 4 days. When it has done working stop it up. Bottle it in 6 months. Do not put the flowers into the barrel.

We intend putting the flowers in a Bag next time — They were so much trouble the last

Miss C Dethick

Elderflower wine recipe.

a hot tasty drink is a beneficial treatment for relief of most symptoms of common cold and flu' because of the powerful placebo and physiological effects on salivation and airway secretions.[88] As was typical, Ann laboriously made hedgerow wines, mead, beer and sloe gin for the family to consume at home. Could it be that Ann followed a family pattern of self-soothing with alcohol?

Recipe for making Mead.

Cut HoneyComb fine & place in earthen vessel with enough water to cover. Let it remain 3 days, then strain through a sieve. See if liquid is strong enough to carry a new laid egg, if not more honey to needed until the liquid is of that strength. Take egg out & put a few cloves in and a little whole ginger. Place in Copper & boil ½ hour. When Cold enough, work with a little New Yeast (home brewed best) Let it remain 3 days then place in big bottle or vessel until used. (E.C.)

Mead recipe.

The daily life of a working-class housewife

Despite her mental health problems, Ann was responsible for her family's health and nutrition. She also made, repaired, and cleaned their clothing and bedding, and kept their home clean and free from infection. Yet Ann had access to the most basic implements and ingredients. Although Walter's working-

Furniture polish recipe.

class family were comparatively well-off, health remedies, meals, cleaning products, towels, curtains, rugs, and all of their clothes were fashioned by Ann, either reworking them from existing items or making them from scratch. Unlike her middle-class counterparts, Ann was expected to manage her duties without the aid of a servant. If she was lucky, after Walter's birth, Ann might have had her ten-year-old niece, Rose Ann, lend a hand as a mother's help after finishing her chores at home.

Open fires and few appliances meant housework was heavy, isolating work, and the hours were long. It was usual for the housewife to rise before her husband to give him his breakfast and ready his food and drink to take to work. If Ann had a cooking range, instead of an open fire to cook on, her first job was to clean the range, except the front bars, while the fire was drawing up.[89] To keep the appliance in working order, Ann cleaned the whole of it, including the boiler and oven, once a week. The water levels in the boiler had to be replenished daily. Once Ann was satisfied with the water, she put the kettle on to boil, set the porridge to cook, and laid the table for breakfast. Used tea leaves from yesterday's breakfast were scattered on the floor to help collect the dust. If Ann had a rag-rug in front of the fire, now would be the time to shake it outside before sweeping the front step.[90] After breakfast, Ann aired the bedding, turned the mattresses, emptied the slops, and rinsed the chamber pots.

It was recommended that the floors were washed three times a week, less frequently in winter.[91] Any pieces of carpet Ann may have had needed regular cleaning. Candle drippings were scraped off first. Then the area was cleaned with a brush and chilly water. Next, a bar of homemade soap was melted into scalding water, and the floor scoured using as little water as possible. The entire area was gone over with a sponge removing the soap and dirt. The sponge was rinsed well before being dipped into a pail of cold vinegar water, and the whole carpet was wiped a third time.[92] The dirt produced by coal fires meant dusting and polishing was done daily and rooms cleaned from top to bottom once a week. This cleaning involved lifting any floor covering, beating it, brushing down the walls and curtains or blinds, washing the paintwork and cleaning the windows.[93]

Between the demanding jobs around the house, Ann fed the children and kept them clean, prepared a midday meal, then an evening meal. If Stephen could not get home for lunch, Ann sent him a wooden box with a lidded dish inside surrounded by straw to keep the food warm. After the evening meal, which usually started around 5 p.m., Ann cleared away, perhaps preparing a lunch for Stephen for the next day and washed and dried the utensils and pans. Now she might have time to sit and either mend or make bedding or clothing for one of the family. The last job was to rake out the kitchen fire and lay it ready for the morning. If a maid-of-all-work was expected to retire to bed no earlier than 10 p.m. it is probable the working-class housewife would not get to bed sooner.[94]

The weekly washing, drying, and ironing took the working-class housewife three days per week. On Sunday, Ann soaked Walter's cloth nappies and sorted and soaked the other washing. On Monday, the nappies were plunged into a hefty pot of boiling water set on the range or an open fire. Pounding was the next task. Then, like the clothes and bedding, they were rinsed four times, hand-wrung and heaved through a mangle. After some time drying on an outside line, clothes horse, or an airer on a pulley system, the washing was rolled up, at a specific level of dampness. This made Tuesday's job of ironing as easy as possible.

To remove the creases from fabric Ann used heavy flat pieces of cast-iron metal with a handle attached. While she ironed with one another was kept hot by a fire or cooking range. When she had finished, the laundry was aired again. The irons had to be kept immaculately clean, sand-papered, and polished. They were stored away from burning fuel and were regularly, but lightly, greased to avoid rusting. An application of beeswax on the base prevented the iron from sticking to starched collars, cuffs, and aprons. No wonder the better-off roasted a large joint on a Sunday; it provided meat for the family's main meal until Wednesday. It is sobering to think all Ann's chores were probably completed without even a cold-water tap in the house.[95] Industrialisation gradually brought household products into the home. From 1884 Ann could buy Sunlight Soap, a laundry block, to wash the nappies, clothes, and bedding. Its recipe contained copra or pine kernel oil, which lathered more easily than the traditional soaps Ann laboriously made at home from animal fats. I expect Ann was grateful for the improved facilities her home in the Tank Yard provided.

Family tree

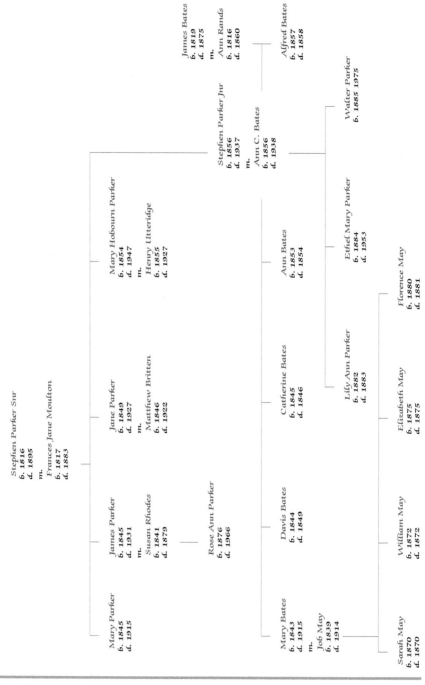

A New Life in Thorney

In March 1892 Walter's pa, Stephen, left the uncertainty of the building trade to take up a responsible post managing the water and sewer complex in Thorney.[96] The village and the surrounding land belonged to Herbrand Russell, the 11th Duke of Bedford.[97] Formerly a gravel island surrounded by low marshland, Thorney came into being after the 4th Earl of Bedford financed the draining of 2,000 square acres of fenland around Thorney Abbey. It became known as the 'Bedford Level' and was completed in 1652. Over two centuries later, Herbrand Russell, the 11th Duke of Bedford, wrote:

It was no doubt a pleasure to my predecessors to evolve a pretty village out of the dreary waste of fens, to create a charming river and well-wooded banks, and to make life less malarious [sic]

His Grace the 11th Duke of Bedford, Herbrand Russell (1858–1940). From the Woburn Abbey Collection, with permission from His Grace the 15th Duke of Bedford, Andrew Russell.

> *and less miserable by a complete fresh water drainage and sewage system worked by steam.*[98]

In 1849 Francis Russell, the 7th Duke, carried out an enquiry into the cottages of his labourers on the Bedfordshire and Buckinghamshire estates. He sent the results to the Earl of Chichester, President of the Royal Agricultural Society. He aimed to improve the 'dwellings of the labouring classes' and afford 'them the means of greater cleanliness and comfort in their own homes'.[99] The same year the Duke started the rebuilding of Thorney as a model agricultural village. The *Victoria County History* states that 'there is probably no village in England with a more extensive display of well-designed Victorian cottage architecture'.[100] The 1883 edition of *Kelly's Directory* said that the land 'now ranks amongst the most fertile districts in the kingdom'.[101] The chief crops were wheat and oats, and Thorney became known as one of the breadbaskets of England.[102]

Families had always moved to where there was work, but the Industrial Revolution drastically increased the numbers migrating to the towns and cities. Did Stephen and Ann's families see the move away from their outward-looking, thriving, and affluent community as an odd decision? Maybe Stephen thought it best to move Ann away from the temptation of the Jolly Farmers Inn, run by her sister. As Ann's brother-in-law, Job May, had been fined for serving drinks out of hours, the move may have been prudent.[103] Or did Stephen see it as his duty as breadwinner to take the best opportunity to provide for his wife and children?[104] From Stephen's point of view, it might be less stressful to manage an emotionally fragile, depressed, alcoholic wife in the smaller village of Thorney as an employee. With no state pension or welfare system as we know it, Stephen knew he would have to squirrel away enough money to keep him and Ann out of the workhouse, should they be unable to work until their deaths.

Stephen's new job was to manage the comprehensive village water, drainage, and sewage system, all controlled from the Tank Yard complex. He reported to the Duke's steward. In the Tank Yard, as author Trevor Bevis explained, hidden from view, was an ingenious feature of Victorian industrial engineering.

Walter Parker & his family outside the engineer's cottage, The Tank Yard, 6 April 1896.
I found this amongst my mother's papers after her death. I did not know the family or the location until I visited the Thorney Museum. Unlike his younger sister, Lucy, Walter is not sitting formally. Instead, there is a chair back between him and us. With his cap thrown carelessly down and feet barely touching the ground, Walter seems poised to move as soon as we look away from his image. Top row (left to right): Walter's parents, Stephen (aged 40) and Ann (40). Bottom row (left to right): Ethel (12), Lucy (6), Lily (9) and Walter (10). Photograph from the author's collection.

A stepped reservoir descends like an inverted pyramid from a quadrangle of slate roofs and terminates several feet below ground level. It collected rainwater from the roofs and into it could be pumped thousands of gallons of water from the river. The water was purified through a filtration system before being pumped into the lower reservoir.[105]

A steam-powered beam engine served a dual purpose: it pumped the water needed in the village, and once the human

The Tank Yard, c1896.
I believe Walter appears by the window of the corner house. (The figure is clearer in a larger image.) From the Culpin collection of Thorney postcards and photographs.

waste was treated, it provided a fertiliser that was sprayed onto the estate fields. Such sustainable, cutting-edge technology came at a price. According to the 11th Duke of Bedford's accounts, the works drained the estate of £351 [£45,243] a year, so a trustworthy man to manage it was a must.[106]

Walter's pa was also the leading fireman in the village. The fire station, part of the Tank Yard, was another building paid for by the Duke. On hearing of a fire, it was Stephen who rang the bell to call men from the fields. He then ran to catch the horse and harness it to the fire engine hoping they would reach the blaze in time to save people, crops, and property from the flames. Cousin Mary told me her grandfather was the 'obvious

Horse drawn fire pump, Thorney, 1908.
Photograph supplied by John Clark, Chris Lane and the Thorney Society.

man for the job', partly because he was in the Tank Yard, but also because he could alert the men faster than most as 'in the early days he was the only one in the village to own a bicycle'.

In 1881 the parish spanned 17,590 acres, with a rateable value of £28,729 [£3,464,229]. It was home to 2,055 people.[107] The purpose of Thorney was to be a larder, providing food for the Duke, his family and estate workers in Woburn.[108] Travelling with his family by wagon towards Thorney, six-year-old Walter saw the 96-ft high Jacobean brick-tower long before he arrived at the village. As the wagon trundled into the walled Tank Yard, I can picture

The Tank Yard from afar.
From the Culpin collection of Thorney postcards and photographs.

**Walter, his ma & his sisters,
The Tank Yard, 1896.**

*Walter's home was the engineer's cottage, a typical
Thorney two-storey cottage with cast-iron windows.
It is now the Thorney Museum. In this photograph,
Walter can be seen on the far right, with sisters
Lily, Lucy and Ethel watching the photographer.
Walter appears to be around ten years old and
carrying a toolcase. Standing outside their home,
Walter's ma appears separate from her children.
Photograph taken from the author's collection.*

**Ben Jeff, in the carpenter's shop
in the Tank Yard, c1950/1951.**

*Ben was 74 years old when he appeared in this
photograph. He had been working in this workshop
since 1898/99. Stephen and Walter Parker knew him
and the workshop well. From the Culpin collection
of Thorney postcards and photographs.*

Walter feeling small as he craned his neck to look up at the tallest building he had seen. After a bone-rattling journey of twenty miles, Walter was likely feeling stiff and impatient to explore.

Walter's new home was the engineer's cottage, also known as the pump keeper's cottage. It was a three-bedroom house with cast-iron window frames, on the corner of the Tank Yard complex. The house, set apart from the rest of the Duke's cottages, came with Stephen's recent post. Was it a novelty for Walter to sleep in a separate room from his sisters? At least Walter's bedroom offered him a release from watchful eyes. Whatever he felt about sleeping alone, we can imagine his delight when he discovered his new home was lit by gas and had a cold-water tap in the kitchen – no need to haul water for his ma from a shared pump.[109]

I expect Stephen gave his children a tour of the industrial complex in the Tank Yard. This included a blacksmith's shop, craftsmen's workshops (including a wheelwright), timber store, and sawmill. He may have pointed out the estate offices some thirty paces from the Parkers' front door, with its 'strong room' with bars on the windows and a 'whistling tube' system, whereby a speaking tube was used to communicate between the offices and the document storage rooms.[110] Walter also became familiar with the two impressive 25 horse-power engines installed in the cellars

Purpose built estate offices in the Tank Yard a few steps from Walter's front door by Dexter Morgan Photography, 2019.

Bedford Hall Pump.
One of two engines installed in the cellars of Bedford Hall that pumped the water to the tank in the tower in the Tank Yard. Photograph from the Thorney Museum, believed to be out of copyright.

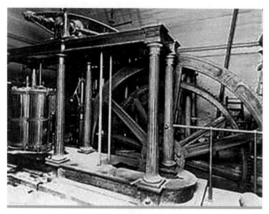

Bedford Hall Pump.
The second of the engines installed in the cellars of Bedford Hall. Photograph from the Thorney Museum, believed to be out of copyright.

of the hall. These pumped water via the Thorney River (fed by the River Nene) to the tank on the sixth floor.

There was no doubting the 7th Duke of Bedford was to be credited for living conditions in Thorney having understood 'It is the duty as well as the wisdom of the landowner to house the labour necessary for his estate'.[111] In their book about the village, the Friends of Thorney Society note that a 'range of cottages' was built to reflect the working status of the tenant. They were intermingled to promote 'good levels of social behaviour'.[112] Octavia Hill, the social reformer and pioneer of social housing born in nearby Wisbech, would have approved. One of the most striking comments on Thorney's architecture and how it reflected social norms was the shepherd's house. It was at number 25 Wisbech Road (since renumbered 140) and had a carefully crafted tongue-and-groove wooden floor instead of the usual brick on earth used for nearby properties.[113]

Each of the cottages on Wisbech Road had outbuildings for washing and summer cooking. As the 11th Duke believed that 'no cottager who is without a pig can be said to be making the best of his opportunities', he included a pigsty in the design.[114] The pig was fattened and killed in late autumn, to be salted or smoked as a source of meat through the winter and early spring. Pig-killing was one of the significant events in the calendar of most rural families. Everything would be used: skin, bristles, bones. Scraps of meat and blood were made into puddings with oatmeal and herbs. The pig's head was transformed into traditional Norfolk pork cheese, also known as brawn. This cheap dish has a salty, savoury, and sweet taste. It was served hot with potato or eaten cold with bread and pickle.

Of the 317 cottages the 7th Duke of Bedford built in the mid-nineteenth century, 210 had a garden big enough for the labourer to grow food. The latest in (outdoor) flushing toilets were part of the scheme, though they used sand, not water, to flush waste. The 11th Duke commented on the cottages' design:

> *No room, saving the third or boys' bedroom, should be built without a fireplace, both on account of ventilation and in case of illness. The boys' bedroom should have a ventilating shaft connected with the chimney, and the family should be induced to keep the shaft open. Though I advocate fireplaces in the other two bedrooms, I am well aware that in practice they are rarely used, and that the occupants often seek to exclude ventilation by blocking up the chimney.*[115]

The 11th Duke could have put profit before what he saw as his duty of care to the estate workers and their families. Instead he claimed he ran the Thorney estate 'to realise in the agricultural population such a standard of moral and physical well-being as would have been unattainable by strict adherence to commercial lines of administration.'[116] He provided cottages at a subsidised rent, equipped the community buildings, supported the Abbey, and part-maintained the school, along with other voluntary payments to improve the lives of those

living on the estate and, it is hoped, 'add to the sum of human happiness'.[117]

Historically, the Dukes provided cottages in much better condition than those 'in neighbouring towns and villages [where] the working class eked out an existence in squalid conditions'.[118] An 1890 pamphlet titled 'Housing for the People' opens with the following lines:

> *The provision of house accommodation for the industrial classes has hitherto been left almost entirely in the hands of private enterprise, with the inevitable result that high rents are extracted for the privilege of occupying squalid dwellings whose very existence is a grave social danger.*[119]

The 11th Duke of Bedford could be justly proud that, rather than abandoning Thorney in 1880 'in despair of making a profit', he enabled the dignified survival of its tenant farmers.[120] Writing of Thorney, the Duke notes: 'the only pleasure that I and my forebears can have derived from Thorney is the kindly feeling that has existed between us and our tenants and the inhabitants of Thorney Town'.[121]

Exploring the village

Six-year-old Walter was always keen to explore the village. Exiting onto Wisbech Road through the carriage archway that existed then between cottages, he saw The Rose & Crown Inn and The Rose & Crown 'taproom', on his right-hand side.[122] The new Rose & Crown Hotel was erected by the 11th Duke of Bedford and was one of the first public houses gained by the People's

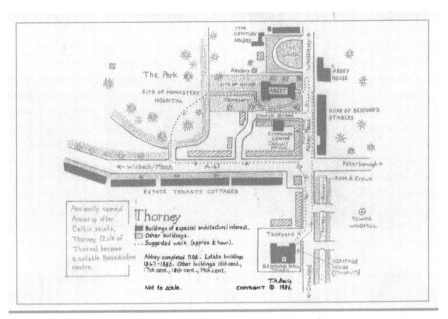

Line drawing of the centre of Thorney by author Trevor Bevis, 1986. With Trevor's kind permission.

Refreshment House Association in 1899.[123] The association paid their managers a salary and did not allow them to profit from alcoholic beverages. The manager was asked to make it a place 'where recreation and social intercourse of a harmless nature may be enjoyed', and 'where refreshments of the best quality may be obtained'

An arch on Wisbech Road, 2015.
It once gave access to the Tank Yard, with the tailor's workshop on one side and Halford's saddler's on the other. From the author's collection.

under conditions that encourage temperance.[124]

When Stephen and his family moved to the village, the inn's manager was Albert Bennett, a Yorkshireman. He was allowed

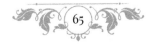

Rose & Crown, Thorney, 1908.
Photograph from the Peterborough Images Archive. www.peterboroughimages.co.uk.

a profit on all trade in food and non-alcoholic drinks, and it was therefore in his interest to encourage a convivial atmosphere in the establishment. He urged his customers to consume tea, coffee, light refreshments, and meals. The 11th Duke, supported this scheme, being of the view that 'the abolition of a paying public-house saves the rates and the State from the creation and maintenance of paupers and criminals'.[125]

Taproom with the Tank Yard tower in the background, 2015.
From the author's collection.

The temperance-supporting public accumulated the People's Refreshment House Association's capital in the form of £1 [£126] shares. In return, shareholders received a dividend out of the profits at a rate not exceeding 5 per cent per annum. Any surplus was given to local endeavours. A board decided how the money was to be split. In 1900 the surplus went to the Thorney Mutual Improvement Association (£30 [£3,790]), the Peterborough Infirmary (£15 [£1,895]), the Thorney Flower Show (£5 [£632])

Taproom by the Rose & Crown, 2015.
From the author's collection.

and the Thorney Foal Show (£5 [£632]).[126] It was the taproom, however, a simple alehouse built in 1850 as part of the 7th Duke of Bedford's model village, where working men went to relax. The 'tap' was in the shadow of the Rose & Crown Inn, and according to Walter's niece, it was here where teetotallers Stephen and Walter Parker came to escape Ann's 'condition'. They played many games of cards and dominoes here.

Wisbech Road.
This Parker shop is not connected to Walter's family.

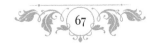

Wisbech Road, Thorney. The tree appears outside what is now no. 74.
Photograph from the Peterborough Images Archive: www.peterboroughimages.co.uk.

Wisbech Road, Thorney.
From the author's collection.

Across from the grocery store on the corner of Wisbech Road and Abbey Place was the post office. In earlier times it

Wisbech Road, Thorney.
From the author's collection.

had been the constable's office and the relieving office (c.1860–70). The relieving officer evaluated the cases of all persons applying for medical or poor relief, allowed emergency relief or entry to the workhouse.[127] Walter also passed the infant and girls' Abbey school on

Staff outside the (Peterborough) Co-operative Society, Thorney.
Photograph from the Peterborough Images Archive: www.peterboroughimages.co.uk.

Church Lane, where he and his sisters Ethel and Lily would soon be enrolled. Further along the road were the Abbey Rooms.[128] In the early days of cinema, Walter's sister Ethel would play the accompaniment for the silent movies. Near to the Abbey is what is now known as the Manor House. Walter knew it as Abbey House.

The interior of the Thorney (Peterborough) Co-operative Society, Thorney.
Photograph from the Peterborough Images Archive: www.peterboroughimages.co.uk.

With his back to the Abbey and The Green, Walter retraced his footsteps to the crossroads. To his left was the modern Primitive Methodist chapel on The Causeway, constructed in 1886. Just before the outside entrance to the yard, Walter reached the boys' school. At seven

John Amps Stores, at the crossroads, Thorney.
The store was opened in 1891 by John Amps who moved to open a similar store on Market Place in Oundle in 1901. Amps Grocers on the crossroads at Thorney. Photograph from the Peterborough Images Archive: www.peterboroughimages.co.uk.

William 'Billy' Amps shop, at the crossroads, Thorney, c1901.
He remained here until c. 1922. Photograph from the Peterborough Images Archive: www.peterboroughimages.co.uk.

years old, he would leave the infant school to follow a syllabus suitable for an agricultural worker. His tour of the village would not be complete without visiting the railway station. Although Thorney was a village, the Peterborough and Sutton Bridge line had connected the Thorneyites with the world since 1866. It also brought hundreds of visitors to village events. The railway line

William Amps Stores, at the crossroads, Thorney.

Old Post Office Buildings, Thorney.

was so close to the Tank Yard that the sound of the steam engines punctuated Walter's youth. When his ma had too much to drink, did he dream of climbing aboard a train to escape to the unknown?

Abbey Place, Thorney, 1906.
Photograph from the Peterborough Images Archive: www.peterboroughimages.co.uk.

The infants' and girls' school,
Church Street, Thorney.

The Church of St Mary and St
Botolph, once part of Thorney
Abbey, 2014.
From the author's collection.

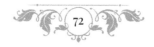

Abbey Green, Thorney.
From the author's collection.

~~> VIEW OF THE ABBEY AND HIGH STREET, THORNEY. <~~

Thorney Abbey & High Street, Thorney.
From the author's collection.

Abbey House, Thorney (misnamed Morton Hall).

Sixteenth century Thorney Abbey House. The single-storey part of the house (on the left with a door) was the original estate office until the new estate office was built in the Tank Yard. (A seventeenth century addition to Thorney Abbey House was built behind the original house.) From the Culpin collection of Thorney postcards and photographs.

Abbey House, Thorney.

Thorney Abbey House. With permission from John Clark, Chris Lane and The Thorney Society

Abbey Place, Thorney, 1907.

Crowd at the crossroads, Thorney.

A large crowd of curious locals watch the photographer at work as he captures the crossroads in Thorney in the early 1900s. Photograph from the Peterborough Images Archive: www.peterboroughimages.co.uk.

Boys' School Station Road, Thorney.

Photograph supplied with the kind permission of John Clark, Chris Lane and the Thorney Society.

The modern Primitive Methodist chapel on The Causeway, built 1886.
*Photograph supplied with the kind permission of John Clark,
Chris Lane and the Thorney Society.*

Thorney Station, c1920s.
*Undated, but believed to have been taken in the 1920s.
Photograph from the Peterborough Images Archive: www.peterboroughimages.co.uk.*

Thorney Station, c1920s.
Undated, but believed to have been taken in the 1920s.
Photograph from the Peterborough Images Archive:
www.peterboroughimages.co.uk.

Class of 4-4-0s Engine.
This class of 4-4-0s had cylinders of 18.5 inches by 26 inches. The driving wheels were
7 feet in diameter. It was designed for the Midland Railway by S. W. Johnson towards
the end of the 19th century. From the Railway Wonders of the World, Part 37,
first published 11 October 1935.

The Water Tower & Buildings, Thorney.
Postcard given to Walter by his employer with the message, 'To Walter Parker from Mr &
Mrs E W Smith [Edward William Smith] upon leaving Thorney March 6 1907 with our Best
Wishes for Time & Eternity, "In all thy Ways acknowledge Him & He will direct thy Paths".
[The Bible, Proverbs 3:6, King James Version.]

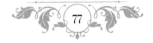

Back in the Tank Yard Walter climbed the steps of the tower. He saw the large cast-iron reservoir tank where the water was stored after it had been filtered, before being piped to each of the cottages. I wonder if the panoramic view from the top floor gave Walter an appreciation of a broad, flat landscape and enormous sky, and whether this stayed with him. It was important to him to climb the stairs one last time, aged ninety, suffering from a heart condition, accompanied by his daughter and grandchildren.

Village hierarchy

As the manager of the water and sewage works, Walter's pa, Stephen, was set apart from the other working families. He was expected to set an example. When Stephen was promoted to estate foreman in 1900, a job previously carried out by a man of a higher social status, he became privy to confidential information. Such a situation could make him, and his family, vulnerable to anyone who was resentful or jealous of how far Stephen had risen 'above his station'. Being the only son, it is likely Walter felt added pressure. Cousin Mary described herself and her sisters as being ostracised by some of their peer group because their grandfather, Stephen, had more disposable income than other families enjoyed.[129] If so, perhaps Walter felt excluded too.

Although the nineteenth century saw opportunities for some men, most working-class people were still constrained by their class and occupations.[130] In addition, people's hard-won reputation was vulnerable to 'talk'. It can be hard to believe that class, gender, and social standing dictated much about people's lives. This included what they ate, when and how it was eaten, how they dressed, what time they got up and went to bed, how long and in what they were educated, what work they did, where they lived and who they married – even how far they travelled.[131]

Growing up in Arkley, near the Hertfordshire town of Barnet in the 1960s and 1970s, I remember an uncomfortable sense of being observed, challenged, and found wanting. Mine was not the intimate and closed community Walter grew up in, but there were claustrophobic moments when I felt pinned down like a moth under glass. Walter probably had ambivalent feelings about leaving Upwell, the village where he was born. His father's new position took him, his ma, and his sisters away from a well-established extended family. Before the move, Walter would have seen his uncles, aunts, and cousins regularly at church, Sunday school, or church events. No train or tram linked Upwell to Thorney. The thirty-six-mile round trip would

James Parker & Family.

James Parker (Walter's uncle, 1845–1931) with his second wife Rachel Dring Wagon née Clark (1835–1903), stepmother to Joel (1876–1958), Rose Ann (1875–1966), Jesse (1874–1955), Josiah (1872–1930), Theophilus (known in the family as Thop/Theo, 1870–1956) and Jabez (1869–1930). Photograph taken in 1886, Upwell. Photographic restoration provided by Simon Barraclough at www.fix-your-pix.co.uk and Claudia d'Souza at www.thephotoalchemist.biz.

not have been a casual undertaking for an adult, and it would have been impossible for a young boy who was missing his cousins to travel there alone.

Walter's aunts had been left behind in Upwell, but his mother's half-sister, Ellen Bates, who had spent time in the Huntingdon workhouse as a child, found her way to Thorney. In 1898, in what was Thorney Abbey, the family gathered to witness Stephen Parker give Ellen away in marriage to George Blyth, a carpet-layer from Hull. The girl who had seemed doomed in the workhouse had found her life partner, though she would move many times over the years.

Although the Royal Mail postal system was reliable, frequent, and cheap, how likely was Stephen to keep in close touch with his family by post? We know Stephen kept ties with his sister Mary, because her daughter, eleven-year-old Frances Utteridge of Upwell, was staying with the Parker family in April when the

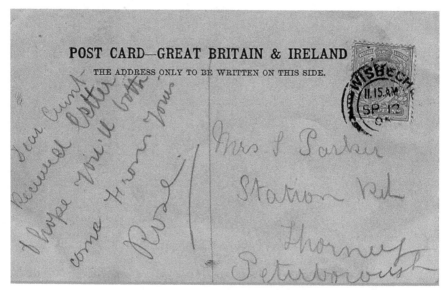

Invitation to Ann Parker from Rose Ann Robb, née Parker.
Postcard from Walter's cousin Rose Ann Robb née Parker. From the author's collection.

1901 census took place. A postcard from Walter's cousin Rose Ann Robb née Parker invites Ann to visit Upwell, so maybe Stephen and Ann returned.

When the Parkers left Upwell, it had a population twice that of Thorney.[132] The tram, river, canal, and road traffic all ensured a lively kaleidoscope of people and goods. Despite the grand setting of the Parkers' new home, Thorney was an agricultural village controlled by the steward in the Duke's name. It may have felt claustrophobic to young Walter. On Sundays, as people came to attend service at the Abbey or the Primitive Methodist chapel, it might have felt a hive of people.[133] But for the rest of the week, Thorney may have appeared a slower, duller village. For Ann, it could have been an isolating and claustrophobic place that drove her ever closer to the whisky bottle. Though having suffered so much loss, it is possible she saw Thorney as a safer place to raise her children. While there is a lot we cannot know, the questions we consider could offer some insight into Walter's character and his decision to leave, like his father before him, the place where he had grown up.

Family tree

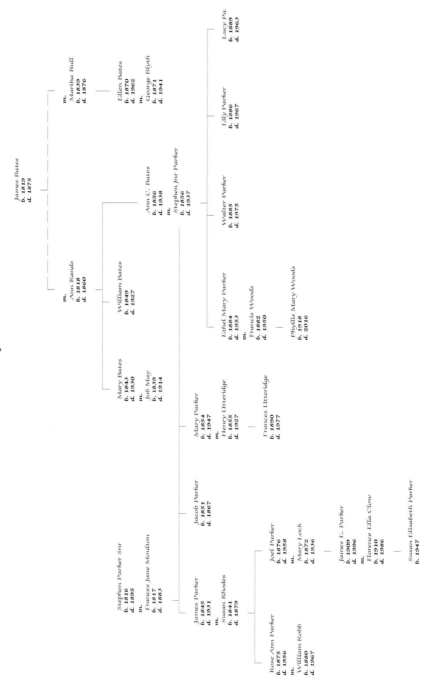

CHAPTER 4

An Alcoholic
in the Family

For generations, the Parker's life had centred on agriculture, ebbing, and flowing with the seasons. It was often a hand-to-mouth existence, and most of those living beyond the bounds of a country estate could not expect to earn a consistent wage throughout the year. The cost of candlelight and keeping a fire burning was prohibitive.[134] 'Early to bed and early to rise' helped workers pace themselves and make the most of natural light. It would have been difficult to pursue personal interests, particularly within the setting of a tiny, damp, dimly lit, cold, and overcrowded cottage. Space was at a premium, so children were 'topped and tailed' in bed. Many working-class families slept in one room with a ragged curtain providing a visual separation between the adults and children.

In exchange for predictable wages numerous families moved away from the land. The rapid and widespread industrialisation led to new working patterns. Adults and many children became tethered to the modern factory machines:

Whilst the engine runs the people must work – men, women and children are yoked together with iron and steam. The

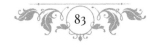

animal machine breakable in the best case, subject to a thousand sources of suffering... is chained fast to the iron machine which knows no suffering and no weariness.[135]

In the industrial north, coal combustion led to widespread respiratory illnesses, slower growth during childhood, and shorter adult stature.[136] Walter was fortunate to have clean, unpolluted air. Technology changed life at a slower rate in agriculture, but as a farm labourer, Walter's work was aided by the new steam-powered tractor and the thresher.

Alongside the new work patterns came excessive beer drinking. It was hoped that The Beer House Act of 1830 would reduce the consumption of spirits, particularly gin. The Act was intended to encourage the small entrepreneur to open premises where only home-brewed beer was offered.[137] However, it resulted in an explosion of small home-based enterprises. Any person whose name was on the rate-book might open their house as a beer shop on payment of two guineas per annum [£235] to the local office of excise, which was inundated with householders keen to cash in.[138]

The hope that the new legislation would cause fewer people drinking spirits was crushed as, after a slight check, the consumption of spirits soon escalated. Sydney Smith, a member of the Whig party who had been ordained in 1796, wrote: 'The new Beer Bill has begun its operations. Everybody is drunk. Those who are not singing are sprawling. The sovereign people are in a beastly state'.[139] As early as 1833 a Parliamentary Select Committee concluded that 'considerable evils' had arisen from the looser licensing law. The 1834 report to the House of Commons Committee on Drunkenness stated that there was one beer house for every twenty families; no other Act of Parliament had had so catastrophic an effect. Alcohol was an affordable escape from the treadmill of work and the misery of cold, dark, and overcrowded dwellings. Increasingly, the beer houses were linked to drunkenness in working-class men. Long-term heavy drinking was on the rise.

By 1869, tens of thousands of people had been prosecuted for drunkenness and drunk and disorderly behaviour. The government's response was to introduce the Licensing Act of 1872, according to which public houses had to shut by midnight in towns and by eleven o'clock in country areas. It also became an offence to serve spirits to those apparently under the age of sixteen and to sell intoxicating liquor to someone who appeared drunk.[140]

Women and alcohol

Although women's alcoholism was recognised in the nineteenth century, it would appear that most women were associated with fighting for temperance or teetotalism or were the victims of male drunkenness. In 1878 a female writer expressed a popular opinion when she wrote that a man should be excused of domestic abuse if he had the 'universally condemned creature, the drunken wife'.[141] However dated this view may appear, a recent study has shown that both men and women still dehumanise drunken women.[142]

While scholarly and other literature mainly concentrated on the inebriation of working-class men, the Parker family – like many others – suffered an alcoholic wife and mother.[143] George Vaillant, an American psychiatrist and Professor at Harvard Medical School, is a leading researcher in this subject. He writes that genetic loading (the average number of lethal mutations per individual in a population) 'is an important predictor of whether an individual develops alcoholism'. A challenging childhood environment 'is an important predictor of when an individual loses control of alcohol'.[144]

Ann became addicted to alcohol, but the trigger is not known. As suggested in a study paper published by the World Health Organisation, Ann's bereavements or fear for her children's lives may have made her more vulnerable to mental ill-health.[145] If so, it is unlikely she had access to adequate medical care. Treatment for depression, or any mental illness was stigmatised and was to be avoided, if possible, especially for the working class.[146] Even if the family could afford medical help for Ann, it would have involved a lengthy stay in an asylum, miles from home. In these institutions, 'rigid routine... standardising work, leisure and exercise [were used] in attempts to stabilise the minds of the patients'. Women patients had little choice in their employment which reflected their roles outside the asylum.[147] If it were productive work, it would likely be in the laundry working from 6.30 a.m. to late afternoon six days a week. In contrast, the upper class insane were far more likely to be given massages, rest cure and repeated water baths.[148] An alternative was meaningless needlework or sorting coloured beans into different piles only for them to be presented mixed up again in the morning.[149]

Although there were regional differences in remedies used to treat mental ill health, enemas, laxatives, opiates, rest, alcohol, sedating medications, Turkish baths, packing people in wet-sheet and electric shock therapy were common.[150] In some areas gynaecological surgery, including clitoridectomy, hysterectomy and the removal of the labia were carried out in the belief it would cure illness of the mind.[151] Surgeon

Baker Brown became obsessed with the removal of the clitoris as a treatment for mental illness in London in the 1860s.[152] Thankfully, by 1895 the British medical community had firmly concluded that the removal of the clitoris to treat melancholy and other mental illnesses was 'odious and unscientific'.[153] The separation from friends, relatives and former associations was common. Sometimes it was part of the treatment plan, but not necessarily communicated to the patient.[154]

Rather than receive a helping hand, Ann would have been aware of the community view: 'Alcohol consumption was a waste of money, a waste of potential labour, and a waste of the maternal gifts that a woman 'naturally' possessed. The body of the female alcoholic was by definition, wasted'.[155]

Historian and social scientist Thora Hands wrote, 'Although thought to exist mainly among the labouring population, the drunkard did not respect other social boundaries and breached gender, age, region, religion and ethnicity. The drunkard was viewed as a social pest and a danger to civilised and progressive society'.[156] However, for a woman, especially a mother, to succumb was seen as abhorrent and against her maternal nature. The legal and social consequences of being inebriated were more damaging for women than for men.[157] Female alcoholics held a special place in the popular imagination as a villainous fallen woman; not only a threat to her own body and those of her children but also to the British nation.[158]

Victorian society wrestled with understanding the roots of alcoholism. Some squarely blamed repeated inebriation on the 'lazy drunkard' and were keen to condemn and punish. Others, like social reformer Frances Power Cobbe, saw alcoholism as the effect of abysmal ill-treatment:

> *How many have sunk into the habit because... degraded in soul by contempt and abuse, they have not left in them one spark of that self-respect which enables a human being to resist the temptation to drown care and remembrance in the dread forgetfulness of strong drink?*[159]

Sigmund Freud, born a year before Walter's mother, defined the 'id' as the unorganised part of the personality. He explained it contained basic, instinctual drives that indiscriminately seek to avoid pain.[160] Could the 'id' hold the elusive answer to Ann's excessive drinking? Or, as the American journalist and philanthropist Charles Dana asked in 1909, might alcohol itself cause madness?[161] Alcoholism, particularly in women, was thought of and treated as madness or moral insanity, defined as 'deviance from socially accepted behaviour'.[162] However, Thora Hands points out that women known to be drunk in public or secret drinkers were also seen as deviant and immoral because they were consuming alcohol without the consent of their husbands.[163]

Ann bought spirits as part of her shopping from a nearby licensed grocer. Evidence that middle-class women, unable to purchase their drinks in a public house, purchased alcohol for their secret drinking from licensed stores appeared as part of the 1877 Select Committee of the House of Lords on Intemperance (1877 enquiry). During 1877 the *Lancet* ran a series of articles relating to licensed grocers where doctors claimed this practice was commonplace. In one statement, the conclusion was that 'the grocer and the 'foolish' wife had colluded in this deceit'.[164] However, the central dilemma was apparently 'deciding if licensed grocers actively encouraged, either by their very existence or in collusion with women, the practice of secret domestic drinking.'[165] While some saw furtive drinking as foolish, the doctors writing in the *Lancet* claimed the grocery trade is wholly removed from police supervision and is a direct incentive to "secret drinking". It continued that hidden consumption was a practice more detrimental to the health and morals and social prosperity of the community than ordinary trade in intoxicating liquors'.[166]

The cause of alcohol use disorder is still unknown. It is thought to be a complicated blend of genetic, physical, psychological, environmental, and social factors that can be different for each addict. For Ann, alcoholism was only just beginning to be seen as something which could be treated, rather than a shameful failure to resist temptation.[167] Most Victorian doctors believed that individuals could conquer it with willpower and religion.[168] Julia Skelly, faculty lecturer at the Department of Art History and Communication Studies at McGill University writes that some middle-class women 'voiced their willingness to help lower-class female drinkers. These offers of assistance were often characterised by the middle-class women's sense of moral superiority'.[169] It was not only the middle class that took a stance. On 5 August 1892, this remark was recorded in the Thorney Infant and Girls' School log: 'Several children away on Monday for Temperance Demonstrations at Peterborough'.

One can imagine the humiliation Walter and his siblings felt at having an alcoholic mother. Contemporary opinions on the subject of alcoholism were replete with moralistic overtones. Emma Griffin notes in her book, which was informed by over 600 autobiographies, that, 'drinking was quite easily incorporated into narratives about fathers; but alcoholic mothers were an object of shame'.[170] Mothers heavy drinking and their neglect and mismanagement of their infants figured in many Old Bailey cases, for their dereliction had dire consequences for their families'.[171] Norman Kerr was the president of the British Society for the Study and Cure of Inebriety.

He stated in a lecture of 1893 that 'intemperance has a physical and pathological as well as a legal, moral and spiritual aspect'.[172] Concern grew for the children of female alcoholics, and a disproportionate number of women were incarcerated.

From the 1870s and 1880s in Britain and America, specialist journals and societies developed and disseminated a 'disease model' of inebriety, emphasising the physiological effects of alcohol.[173] But by the late 1890s, those who subscribed to degeneration theory (the transmission of alcoholism and insanity to future generations through biological factors, toxic environmental influences or moral vices) believed that social, ethical and medical problems would increase in each generation, finally resulting in the extinction of that family.[174]

The risk of public inebriation

The enforcement of the 1872 licensing laws would reduce public drunkenness and disorderly conduct. It was a successful act of social engineering, but it was also deeply unpopular with those who felt their freedoms were being curtailed. On the other hand, there can be little doubt that widespread alcoholism was a concern for the Victorian authorities. Police records show that it was not rare.[175] A fifth to a quarter of those arrested for drunkenness were women. What is more, because of the nature of police records the number of people who suffered from addiction was probably much higher.

The consequences of arrest were considerable. Under the Habitual Inebriates Act of 1898, if charged with drunkenness, women could be confined in detoxification homes for as long as three years, if they had been convicted at least four times over twelve months. The 1902 Licensing Act allowed a magistrate to send an 'inebriate' wife to a reformatory for specialist help.[176] Despite the best intentions behind Inebriate Reformatories and the work of the After-care Association, homes did not always meet the 1898 General Regulations for the Management and Discipline of Certified Inebriate Reformatories:

> *It shall be the duty of all officers to treat inmates with kindness and humanity, to listen patiently to and report their complaints or grievances, and at the same time to be firm in maintaining order and discipline.*[177]

Somewhere between care-home, asylum and prison, state reformatories were viewed as the best means of isolating, controlling, and reforming 'inebriate' women.[178] However, there were not enough state places because local authorities were reluctant to fund treatment. As a result, many dubious unlicensed homes were opened. These were not regulated or inspected. An example was a commercial enterprise posing as a charity. St James's Home for Female Inebriates in Kennington, London, used the unfortunates who were admitted as slaves in the laundry. According to the case that was brought against the owners, many inmates were forced to work for as much as eighteen hours a day on a diet of bread and water.

> *Women entering the Home were told they would not be allowed to leave or see visitors without the permission of the 'Lady Superior'... and that the shortest time many could expect to remain was 12 months... 'Better class' private patients passed their time producing fine needlework, but most women worked in the St James's Sanitary Steam Laundry.*[179]

An article about the 'inebriates' homes' appeared in the Parkers' local weekly paper, the *Peterborough and Huntingdonshire Standard*, in February 1907. It is difficult to believe Stephen and Ann were unaware of these detoxification homes, or their reputation. According to Ann's granddaughter, Mary, Ann avoided arrest by inviting the local policeman to drink with her.[180] Cousin Mary further explained that the two sat on a bench made for Ann by her husband, Stephen, with the excuse, 'she can rest while hanging the washing.' Both Stephen and Ann would have been aware of the law that forbade drunkenness in a public place from the newspaper reports, such as the case of Martha Clerke brought before the Whittlesey Petty Sessions in 1892.[181]

Mental health: intergenerational loss, trauma, and depression

Ann's formative years were threaded with tragedy and we can speculate that the ensuing years of her mother's consumptive disease were a frightening and anxious time. Growing up it would be natural if Ann were fearful for herself or her father's survival. Scientists have linked the oxytocin receptor gene to optimism, self-esteem and 'mastery', the belief that one has control over one's own life.[182] These three characteristics are seen as critical psychological resources for coping well with stress and depression.[183] Reading between the records, we can surmise that Ann's family lived on the edge of crisis for many years, and probably could not provide the nurturing environment she needed.[184] This experience was far from unique. Most of us have ancestors with agricultural roots who lived hand-to-mouth and may have passed on a damaging psychological and a physiological inheritance.

Denial, avoidance, silence, procrastination, projection onto others and dissociation are ways individuals, families, organisations, societies and even nations can cope with overwhelming experiences.[185] While pain, misery and anguish may be suppressed in those desperately clinging on to physical and emotional survival, their offspring and the generations that follow can feel stalked by a dread or fear they cannot name. Indeed, research suggests that when left unattended, the traumas suffered by one generation continue to be visited upon successive ones.[186] It is, therefore, possible that emotions not explained by the individual's own experiences may stand for the intergenerational transmission of unresolved loss, conflict or trauma unwittingly passed on as a psychological inheritance.[187]

Before we become too despondent, we should remember that while there is a genetic connection to psychological states, genes predict behaviour; they do not determine it. The good news is that even without psychological intervention, positive development can continue throughout our lives. So early experiences need not dictate our destiny; there is always the hope that other factors in our environment can steer us in a positive direction. Insight into our upbringing and our emotions allows us to bring to light the invisible threads that were not verbalised but hidden in shame or kept as secrets. It can enable us to challenge unconscious repetitions, and allow us to break the chain, passing on a healthier legacy. In short, we have the power to restructure our brains, improve our quality of life and the lives of those that come after us.

Ann did not recover from what I believe was crippling depression, a mood disorder that Freud called 'melancholy' in 1911. His use of the word was not original (as is made clear by Dürer's engraving 'Melancholia', produced in 1514).[188] Freud described its cause as an incomplete form of mourning.[189] Genetic research shows us that the same genes and neural pathways that can make us more vulnerable to depression are also involved in anxiety, alcoholism and suicide.[190] Feasibly, Ann's misuse of alcohol could have been an attempt to self-medicate untreated depression following the unresolved catastrophic loss of her first-born daughter. Research has shown that alcohol use disorder is predated by either anxiety or depression in 45 per cent of sufferers.[191]

Unavoidable, inescapable, and overwhelming suffering and loss in childhood can weaken resilience and lead to depressive episodes. It is also common for depression to be passed on from generation to generation.[192] Genetic factors have been found to influence the risk, in part, by altering the sensitivity of individuals to the depression-inducing effect of stressful life events.[193] Unsurprisingly, genetic and environmental factors are present in depression too.[194] Ann's life had been such that we could predict she would struggle with negative thinking, which worsens the effects of a depressed mood.[195]

A likely consequence of Ann's addiction was an inability to react appropriately to her children. A study of mothers with unresolved trauma, showed that the amygdala, the part of the brain which processes emotion, memory, and emotional dysfunction, was turned off when the mother was looking at her child's distressed face. The observation of blunted amygdala response could contribute to an account of the transgenerational transmission of trauma. We can speculate that the blunting of response is maintained because it protects the mother from re-experiencing her trauma. Yet, this leaves the infant psychologically 'alone', with no one to share or mitigate his emotional pain.'[196] The price paid by the children of traumatised parents can be confusing as they can struggle with debilitating depression, unexplained grief, and an increased vulnerability to stress, without understanding the cause.[197] Mothers who had addiction problems also show a diminished response when viewing their child's happy face. Yet, when they saw unknown children, their responses compared to those of mothers who did not have an addiction problem.[198]

Ann was a long way from the array of therapies we use to treat anxiety and depression. Eye movement desensitisation and reprocessing therapy (EMDR) can help heal survivors of trauma. Cognitive behavioural therapies (CBT), including Ellis's Rational Emotive Therapy, encourages people to recognise their negative thoughts and replace them with more realistic outlooks. Or the new view of human nature offered by Lisa Feldman Barrett, Professor of Psychology at Northeastern University. Barrett shows us how our 'brain operates by prediction and construction and rewires itself through experience'.[199] Her work, using neuroscience research, gives us a practical toolbox enabling us to master our emotions for a significantly healthier and more meaningful life. (These methods are considered as, or more, effective than medicating the brain.[200]) Psychiatric treatment was also limited for the following generation. Ann's niece, Ada Mary Walton née Bates, was diagnosed with postnatal psychosis. She was admitted to an asylum five months after the birth of her fifth child and died of epilepsy aged thirty-one just before Christmas 1902, in the Three Counties Asylum at Stotfold, sixty miles away from the family home.[201] Although living with an adult with untreated mental illness negatively affects a child's mental health, this is particularly true if the child is carrying a higher genetic risk. It seems possible Walter's relationship with his ma impaired his ability to form healthy attachments.[202] We do not know Ann's daughters' psychological inheritance, but their suffering poorer mental health seems almost inevitable.[203]

Male trauma also affects psychological inheritance. Data shows that paternal hardship as a prisoner of war during the American Civil War could affect the lifespan of sons born after the traumatising event. Importantly, the same study showed the effect could be 'neutralized before the child is even born – by the nutrients a mother ingests during pregnancy'.[204] Ann's youngest, Lucy, was perceived by her grandson, John Malyon, as a rigid, cold woman who was not much interested in her grandchildren.

However, this could also describe a woman battling demons that would not lie quietly. Lucy had been isolated by tuberculosis in her youth. She was kept at home with a depressed alcoholic mother who was likely fearful that Lucy would die or pass on the infection to other members of the family.

Lucy Malyon, née Parker, holding her grandson, John Malyon, with John's mum Gertrude Doris née Blank, known as Doris.
Photograph from John Malyon's collection.

Lucy escaped into marriage during the First World War, but it did not end happily. Her husband, Frederick Charles Malyon, tragically took his own life in the 1930s. According to Lucy's niece, my Cousin Mary, this was because he could not face the consequences of his extramarital affair. Frederick had become a captain in the Royal Army Medical Corps, and he survived Passchendaele. He was a decorated soldier, but he almost certainly returned home at the end of the war emotionally scarred by his experiences.[205] Lucy was left a widow at forty-six years of age. In February 1942, six years after his father's violent death, Lucy's son, Frederick Parker Malyon, a Royal Engineer, was captured and held by the Japanese as a POW.[206] His camp was liberated in September 1945 when he was twenty-five years old. He endured punishment, brutal work, disease, and starvation. Lucy would have needed to be remarkably resilient to have avoided mental health problems.[207]

Mental ill-health continued in the Parker family. In 2015 Cousin Mary told me her father Francis had had a mental breakdown, triggered by his wife, Ethel, having her Victorian styled long hair cut into a modern bob. Apparently, Francis never forgave her.

Francis Woods, known as Frank, aged 24, 1907.
From the author's collection.

Ethel Parker studio photograph, 1907.
From the author's collection.

As early as 1896 Freud interpreted out of proportion reactions in the following way:

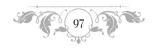

It is not the latest slight–which, in itself, is minimal– that produces the fit of crying, the outburst of despair or the attempt at suicide, in disregard of the axiom that an effect must be proportionate to its cause; the small slight of the present moment has aroused and set working the memories of very many, more intense, earlier slights, behind all of which there lies, in addition, the memory of a serious slight in childhood which has never been overcome.[208]

Mary recalled her parents 'were so unhappy; I had a breakdown too'. Mary explained she became 'very nervous' and developed a fear of her sister 'Rene's cat, Felix, and other animals. Her anxiety grew so intense that 'Rene was forced to give her pet away. Eventually Mary's anxiety lessened to a more manageable level, but she told me she was always an anxious sort, though it might not have looked like it from the outside. She said it was with her husband she felt most herself.

Stephen Charles Skells
(1952–1987), aged 21.
Photograph provided by Stephen's mother, Phyllis Mary Skells née Woods (known as Mary).

Psychiatrist Myrna Weissman's thirty-year study covering three generations concluded that 59 per cent of grandchildren who had two generations of major depression preceding them had either depression or an anxiety disorder.[209] This was borne out when Mary's son (Ann's great-grandson, another Stephen) died by his own hand in 1987, aged thirty-four. Mary outwardly blamed an earlier car accident as being the most significant influence on her son's desperate act, but in her low moments told me she blamed herself. Tellingly, Mary said she could not find release or comfort in talking about her son's death with others because she had believed for so long that such things should not be spoken aloud.

As Victoria Costello reminds us, the inheritance of mental illness does not happen solely through genes. 'Equally important are the habits of mind and behaviour that are culturally endowed to us across oceans and centuries'.[210] I believe if we could talk about our mental health struggles openly and if family mental health history was taken as a matter of course, Stephen Skells' death, and many others, might have been prevented. Some of today's therapists are successfully treating deep-rooted, inherited shadows of buried trauma. These can appear as unexpected illness, immune disorders, pain, as accidents, nightmares, depression, intrusive thoughts, anxiety, or paralysing terror.

The impact of trauma and addiction

I cannot help but wonder what impact Ann's trauma or heavy drinking had on her children. French psychoanalyst Françoise Dolto told psychotherapist Anne Schutzenberger that 'in a family, children and house dogs know everything, always, and particularly when it's left unsaid'. So, we might infer Walter and his siblings, either consciously or unconsciously, understood their family dynamic.[211]

Addicts commonly exhibit mood swings along with inconsistent and erratic behaviour. According to Marni Low, a Certified Alcohol and Substance Abuse Counsellor, when drug or alcohol abuse exists in a family, 'family rules, roles and relationships are established and organized around the alcoholic and/or other substances, in an effort to maintain the family's homeostasis and balance'.[212]

An addict's family often develops rules such as, 'Don't talk, don't feel, don't trust'. The rules are rarely spoken but can be absorbed along with a belief: 'This is what we do in our family'. Individual family members can believe they have become adept at managing the alcoholic's behaviour. They can believe they are protecting the 'shameful' secret of dependence. But instead the behaviour can lead to a cycle of insecure attachment, a predisposition to addiction and learnt, damaging co-dependent patterns of behaviour that, unchallenged, may become part of the next generation's inheritance.[213]

Psychotherapist Ross Rosenberg described co-dependency as a person giving up their power and control to individuals who are often addicts. The positive intent of this 'enabling' can be to end the dependency on the drug, by 'helping' in some way. However, unhealthy co-dependency can result in family and friends making it possible for the addiction to continue. As I understand it, the alcoholic often relies heavily on loyal, flexible, enabling carers with poor boundaries, who become 'rescuers' in reaction to the dependent's victim stance. The rescuer tries to keep peace and balance in the family, while the addict swings between verbal or physical blame or a controlling manner and needy dependence. Co-dependency theory is considered controversial by some. Others argue it describes the result of trauma or poor attachment, yet it appears to offer many a compelling way to make sense of their experience.[214] Cousin Mary's description of Stephen and Ann's relationship sounded like a co-dependent 'dance' with Stephen adapting to

whatever Ann appeared to need from him.

To manage the stress of their dysfunctional home life one school of thought suggests that Walter and his siblings might take on one of four roles in the family: the Hero, the Scapegoat, the Lost Child, or the Mascot.[215] In this model the Hero, often the eldest, takes responsibility and is usually a high achiever, a perfectionist, and/or a people pleaser. The Scapegoat is rebellious and disruptive and takes the spotlight away from the alcoholic parent.

Stephen and Ann Parker.
The traditional pose does not reflect their relationship as their granddaughter Mary understood it. Neither are engaging with the photographer. Ann appears absent and her hands, even in a still image, appear restless.
From the author's collection.

Meanwhile, the Lost Child adapts by unknowingly repressing their thoughts, feelings, and needs. They withdraw into themselves and appear to need less adult attention, are non-demanding and are often overlooked. Some children plan their escape from a dysfunctional parental situation in which they feel anxiously trapped. They may grow up to avoid intimate relationships, to guard against anxiety or abandonment, and be fearful of risk or initiative. The Mascot is the family clown who takes attention away from the dysfunction. They try to make people laugh despite the unaddressed psychological pain within the family. I believe Walter, a shy, quiet lad, became the Lost Child who emotionally was largely left to himself. A further family role is that of the Caretaker or Enabler who makes all the other roles possible. They try to keep everyone happy and the family in balance, usually at the expense of their own needs. According to Cousin Mary's description of her grandfather, this role was fulfilled by Stephen. 'He would do anything for anybody' and endeavoured to present the family to the village as one that was coping. Attachment theory, first proposed by John Bowlby in 1969, emphasises the importance of an infant's long-lasting emotional connection with a meaningful person who soothes them in times of stress.[216] Ann's development, resilience and long-term wellbeing may, therefore, have been threatened by the death of her mother and siblings and her sister's move to Upwell.

Our infant attachments also shape how we will react to situations and the people around us. This is important in my attempt to understand Walter because the theory explains that a parent who has unresolved loss can become dissociative and display 'a range of perplexing behaviours during parenting, including dissociative-like stilling, distorted and frightening facial and vocal expressions and poorly timed, rough or intrusive caregiving'.[217] The disorganised attachment style that results can lead to 'dramatic effects on a child's emotional development'.[218] It is also known that those dependent upon alcohol rarely have securely attached children. Most addicts manifest immense distrust in their relationships, often avoiding emotional openness and intimacy with others.[219] Although a secure attachment can be gained through positive relationships in later life, our original attachment style often stays with us over our lifetime and can be transmitted in some form or other to subsequent generations.[220] Griffin reminds us that historically 'harsh and distant mothering was not regarded as problematic or abnormal' but was part of a 'widely shared cultural belief within many working-class families that mothers should not overindulge their children'.[221] What chance did Walter and his siblings have to avoid a toxic legacy?

Looking through the lens of attachment theory we can note 'the association between insecure attachment and substance use was especially strong for nicotine/tobacco as compared with other drug classes' and consider that Walter was a lifelong pipe smoker.[222] It is interesting to note that Walter may have defensively withdrawn from others and attempted to achieve a high degree of self-sufficiency.[223] Whether we believe co-dependency or attachment issues cause maladaptive behaviour, the tragedy is that studies repeatedly show that close relationships play a vital part in our happiness, health and general wellbeing.[224]

The transmission of mental health issues across generations is being explored. Some believe that anxiety, panic attacks, depression and self-destructive patterns that have no apparent basis in the present may result from a transferred defence mechanism. I believe we can absorb the patterns of behaviour that have served the previous generations. Three common unconscious defence mechanisms are repression, projection, and splitting. Repression is where we shift out of our conscious mind the awareness of what cannot be coped with. Projection is our way of shifting what we dare not own ourselves onto someone else. When we cannot manage the complex reality of both good and bad existing at the same time, we might cope by splitting parts of our self.

Psychoanalyst Melanie Klein demonstrated how unconscious influences, with roots in pre-verbal infancy, impact adult perception.[225] Psychologist Paula Nicolson agrees that even our earliest experiences are not 'passively accepted – they arouse feelings and can shape how we respond to those feelings throughout our lives'.[226] Nicolson makes the fascinating link with how our conscious, unconscious and social influences are transmitted across generations. Such experiences can deplete our resilience, making it difficult, or maybe even impossible, for some to recover from adversity.

Considering these theories to Ann's case is a rewarding exercise. Ann's granddaughter Mary told me in 2013:

> *Unlike my father's mother, Granny Parker did not touch people, smile, or laugh. She was a difficult woman, with no friends, whose behaviour often left me in confused tears. Granny appeared to be as unhappy as she looked in her photographs.*

Although Ann's demeanour as described by Cousin Mary cannot be symptomatic of an alcohol use disorder, we can surmise that insecure attachment diminished Ann's ability to cope with the tragic death of her first child. It would have been remarkable if Ann had avoided anxiety or depression, either or both of which could have been the precursor to her drinking, possibly triggered by postnatal depression or a genetic inheritance.[227]

Postnatal depression also affects fathers and young women at eighteen whose fathers had experienced depression after their birth were themselves at higher risk.[228] Mental illness in Ann's father, James could have increased Ann's chances of poor mental health. A paternal postnatal depression campaigner by the name of Mark Williams remarked that fathers' depression 'impacts on the whole family [...] often resulting in [them] using negative coping skills, avoiding situations, and feeling anger'.[229]

In a dysfunctional family, the individuals are expected to be fiercely loyal. A culture can become established where the children take care of the adults. A system of 'family bookkeeping' can develop that keeps track of merits and debts. However, justice, as defined by the family, is only ever roughly served. Those who suffer injustices still hurt and the debts can become an inheritance paid for by future generations.[230] Whichever way Walter's family was organised, the most important things were likely hinted at, communicated through body language and facial expressions, or had to be arrived at through cryptic reward and punishment.[231] We cannot witness Walter's first years. Still, I wonder if what his daughter Doreen thought of as his being a 'Victorian' father, i.e. emotionally absent, was as much, if not more, about his psychological inheritance and the coping mechanisms he developed as a child living with a depressed alcoholic parent.

Family tree

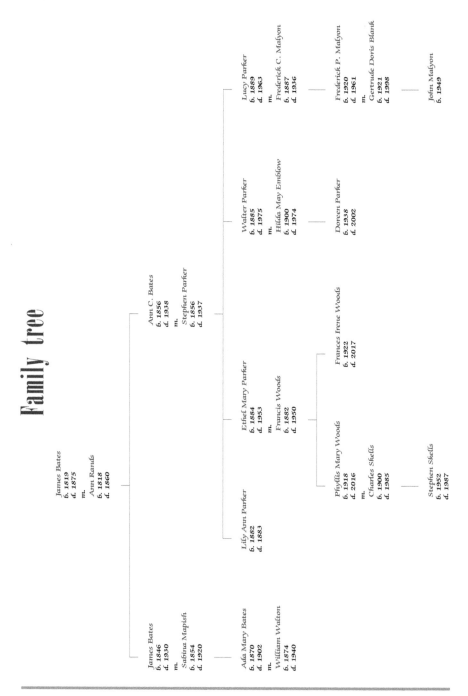

James Bates
b. 1819
d. 1875
m.
Ann Rands
b. 1818
d. 1860

Ann C. Bates
b. 1856
d. 1938
m.
Stephen Parker
b. 1856
d. 1937

Lucy Parker
b. 1889
d. 1963
m.
Frederick C. Mafyon
b. 1887
d. 1936

Frederick P. Mafyon
b. 1920
d. 1961
m.
Gertrude Doris Blank
b. 1921
d. 1998

John Mafyon
b. 1949

Walter Parker
b. 1885
d. 1975
m.
Hilda May Emblow
b. 1900
d. 1974

Doreen Parker
b. 1938
d. 2002

James Bates
b. 1846
d. 1930
m.
Sabina Mapish
b. 1854
d. 1920

Ethel Mary Parker
b. 1884
d. 1953
m.
Francis Woods
b. 1882
d. 1950

Frances Irene Woods
b. 1922
d. 2017

Lily Ann Parker
b. 1882
d. 1883

Phyllis Mary Woods
b. 1918
d. 2016
m.
Charles Skells
b. 1900
d. 1985

Stephen Skells
b. 1952
d. 1987

Ada Mary Bates
b. 1870
d. 1902
m.
William Walton
b. 1874
d. 1940

CHAPTER 5

School and Education

Walter Parker was six years old when he was enrolled at the infant school in Thorney on 28 March 1892, with his five-year-old sister, Lily.[232] They were two of seventy-eight students under the watchful eye of Miss Annie Crabb, the Board School Mistress of the Infant School.[233] Ethel, at eight years old, entered the girls'

Thorney Infant and Girls' School.
*Photograph supplied with the kind permission of John Clark,
Chris Lane and the Thorney Society.*

school next door. It had eighty-nine pupils. Their School Mistress was Miss Laura Crabb, the elder of the two sisters.[234] They shared an assistant, Miss Gray.[235] Annie Peach was the paid monitor.[236] Walter's father, Stephen, must have valued education, as even as late as 1930 only half of five to seven-year-olds attended infant school.[237] It may have helped that he did not have to pay school fees, as these had been abolished the year before.

We are fortunate that headteachers were instructed to keep a logbook to include the 'introduction of new books, apparatus, or courses of instruction, any lesson plans approved by the inspector...absence, illness or any special circumstances affecting the school'.[238] These school journals were read and often commented on by the school inspector. Not all the Thorney school logs have survived, but the Cambridgeshire archive holds logbooks for the girls' school 1863–1895 and 1895–1907, and the infant and girls' school and boys' school 1910–1940.[239] While they are rarely specific to individual children, they can provide snippets of information that paint a vivid picture of school life. Reading them, I was struck by an unchanging rhythm through the school year reminiscent of my school days (1967–1979). Given how similar Mary's experience was to these accounts, I believe these sources can give us a flavour of Walter's time in the boys' school.

The Girl's Schoolroom, 2015.
The wear on the stone has been explained by a village story. Apparently, generations of lads have stood on these stones, hands up to block the light as they peeked at the girls in their classroom.
Photograph taken from the author's collection.

The staff supervised large classes. Walter was taught in a mixed age and ability group. Children often repeated by rote what the teacher, or their assistant, said, or copied from the blackboard. As an infant, Walter used his finger or a wooden skewer to form his first letters and numbers in a tray filled with fine damp sand. Once deemed ready, Walter was given a slate on which to work sums or practise his writing. If a child made a mistake, they wiped the slate clean with a damp rag and started again. In the classroom's silence, we can imagine the screech of slate pencils as the youngsters scraped their lessons.

Walter's youth was preceded by a broader, national debate on the purpose of education. Not long before, in 1870, Gladstone's government had introduced compulsory elementary education for children between the ages of five and thirteen.[240] Widely hailed as a progressive reform, it has since come under criticism as a covert attempt to produce generations of obedient children who cannot think critically, ensuring a steady supply of compliant and submissive workers for Britain's industries. However, the perceived 'opposition' of major employers, industrialists and large landowners to compulsory education is debatable and should not be assumed. Regardless, some employers, such as the Dukes of Bedford, were convinced that:

> *Although there was no legal obligation [...] to educate the children of the labourers, the social obligation to do so was accepted as one of the conditions of ownership [of the estate] and in this spirit was discharged as a matter of duty.*[241]

According to the same 1897 account, all three schools and the church in Thorney drained the Duke's estate of £978 [£126,063] a year; whereas the 1891 Elementary Education Act provided only ten shillings [£151] a year, to be paid as a fee grant by Parliament, for

each child aged three to fifteen attending an elementary school. In 1892 the sum of £15-17s-6d [£2,390] was paid as a quarterly grant.[242]

In Thorney, the purpose of boys' education was to prepare them for work as agricultural labourers for one of the Duke's tenant farmers. They were taught reading, writing and arithmetic competency, (the 'three Rs'), alongside grammar, the acceptance of the teacher's authority and the need for punctuality and conformity. Drawing was made compulsory in boys' schools by the Government Code of 1890 'unless certified impracticable'.[243]

All children attending school were expected to write letters in a clear, legible hand by the time they left.[244] Education was little more than preparation for future adult work, to teach thrift and the required social character – habits of regularity, self-discipline, obedience, and trained effort.[245]

For Walter and his sisters, education was primarily delivered under the Code of Regulations for the 1862 system, where children were examined according to one of six 'standards' in reading, writing and arithmetic. Teachers were expected to get as many children through the exams as possible and, as the educationalist and historian Brian Simon said, 'the most effective way of doing this, especially with very large classes, was by rote learning and drilling'.[246] Children often learnt their reading books off by heart, as did Cousin Mary in the 1920s. The goal was disastrous to learning. Simon writes: 'No system could have been better designed to limit and stultify the educational process.'[247]

Inspectors who supported the principle of the Revised Code reported its deadening and disheartening effects. The need to drill the children to meet the inspection requirements was reflected in the schools' activities throughout the year. Frequent testing became the norm. Some of the improvements of the 1850s in curriculum and method in many schools were cut short.[248] Writing in 1911, former inspector Edmond Holmes described the process as 'that deadly system' which seemed to have been devised for 'the express purpose of arresting growth and strangling life'.[249] Article 108 of the Code of 1885 stated that infants should be instructed suitably for their age, and in the Code of 1889 this phrase was expanded to read 'suitably to their age and capacity'.[250] Teachers were given further guidance in 1893 to follow 'the child's spontaneous activity'.

> *The teacher should pay especial regard to the love of movement, which can alone secure healthy physical conditions; to the observant use of the organs of sense, especially those of sight and touch; and to that eager desire of questioning which intelligent children exhibit. All these should be encouraged under due limitations, and should be developed simultaneously, so that each stage of development may be complete in itself.[251]*

In recognition of young children's needs lessons were interspersed with rest, song, and stories:

> *It is essential, therefore, that the length of the lesson should not, in any case, exceed 30 minutes, and should, as a rule, last only 20 minutes, and that the lessons should be varied in length according to the Section of the school, so that in the babies' room the actual work of the lesson should not be more than a quarter of an hour. Each lesson should also be followed by intervals of rest and song; the subjects of lessons should be varied, beginning in the lowest Section with familiar objects and animals, and interspersed with songs and stories appropriate to the lesson; the spontaneous and co-operative activity of the scholars should form the object and animate the spirit of each lesson'.[252]*

We know from the school logs that Walter and his sisters learnt from readers produced by Blackie & Son Ltd and the Blackwood publishing house, which produced an extensive list of educational texts.[253] Reading practice, recitation and poetry pieces were chosen as suitable for the standard the pupils were working towards using *Green's Poetry Cards* and *My Sunday Friend* by Reverend G. H. Curtis, produced between 1870 and 1884. Children were encouraged to recite the songs, portions of scripture and poetry they learnt at social gatherings as their 'turn'. In 1891 the girls' poetry recitation for Standard II was the thirteen-verse 'The Spring Walk' by Thomas Miller.[254] It starts:

> We had a pleasant walk today,
> Over the meadows and far away,
> Across the bridge by the water-mill,
> By the woodside, and up the hill;
> And if you listen to what I say,
> I'll tell you what we saw to-day.

For Standard III the girls were expected to learn William Wordsworth poem 'The Idle Shepherd Boys'.[255] It has nine long verses and begins:

> The valley rings with mirth and joy;
> Among the hills the echoes play
> A never, never ending song,
> To welcome in the May.

Older children were instructed in history and geography. Modelling, drawing, painting, scripture and times-tables were also part of the curriculum.[256] An art master from Wisbech visited the girl's school to 'advise about drawing'.[257] If the weather remained dry, 'games' took place on Friday afternoons. Physical education, or 'drill', was Walter's favourite part of the week, and was carefully thought out.[258]

Physical exercises are best carried on simultaneously with the development of the reasoning faculties, in the pauses which are needful for the repose of these faculties; they afford that relief which is so essential when the mind has been actively engaged. The means in use at some of the infants' schools, and others that are recommended, are, 1st, a well-ventilated and lofty school-room; 2nd, muscular motion, introduced both into their lessons and their amusements; 3rd, easy gymnastic exercises, adapted both for the open air and for the school-room; 4th, social games, or plays; 5th, useful employments, to accustom them early to habits of industry. ...we would also suggest an open shed, for shelter and exercise in wet weather.[259]

The school logs show that the Church of England ministers were regular visitors to the infant and girls' schools. The Reverend William Symons was recorded as visiting several times a week to listen to the children read or recite. Walter received scripture lessons twice a week. These were delivered in turn by the church leaders from the Abbey and the chapel. After each lesson, it would not be unusual for the children to be given a lecture on morals and behaviour.

As in my classroom, the children could not talk during lessons, and a log tells us of a girl being punished for 'writing a note to a boy and speaking untruths'.[260] We also learn the schoolroom was heated by an open fire, without a guard, over which an older pupil was trusted to make watery cocoa for the children on bitter days. One February, to keep pupils warm, the teachers set the children 'marching to promote circulation'.[261] The teachers monitored the temperature carefully. For example, the school temperature was below 45 degrees *Fahrenheit [7 degrees Celsius]* at 9 a.m. for 44 days, or below 50 degrees *Fahrenheit [10 degrees Celsius]* at 10 a.m. for 39 days.[262] Yet for decades the

school was closed periodically because the rooms were deemed too cold for the children to concentrate on learning.

Walter reached an average Standard III when he left the schoolroom on 27 May 1898, having just turned thirteen. Standard III comprised:

Reading	A short paragraph from an elementary reading book used in the school.
Writing	A sentence from the same, slowly read once, and then dictated in single words.
Arithmetic	A sum in any simple rule as far as short division, (inclusive)[263]

A farmer gave one thousand and eighteen pounds four shillings for five cows. The price of one of them was £409, 12s. 6d., another cost £117, 3s. 8d., and two others cost £99 each. What did he pay for the fifth cow?

Add: 19s. 10d + £4004 2 0¾ + £950 17 8½ + £2,012,019 3 11 + £504,640 18 9¾ + £7 15 8¼

A bricklayer puts by 3s. 9d. a week out of his wages, and he spends £1, 11s. 6d. a week: how much does he earn?

Compound Subtraction

£	s.	d.
20,710	14	2½
4,983	17	3¾
15,726	16	7¾

When you have finished each sum add the number you have subtracted and the remainder together; if your sum is right; the total of these two is the top line of the sum. It is not necessary to do this with pen or pencil; just run it over in your mind, noticing whether it is right or not as you go along.[264]

Girls' education

According to the 1901 curriculum, it would appear that the lessons for standards I, II and III for the year ending February 1901 concentrated on the three kingdoms of nature, including:

Animal Kingdom.
- I   Beast of burden. Horse. Camel. Elephant.
- II   Beast & Bird of Prey. Lion. Tiger. Eagle. Owl.
- III   Domestic animals. Dog. Cat.
- IV   Animals used for food. Cows. Sheep. Pigs. Fowls.

Vegetable Kingdom.
- I   Grain. Corn. Wheat.
- II   Trees. Oak. Chestnut.
- III   Flowers. Buttercup. Daisy.

Mineral Kingdom.
  Minerals. A mine: Coal. Slate. Salt.[265]

Rain, clouds, snow, and sun were covered under 'Natural phenomena'. Rainbows, flowers, and holidays were suggested as suitable subjects for conversational lessons. Standard III covered much of the same ground, presumably in more depth. Under item IV, the conversational lesson was 'The Tea-Service and Dinner Service'.[266] I assume 'appropriate' behaviour and manners were touched on here. The instruction included: 'Sitting room furniture, dish, plate, glass, cup and saucer, milk, butter, salt, sponge'.[267] A doll's tea party seems incongruous, but it could have served those girls whose home life did not recognise this societal norm. The last item in the 1901 Syllabus for Girls appears to be 'money'. Pupils were given lessons on thrift; for example, by one of the Thorney ministers, Reverend Doubleday in 1894.[268]

Ethel Parker's school photo, 1894.
Ethel is in the first long row – bottom, far left.
Photograph kindly supplied by the Thorney Museum (Eric Rayner).

Thorney school for girls, Church Street, c1890.
From the author's collection.

Walter's sisters were taught skills that were expected of working-class women: needlework, knitting and crochet. In 1892 materials costing £2-1s-5d [£328] were bought by the school. The work produced was sold to support it. The girls sold items to the value of £17-10s-5d [£2,300], while the efforts of the infant girls raised a further £3-9s-5d [£520]. The girls' endeavours were often inspected by women from prosperous families, like Mrs and Miss Topham and Mrs and Miss Maxwell, who called to see the children's needlework on 17 March 1893. The 'sales-of-work' raised enough to pay Miss Annie Crabb her annual salary of £17-10s [£2,293].[269]

Making the traditional Thorney lace was a popular pastime for girls. Ethel, Lily and Lucy were also taught first aid, washing, folding, cooking, and housekeeping. Female pupils were often expected to keep the school clean as part of their 'education'. On 22 November 1894, a pupil-teacher gave the girls 'a lesson on domestic service'.[270]

The school day, attendance, and wider learning

Walter's school day started before 9 a.m., with the teacher calling out pupils' names and marking the register. A Bible reading and the singing of a hymn followed. Referring to the 9th Duke, the 11th Duke wrote: 'He held that the minds of children were greatly affected by their physical environment, and he sought to give them bright and healthy surroundings in their homes and schoolrooms.'[271] The high-ceilinged schoolroom (which measured 37 feet long and 18 feet wide, with the roof apex 23 feet high) may have been bright, but I know from my visits that the high windows, which allowed for colourful, instructive posters on the walls, stopped the children staring outward.[272] A curtain separated the infant classes from the older girls' classes.[273]

Walter and his sisters ate their main meal at midday (called dinner) at home, probably with both their parents. So, Walter's generation had an extended meal break to allow the pupils time to travel home. Those who lived too far away to make it home and back in time would stay in the classroom and eat a hunk of bread with a wedge of cheese or, more commonly, bread spread with salted dripping (fat that has melted and dripped from roasting meat, eaten cold as a spread). Walter returned for the afternoon session at 1.45 p.m. Walter's day finished with a prayer at 4 p.m., when the teacher dismissed him.

Schools strived for high attendance, and the reasons children were absent had to be logged, along with an overall percentage for attendance. The numbers in school were important, as they affected the school's income from the local board. It was usual for children to be sent home if they arrived late. This was effective as school attendance determined when the children could legally start work. An attendance officer acted as a liaison between the school and home.

> *These were frequently part-time and badly paid posts and attendance officers also faced hostility and abuse from parents who resented their interference in family affairs. Unsurprisingly attendance officers were not always diligent in carrying out their duties.*[274]

Pupils who walked over a mile each way were given some leeway as they had to cover rough ground which was difficult for short legs especially after snow, heavy rain or when there were strong winds. Absence from school because of awful weather may seem strange to us now, but Victorian mothers understood what science now confirms: their families were more at risk of illness after exposure to frigid temperatures.[275]

Agricultural work could also keep children out of school, for example:

> *Attendance poor: children absent for potato picking.*[276]
> *Annie Brown returned from field work on Tuesday morning.*[277]

According to the 1880 Education Act:

> *Legal exemption [from school] could only [be] granted on a part-time basis if the child had passed the age of ten and if the specified number of attendances had been made. Complete exemption below the age of fourteen depended upon the child passing his 'Labour certificate' at the standard laid down by the education bylaws in his own school district. This was commonly Standard IV or Standard V. Otherwise exemption could be given to a child of thirteen who had 250 attendances, per annum, in the previous five years.*[278]

Therefore, those who had been examined and obtained a labour certificate could leave school and start work before they reached thirteen years of age.[279]

Walter transferred from the infant school to the boys' school at the age of seven. The headmaster was Alfred Law.[280] When the school was opened, in 1875, it was expected to accommodate 120 boys. It later had an average attendance of forty-eight boys in the compact space. Even with less than half its expected capacity, a log entry commented on 'foul air' and recommended better ventilation.[281] The need for instruction in the theory and practice of agriculture was not recognised until the Education Act until 1902. By 1901 however it could be argued the change came too late because the number of males aged ten and over employed in agriculture had fallen to 9.5 per cent, even though 23 per cent of the population was rural.[282] Rural teachers were encouraged to attend summer schools in Cambridge or winter schools in Norwich, yet still 'only 8 per cent of boys' schools had gardening'.[283]

I believe the boys were given similar instruction on thrift as that given to the girls. It would have been an opportunity to highlight one of the values men lived by, as laid down in an 1866 book by best-selling author Samuel Smiles (1812–1904):

> *Every man ought to so contrive as to live within his means. This practice is at the very essence of honesty. For, if a man does not manage honestly to live within his own means, he must necessarily be living dishonestly, upon the means of someone else.*[284]

Direction on frugality also highlighted the importance of saving for a 'rainy day'. In 1898 the mayor of Peterborough, at a meeting to float a new building society, extolled the virtues of financial planning to all working men:

> *[Some men] persistently fool their money away without having first endeavoured to make some provision for the future... He urged every young working man to religiously put something by before he gratified every little whim and fancy.*[285]

As was typical, living independently in a thrifty manner and saving were valued and essential lifelong pursuits for Walter.

I believe Stephen took his responsibility towards Walter seriously and did not leave his education solely in the hands of teachers. Cousin Mary talked of her grandfather's tireless encouragement saying that he asked 'intelligent questions'. Mary explained, he was keen on bettering himself and wanted us to make the best of our opportunities and our education. Stephen's attitude tallies with working-class efforts in self-improvement captured by Smiles. In *Self-Help: With Illustrations of Character and Conduct*, Smiles stresses the importance of character, thrift and perseverance, but also celebrates civility, independence and individuality.[286] The book aimed to show men how best to take advantage of the changes being brought about by the Industrial Revolution.

Influential social reformer Octavia Hill was also a passionate believer that the poor should be encouraged to help themselves, and that philanthropic efforts should be avoided because they create dependency.[287] A letter to a fellow worker in 1890 reads:

> *We have made many mistakes with our alms: Eaten out the heart of the independent, bolstered up the drunkard in his indulgence, subsidised wages, discouraged thrift, assumed that many of the most ordinary wants of a working man's family must be met by our wretched and intermittent doles.*[288]

I like to think Stephen actively promoted free, independent thinking in all his children and grandchildren. Still, I wonder if Walter, as the only son, was particularly encouraged to grab any learning opportunity, to think for himself and escape the family dynamic. Mary told me that Stephen was an active member of both the reading and newsroom, and it seems probable that he was part of the Thorney Mutual Improvement Society referred to in the *Kelly's Directory* of 1883.[289]

The impression of Stephen I received from Cousin Mary leads me to consider whether Walter's attachment to his pa, or elements of Stephen's personality, mitigated some of the damage inflicted by his wife's alcoholism.[290] A voracious reader, Stephen could have found parenting guidance in the 1838 publication of *Young Men; or an Appeal to the Several Classes of Society in Their Behalf* by the Reverend Stephen Davies, which remains in the reading room collection in the Thorney Museum. Did Stephen take to heart the directive that 'a select library should be formed for the use of the young men, and the respective families'?[291] Certainly, Cousin Mary said Stephen was proud of his well-filled, handcrafted bookcases. Perhaps he

The Men's Reading Room, Whittlesey Road, Thorney.
Photograph supplied with the kind permission of John Clark,
Chris Lane and the Thorney Society.

asked himself 'in what way, and by what means he [could], as a parent, most effectively promote the welfare of young men in his own family'.[292]

While Stephen may have found some instructions in *Young Men*, old-fashioned parents have often turned to the previous generation when seeking guidance for raising children. Stephen's energy, questioning way and willingness to take responsibility to bring about change could have found fertile ground in Walter. Such notions are unproven, yet I believe them worth considering, as Stephen would have been a powerful influence on Walter's developing values, and his way of thinking about the world and his place in it.

Expectations of children and their responsibilities

Young people were expected to conform to particular standards of behaviour and morals.[293] According to *The Boy Makes The Man: A Book Of Anecdotes And Examples For The Use Of Youth* the Victorians believed thoroughness should be the maxim of 'every brave English youth'. 'Until a thing is done keep doing. Let no obstacles daunt you and let repeated failure spur you to repeated effort.'[294] Such sustained effort was thought necessary because:

> *The world judges us by our conduct; it has neither the time nor the inclination to study our character; moreover, it assumes that our conduct is necessarily the reflex of our character.*[295]

Walter, in his village controlled by the Duke's men, was expected to be unquestioningly respectful, and well-mannered, especially to his 'elders and betters'. This expectation is illustrated by the many moral stories and poems published for children during Queen Victoria's reign, of which the following was a well-known example:

Table Rules for Little Folks

by
Eliza R. Snow Smith[296]

In silence I must take my seat,
And give God thanks, before I eat
Must for my food, in silence wait
Till I am asked to hand my plate.
I must not scold, nor whine, nor pout,
Nor move my chair or plate about.
With knife, or fork or anything,
I must not play, nor must I sing.

I must not speak a useless word
For children should be seen – not heard.
I must not say, 'The bread is old' –
'The meat is hot' – 'the milk is cold.'
I must not cry for this, or that,
Nor murmur if my meat is fat;
My mouth with food I must not crowd,
Nor while I'm eating, speak aloud.

The table-cloth I must not spoil,
Nor with my food my fingers soil –
Must keep my seat, when I have done,

Nor round the table sport or run;
When told to rise, then I must put
My chair away, with noiseless foot,
And lift my heart to God above,
In praise for all his wondrous love.

However, such poems may have been holding up an ideal, for Ruth Colton, an Early Career Research Fellow at the University of Manchester, discovered, in her research in public parks, that children, at least city ones, did not always live up to these standards of behaviour. Cycling, rounders, cricket, and football were only allowed at certain times of the year and in particular parks. The Parks Committee minutes contain many accounts of prosecutions for various offences, and many adults fell foul of the overly judicious enforcement of these rules. Stealing cherries, damaging trees, and fishing in the park lakes were usually offences committed by children and therefore not severely prosecuted.[297] If the poem describes expectation, I would understand if Walter and his peers preferred to be outside away from watching eyes. But, before Walter could escape the cottage, convention dictated that he had to contribute meaningfully to the running of the household.

Helping with chores was a practical measure which had an effect on children's progress. According to Erickson's stages of development, at ages six to twelve, children engaging in activities with others builds competence. They learn how to move from 'can't do' to 'can do'. By succeeding at household tasks, children gain new skills and knowledge and learn the virtues of method and competence. If a child cannot take part in activities with others and gain skills, followers of Erikson suggest the child can develop a sense of inferiority. If the child believes they are making too many mistakes, they may experience shame, which inhibits further initiative.

Walter and his peers brought in the coal for the fire and oven, cleaned and shopped, along with fetching and carrying. Foraging throughout the year for wild herbs, watercress, raspberries, plums, blackberries, crab apples, violets, rose leaves, hips and mushrooms was also part of a Thorney childhood. Children were expected to help manage the compost heap, lift stones from the soil, plant seeds, water, and pick crops. As Walter grew older, he was trusted to climb the clock tower once a week to wind the village timepiece, and to help his father maintain the pumps in the Tank Yard.

The Bedford Hall Clock, the Tank Yard.
Photograph supplied with the kind permission of John Clark,
Chris Lane and the Thorney Society.

Watching his pa plan and carry out carpentry projects gave Walter a sense of what could be achieved. Stephen was an active member of the Horticultural Society and rented an allotment where Walter helped grow food for the table. Many enterprising boys shovelled horse manure from the roads to sell or enrich the earth in their family allotments. Children collected snails, sow thistle, dandelion and choice grass to supplement the barley meal and pot-liquor made of boiled potato peelings and vegetable trimmings to be fed to their pig.

Older boys and girls still at school were often used at fixed wages in their time off. They helped with the turnip hoeing and took the elevenses and fourses into the fields. Some boys were given the responsibility to lead the wagon horses. At harvest time, both boys and girls were employed as bind-pullers. The bind-puller worked with a tier-up (the man or woman who came after the reaper) and tied the wheat, oat, or barley into sheaves. When the cradle or horns attachment was used with the scythe, it would leave the wheat or oats that had been cut leaning against the standing crop.[298] The tier-up put his foot underneath a bunch of grain to help him lift it into his arms. Meanwhile, the boy or girl acting as his bind-puller pulled out three sheaves from a bunch lying nearby and would be ready to hand these to the tier-up when he was ready to make his knot.[299]

Many women and children gathered the stalks left after the harvest (a practice known as gleaning). The grain was bound into miniature sheaves and dropped into a linen bag carried by many of the gleaners. This grain would be added to any the family had grown on their allotment and stored until it could be threshed. The long summer break was pragmatically created to release children to help their families with the main harvest. This gave the recess the name of Harvest Holiday. In England we no longer refer to it as such, but it remains the longest vacation of the school year.[300]

Ever practical, the school boards timed other holidays to allow the gathering of food. Cousin Sue fondly remembers her time picking strawberries in Upwell, having been released from primary school with her peers for the task.[301] Sue told me the whole village smelled enticingly of the ripe fruit. But important as the work was, it was not considered all that was needed for a balanced life. Sermons reminded people of the need for

*Strawberries picked in the Upwell area being loaded
for the Bradford market at Wisbech East, Somers Road, Wisbech.*
Wisbech East, Somers Road entrance with the weighbridge office on the right:
Strawberries picked in the Upwell area being loaded for Bradford market.
The art of stacking strawberries was to build the strawberry 'chips' into pyramids
that did not topple when shunted.
Facebook: Wisbech and Surrounding Villages Old Photos.

*Strawberries picked in Upwell being unloaded at Wisbech East,
Somers Road, Wisbech.*
The Wisbech East, Somers Road entrance with the weighbridge office on the right.
Facebook: Wisbech and Surrounding Villages Old Photos.

regular periods of rest and renewal. Sir James Sawyer, a well-known physician of Birmingham, explained in a local newspaper that one secret of longevity is a 'change in occupation'.[302] We therefore look next at Walter's leisure opportunities.

Family tree

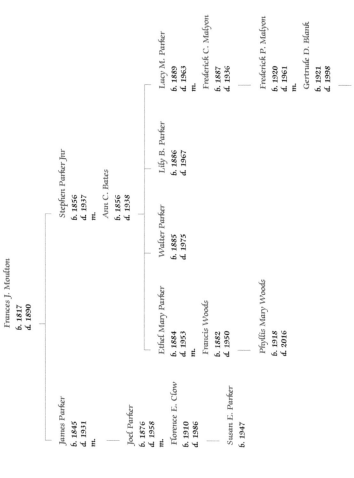

Stephen Parker Snr
b. 1816
d. 1895
m.

Frances J. Moulton
b. 1817
d. 1890

James Parker
b. 1845
d. 1931
m.

Joel Parker
b. 1876
d. 1958
m.

Florence E. Clow
b. 1910
d. 1986

Susan E. Parker
b. 1947

Stephen Parker Jnr
b. 1856
d. 1937
m.

Ann C. Bates
b. 1856
d. 1938

Ethel Mary Parker
b. 1884
d. 1953
m.

Francis Woods
b. 1882
d. 1950

Phyllis Mary Woods
b. 1918
d. 2016

Walter Parker
b. 1885
d. 1975

Lily B. Parker
b. 1886
d. 1967

Lucy M. Parker
b. 1889
d. 1963
m.

Frederick C. Malyon
b. 1887
d. 1936

Frederick P. Malyon
b. 1920
d. 1961
m.

Gertrude D. Blank
b. 1921
d. 1998

John Malyon
b. 1949

https://tinyurl.com/y6fhjf7p

https://tinyurl.com/yywtnoyq

CHAPTER 6

Traditional Games and Pastimes

The dark winter afternoons saw Walter and his sisters cooped up in the kitchen, taking turns to sit close to the range, where they roasted one side of their body while the other side froze. Thrown together, they played games. Draughts, chess, dominoes and long, complicated card games might have helped them forget Ann's challenging behaviour. Cribbage, or crib, was a favourite game of Walter's and he made many boards.[303] Originally a pub game, cribbage can be played quickly. While it is usually played by two players, it can be played by three or four. The object of the game is to complete two circuits of the cribbage board before your opponent. Points are collected by combining cards together to make 'runs' or scoring combinations. You need to reach 61 or 121 points to win the game. While the mathematics are simple, cribbage is a game of tactics and strategy. Sometimes you try to score points; at others, your goal is to stop your opponent from scoring; every game is subtly different. The family used spent matches for counting the points earned.

The Parker children may also have played 'Snakes and Ladders' and 'Tiddlywinks'. Snakes and Ladders originated in India and was released in England in 1892 when Walter was

Snakes and Ladders.

*Photograph with permission from the
Forgotten Toy Shop.*

six years old. It caught on quickly. The affordable game was redesigned to reflect Christian virtues and morals, with each snake or ladder linking causes to effects.[304] Buttons or stones were used as counters. Tiddlywinks was invented by Joseph Assheton Fincher who filed a patent for it in 1888. It had been an adult craze, but by 1892 it was described as a 'favourite' children's game and sold for 8 1/2d [£4.58].[305] It requires an impressive amount of perseverance to become a skilled player. The two key ingredients of Tiddlywinks rules have changed little since 1890:

The offensive shot is shooting a wink toward a target and having the wink land on or in the target. In modern terms, when a wink lands inside the targeted cup, it is deemed potted and earns more points. The defensive shot is shooting a wink so it lands on top of an opponent wink. The opponent wink cannot be used by the opponent while it is covered....In rules from the 1890s, it was not proper to intentionally cover an opponent's wink with yours, but if it did happen, perhaps accidentally, the opponent still was not allowed to shoot his wink.[306]

Gas light was particularly suited to shadow shows acted out on the lime-washed walls.[307] Gas lit homes had come to many of Thorney's cottages by 1860. This was early, considering that the new Houses of Parliament were fitted with a gas supply in 1859. All over the country, 'smaller towns and villages [remained lit] by candles and oil lamps'.[308] Suggested finger positions to create animal shapes were often printed in comic strips. These were distributed by the rail network and stocked by newsagents, such as the grocery shop J. Amps'.[309] Some children's comics were sold at half an old penny [£0.27], such as *Comic Cuts* and *Funny Cuts*.[310]

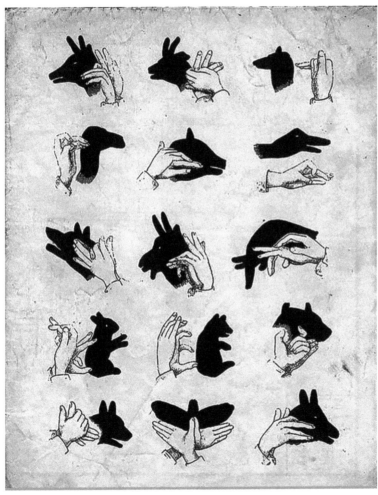

Shadow hands, 1898.
From *Nouveau Larousse illustre; dictionnaire universel encyclopedique.*
Paris: Librairie Larousse.

A love of reading

According to Cousin Mary, Walter's pa was passionate about reading for pleasure and education. I wonder if Stephen also enjoyed novels, despite the press they received. In 1902 a T. Stoby wrote in the *Peterborough Advertiser*:

> *Novel-reading never made a man, least not a man of the type England, the world, needs to-day, and never will. A good novel is [a] good thing – in its place; that is, for recreation, for inspiration, even in a sense for educational purposes. For some novels may help to do that, though, alas! The majority as provided to-day are more calculated to do the reverse – to wither and emasculate a growing man's powers. For it cannot be too often repeated that the ordinary novel does little or nothing to cultivate the intellectual powers but a great deal to stir up the passions and emotions.*[311]

He went so far as to say, 'That way corruption lies.' However, might have Stephen encouraged Walter, agreeing only with Stoby's suggestion that:

> *A story may give a view of the world, or of a certain aspect of life, well calculated to stir the imagination of [a] boy or a young man just beginning life, and so may give him a start, get him out [of] the old rut, and determine him to try to do something effective in the world.*[312]

Reading novels was considered a suitable pursuit for women, 'and for many cribbed, cabined, and confined as their lives are, with so little outlet for their emotions, they are a wholesome necessity'.[313] The Thorney entry in the *Kelly's Directory* of Cambridgeshire of 1904 tells of the Literary Society, founded in 1854. It had a 'news-room, bagatelle room and a library of 500 volumes'.[314] The library was visited by Walter's father, who no doubt

Bagatelle games table.
Antique bagatelle games table chess board top.
Photographer Andreas Praefcke, 2008.

borrowed books to read aloud to his family. This had the added advantage of limiting conversation, which could have been useful when his wife was drunk.[315]

Walter was a lifelong, voracious reader. I can picture him devouring stories that transported him to another time or place. Books such as *Robinson Crusoe* by Daniel Defoe[316] (first published in 1719), the coming of age tale *Treasure Island* by Robert Louis Stevenson (published in book form in 1883), *The Time Machine, The Invisible Man* and *The War of the*

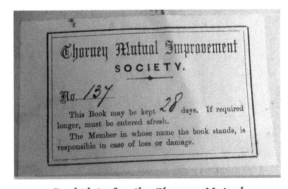

Bookplate for the Thorney Mutual Improvement Society.
From the author's collection.

Worlds by H. G. Wells, or Dracula by Bram Stoker (all published in the 1890s) might have found their way into the Parker home or the novel section of the Thorney Mutual Improvement Society. The

Sherlock Holmes stories by Arthur Conan Doyle were published in Walter's youth in *The Strand* magazine. The adventures of Captain James Cook, George Everest, David Livingstone, Robert Scott, and Ernest Shackleton were in enormous demand. These, along with encyclopaedia entries about faraway places, might have encouraged Walter to imagine a different life and later might have influenced his decision to travel.

The Boy's Own Paper, 11 April 1891.
Photographer Michael Maggs; in the public domain via Wikimedia Commons.

While his pa pored over the local newspapers, Walter may have preferred the *Boy's Own Paper*. This publication carried improbable or daring adventure stories with well-intentioned heroes trying to right wrongs, alongside pieces on nature and sports, including ice-skating, and games and puzzles. If Walter wanted more stimulation then Peterborough, with its lending and reference library, was a bicycle ride away.[317]

Outdoor pastimes

Once his daily chores were done, Walter was expected to be out from under adult feet and in the fresh air. In the Fens, Walter was surrounded by wildlife in a unique ecosystem. The nearby Wash harboured fish, seals, and wading birds. At varying

Peterborough library.

The public opening of the Peterborough Library reading room was on the 29 September 1892, followed by the lending and reference libraries on 10 April 1893.
From the author's collection.

times of the year, it was home to migrating birds, some from as far away as the Arctic Circle. Eel catchers glided silently through the waterways, checking their baited willow hives for the snake-like fish, as they had done for millennia.[318] Owls, hawks, kestrels and marsh harriers flew above, while roe deer, foxes, badgers and hares roamed the area. In 1900 the 11th Duke of Bedford introduced the Muntjac deer to the Thorney estate.[319] Walter's imagination could run riot in the natural landscape big enough to get lost in. Away

Eel fisherman.
The Norfolk Broads.
From the author's collection.

from prying eyes, there were daredevil dares to undertake, war games to enact, trees to climb, nests to find, conker games to play, rivers and dykes to swim in, and forts to build and protect. Gangs of children played group games like 'Tag', 'What's the Time, Mr Wolf?' and 'Bulldog', games familiar in my childhood. Rhymes such as 'Ee-ny, mee-ny, min-y, moe, Catch a ti-ger by the toe. If he holl-ers, let him go, *Ee-ny, mee-ny, min-y, moe'* were a way of choosing people to take on roles in a game. This was decided by someone chanting the rhyme and pointing at each child wanting to play. Their finger moved to the next person at the end of each syllable. The last person pointed at when the rhyme ended was 'it'.

As Walter lived in the Tank Yard, he could have had 'first dibs' on any warped barrel straps from the wheelwrights. These could be raced in the way more affluent children raced their hoops and sticks in town and city parks. A childhood favourite of mine, 'Jacks', also known as 'Fivestones' or 'Knucklebones', was played with a small rubber ball and five or ten small objects are thrown up and caught in various ways. The winner is the first person to complete a predefined series of throws.[320] Victorian factories also made affordable games, such as uniform sets of 'Pick Up Sticks'.

Many children made marbles out of clay, though the new, affordable glass marbles were hugely collectable and could change hands several times a day. The most popular marble game played was 'Ring Taw'.[321] Marbles are placed inside a circle, and the players crouched outside while each player took a turn flicking a large shooter into the ring. The goal is to knock out other marbles, which the successful player keeps. The winner is the player with the most marbles at the end of the game.

Skipping games were popular with the girls. No doubt Walter was sometimes pressed into turning one end of a rope, so his sisters could practise the competitive and often complicated skipping steps. The sound of the rope hitting the ground measured out the beat to the rhymes that were chanted, prompting the jump. 'French Ropes' (also known as 'Double Dutch', where two ropes are turned, one following the other) were ubiquitous. Some rhymes were based on international news of the day, like this gruesome British one inspired by an American murder trial in 1892.

> Lizzie Borden took an axe.
> She gave her mother forty whacks.
> After she saw what she had done,
> She gave her father forty-one.
> Lizzie Borden got away.
> For her crime, she did not pay.[322]

There were singing games too, like 'Farmer in the Dell', and others where you wore a blindfold, such as 'Blind Man's Bluff' and 'Pin the Tail on the Donkey'.

Sports

For men and boys, sports of all kinds were prominent. In the late 1890s, women were physically and socially more constrained, though some took up cycling and a few skated competitively.

Skating

I first tried to picture Walter skating after my brother and I saw his old-fashioned 'pattens', or Fen runners, hanging limp

on the back of his cellar door in the 1960s. But it was not until Cousin Mary described him as 'a beautiful skater, bent forward, flying confidently along Thorney Dyke, with his left hand held behind his back' that an image of Walter in his prime came into sharp focus. Skating had been popular in the Fens for centuries, but racing was still mostly the preserve of agricultural labourers, such as Walter became after leaving school. When the temperature dropped, the many straight man-made ditches and flood plains became ideal terrain for competitive skating. They gave the labourers, unable to find work on the frozen land, the opportunity to win a joint of meat, flour, a voucher to spend in a local shop and the admiration of the girls. Women taking a prize were given a new hat, or a length of material.[323]

The hard winters of the last decade of the nineteenth century became known as 'the Fenman's holiday'.[324] Men (and a few women) from all walks of life skated for recreation, to compete and as a means of transport. With a pair of fen runners on their feet, some men took skating tours and covered twenty or more miles a day, along the natural and man-made waterways that connected the villages and towns.

Brothers James 'Fish' Smart and George Smart, came from near Upwell. Jane Winters (one of the fastest female skaters) and the Olympian, Cyril Horn, were born in the village.[325] It is quite possible that Stephen skated with neighbour George Smart and George's uncle, William 'Turkey' Smart. The Birmingham Daily Post reported:

> *Turkey Smart was a typical fen skater; his running was both morally and physically as straight as ever a man ought to be. With arched back and head low down, he seemed to deliver his stroke with the strength of an ox, and its power and length was enormous.*[326]

Willam 'Turkey' Smart.
Photograph by J. Kennerell; in the
public domain via Wikimedia Commons.

James 'Fish' Smart, c1890.
Photograph by G. Kennetill; in the public
domain via Wikimedia Commons.

Although speed-skating was practised in other parts of the country, fenmen, with their unique style and combination of stamina and speed, were the acknowledged masters. Lancashire sent three of their top skaters to the Swavesey match in January 1879.[327] On the day, George 'Fish' Smart was found to be the 'best man'. His reward was a badge, a sash, and a cash prize. To stop the champion binge drinking, the committee handed the money over in instalments. The Birmingham Daily Post reported:

> *When in 1879 some swift skaters from Lancashire came down to do battle with the fenmen, they met with decisive defeat. With good-natured candour, one of them said: "We are the best men in our parts; but we run. These fenmen flee."*[328]

English speed skates, c1890.
Photograph by the Marsden Brothers;
from the Virtual Ice Skates Museum:
www.iceskatesmuseum.com.

While champions might achieve a mile in two minutes, the ordinary fast skaters, who peaked aged twenty-two, covered one mile in three and a half to four minutes.[329] Naturally, Stephen taught his son to skate; though in Upwell, Walter took to the ice with his uncles and cousins too. While loved for its own sake, skating helped him to escape the claustrophobic atmosphere that can engulf those at close quarters with an alcoholic. There was also the added perk that a match gave children a half-day off from school.[330] No doubt Walter knew the 'thrilling delight of a long moonlight spin... such as the skaters of fen districts look forward to—the air crisp and clear, the sky twinkling with frosty silvery points, the only sound the soft ringing music of the polished blade against the smooth, dark ice'.[331]

Many found it thrilling when the Fens froze, but some parents were fearful. Skating was a risky pastime; accidents and attempted rescues were commonplace. In 1902 the *Peterborough Standard* reported that an eleven-year-old had drowned, having gone through and under a patch of ice, with his would-be rescuers unable to reach him. The author of the report commented it 'did not appear to act as a warning to [the] many children who amused themselves by sliding in the vicinity of the bridge'.[332] Others took the precaution of carrying a skating-pole with them. These could be used to hold their position if they fell through the ice until rescue arrived.[333] Despite (or maybe because of) the danger, Fen skating remained an avidly followed spectator sport. Railways ran special excursions and old champions put on exhibition races. Thousands turned out to watch legendary skaters and, like the frost fairs of the early 1800s, stalls selling roasted chestnuts, hot baked potatoes and drinks were set up near the ice. People rented out their kitchen chairs, and retired skaters put their experience to good use by fixing people's skates for a few pence.[334] In a flight of fancy, I can see Walter reading the local coverage of the Amateur Championship of Great Britain and British Professional Championship of 17 February 1900 and talking to his friends about each man's form, in the way young men might have spoken about athletes throughout history.

Cycling

The 'whippet' safety cycle was invented in the year of Walter's birth, 1885.[335] But it was not until the introduction of the pneumatic tyre and changes in the chain drive (which made pedalling and navigating corners easier) that cycling became a practical proposition. As lighter, simpler, and therefore cheaper machines were introduced, the bicycle came within reach of the working class. We know that Stephen owned one of the first bicycles in the village and that Ethel was riding a bike in 1900. So, I was flabbergasted by the mention of a 'condition' named 'bicycle-face' in a 1900 copy of the *Cambridge Daily News*.[336] The *Worcester Journal* of 1896 had previously spelt out:

> *Bicycles are responsible for many things in our social life. A doctor has [described] the bicycle face. Anxious, weary worn, haggard looks are due to the bicycle. So much anxiety is developed in learning to ride, and afterwards in avoiding accidents that it...affects the muscles of the face, and the care worn expression is retained during the other hours of life. At least the doctor – an M.D. London – says so, and he ought to know.[337]*

According to another report, young women were concealing the harmful effects of cycling and were 'lured to attempt a task beyond their physical powers'.[338] Yet the columnist suggests that Dr Shadwell, whose alarmist article 'The Hidden Dangers of Cycling' appeared in London's *National Review,* suffered a sort 'of colour blindness. He said this blinkered view would render him a dangerous person to be entrusted with the care of patients'.[339] Presumably, when Walter's sister Lily was photographed posed next to her bicycle, c.1900, people had dismissed Dr Shadwell's view that the 'case against the bicycle is that nervous exhaustion is the natural and necessary result of cycling'.[340]

Lily Parker with her bicycle, c1900.
Walter's sister Lily is smartly dressed and ready to ride, with a bag strapped to her waist (much more stylish than the 'bum bag' I wore on holidays in the 1990s). The bike had a chain cover to stop her long skirt being caught in the oily machinery. Mudguards protected her clothes from dirty rainwater mixed with the horse manure frequently found on the roads and tracks. From the author's collection.

Abraham Moores with his bicycle c1900.
Believed to be Lily's future father-in-law, Abraham Moores, c. 1904, Thorney.
The gentleman is formally dressed. His dark, three-piece wool suit, fob watch and bowler
hat were considered suitable riding gear. Intriguingly, the gentleman does not have a
bicycle lamp. Presumably, he soon fitted a light, as people were fined for failing to do so.
With no rack, it would seem he used a knapsack, not considered seemly for a woman.
From the author's collection.

Given Walter's family's cycling activities, and that Walter rode a motorcycle in the 1930s, it seems inevitable that Walter was a cyclist too. The Parkers were not alone. The beginning of the twentieth century brought in a bicycle craze that swept the country. Cycling emancipated many women, gave birth to an exciting form of recreation, and allowed (predominantly men) a broader geographical area in which to make a living.

Walter's work meant he was fit enough to ride long distances. I can imagine the thrill and taste of freedom cycling could bring. The *Peterborough Cycling Club* was formed in 1873. As Walter

A courting couple, posted 1906.
From Ethel Parker's postcard collection
(in the author's keeping).

lived only ten miles away, I can speculate he took part in the twenty-five-mile championship of the Peterborough Cycling Club which started from the Peterborough Cricket Ground, at 5.30 p.m. Thursday, 7 September 1899.[341]

Fishing was a way that older children and youths provided for the table while escaping the control of adults. We know from tales told by Cousin 'Rene in 2015 that Walter was a talented fisherman. Like many human endeavours, it had become competitive, and at weekends men came to Thorney's riverbanks from as far as Sheffield, 110 miles away, hoping to out-fish the locals and other visitors.[342] The local newspapers often reported on how they fared, as in 1900: 'A good catch of bream was had in the Thorney River taking seventeen fish averaging 2½ lbs each.'[343]

Team games were also popular, and Thorney fielded teams for quoits, cricket and football and took part in leagues with the surrounding villages. Quoits is a game in which players toss rings of metal, rope or rubber at a stake, aiming for the rings to land over the stake or as close to it as possible. It is

An example of a quoits team (Benhall, East Sussex), date unknown.
Permission to reproduce this image kindly given by the owner Richard Bloomfield
in association with Benhall & Sternfield History group.

related to an earlier pub game where one threw a horseshoe at a pin in the ground. A form of it can be seen at funfairs and tombola stalls, where one has to throw a hoop and settle it cleanly over an object to win a prize.

An example of a quoits set. (From Ketton Village, East Midlands.)
Quoit bed with iron pin and discs set in a 3ft square clay bed. Each disc weighed around 9lbs. The throwing line was 18 yards away.
Permission given by Ketton Parish Council.

The version played in Thorney was probably the modified East Anglian game, which had slightly different rules to the 'long game'. According to Steve Clarke and Sid Watkinson, whose grandfather was champion of England in 1904:

> *The East Anglian game is unique in that ringers score a clean two points regardless of the opponent's efforts and are immediately removed prior to the next throw. Apparently, quoits on their backs and quoits that land inclined in a backwards direction are discounted and removed immediately. The quoits tend to be smaller than those used in the Scottish and Welsh games, but the distance is maintained at 18 yards.*[344]

I believe the 'S. Parker' who appeared in a winners' list and various match reports over the years was Walter's pa.[345]

> *The annual competition in connection with the Thorney Quoit Club, for prizes, took place on Saturday. This was much interfered with by rain, so much so that the two last heats had to be postponed. The three members left in the running are Messrs. J. Fletcher, S. Parker, and A. Browning.*[346]

Quoits was a focal point in the family. Cousin Mary told me that her parents, Ethel (Walter's sister and Stephen's eldest daughter) and Frank Woods, often talked about the local matches of their past. Traditional games, sport, and cycling ebbed and flowed throughout the year, but they were not the only leisure pursuits. Village life also had an abundance of entertainments, parades, learning for pleasure, brass bands, songs, and special children's treats.

Family tree

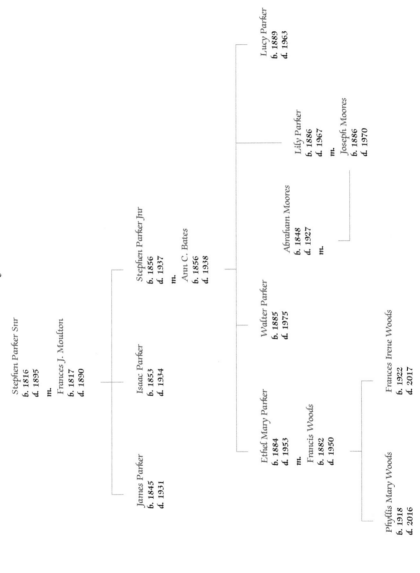

Stephen Parker Snr
b. 1816
d. 1895
m.
Frances J. Moulton
b. 1817
d. 1890

James Parker
b. 1845
d. 1931

Isaac Parker
b. 1853
d. 1934

Stephen Parker Jnr
b. 1856
d. 1937
m.
Ann C. Bates
b. 1856
d. 1938

Lucy Parker
b. 1889
d. 1963

Lily Parker
b. 1886
d. 1967
m.
Joseph Moores
b. 1886
d. 1970

Abraham Moores
b. 1848
d. 1927
m.

Walter Parker
b. 1885
d. 1975

Ethel Mary Parker
b. 1884
d. 1953
m.
Francis Woods
b. 1882
d. 1950

Frances Irene Woods
b. 1922
d. 2017

Phyllis Mary Woods
b. 1918
d. 2016

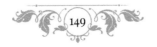

CHAPTER 7

Thorney Village Life

The nineteenth century brought about radical social change, giving rise to the new middle class. Using libraries, taking part in organised sport, and the growing of fruit, vegetables and flowers were all thought of as a productive use of time. Music was considered a force for the 'moral elevation of working people'.[347] Village life gave its residents a social cohesion important for physical and mental wellbeing.[348]

Newspapers can give us a context of a time and society that may feel far removed from our own. Scanning the Parker family's local papers, the *Peterborough and Huntingdonshire Standard, Peterborough Advertiser and South Midland Times* and *Peterborough Stamford Mercury*, gave me a vibrant glimpse of some of the activities available. No wonder Walter's niece told me, 'I wouldn't have liked to live in a town or city. Whatever would one find to do?'[349] The papers also make engrossing reading, possibly because they reflect a time both beguilingly different and reassuringly familiar. People's primary concerns, interests and focus seem unchanged. The press reported on the movements of the royal family, the Duke and Duchess of Bedford, war around the globe, and fear of Russia.[350] Articles about health and the need

to improve education also appeared regularly. Each week there was a column on current events for each village or area. Railway excursions and weekly clubs were common, alongside the annual fetes and treats that filled the Thorneyites' calendar.

Walter and his family lived in a central location, just steps away from much of what happened in Thorney. The fetes, fairs, shows and other social events meant a great deal of work for a small number of people. In Thorney, one of those people was Stephen. With an unhappy, alcoholic wife at home, Stephen had a reason to seek the company of others. But Cousin Mary described her grandfather as a man with the skills and personality to help, support and be interested in much that was going on throughout the village. This was valuable as such committees could be bitterly challenging, especially when egos, jealousies and fragile personalities met bad weather, discord, and financial loss.

Although of a shyer nature than his father, Walter was expected to be at Stephen's side. He watched his pa closely, keen to discover how the latter turned pieces of wood into toys, furniture, or a temporary stage for the musicians for an upcoming fete. It gave Walter practical skills and problem-solving experience, which would pay dividends in his adult life.

The Queen's birthday (and a cousin in jeopardy)

The village of Thorney, like communities all over the country, celebrated Queen Victoria's birthday on 24 May. In 1900, on what was to be the last celebration, the usual events were combined with a fundraising effort to help relieve the besieged inhabitants of Mafeking, a town in South Africa.

Walter undoubtedly saw the flags and banners fluttering from the windows of the village, especially those of the Rose & Crown Inn. According to the *Peterborough Standard* of 26 May, patriotic mottos were 'freely displayed' along the route. A long procession followed the Peterborough Silver Prize Band with people shaking money-collecting buckets alongside representations of Britannia sitting on horse-drawn ambulance wagons and an armoured train. Mounted and foot soldiers fired their guns in 'rapid succession' and fireworks were 'constantly let off'.[351] It was a 'capital turnout'. The same newspaper report mentions Ethel, Walter's sixteen-year-old sister, as part of the parade collecting money on her decorated bicycle.[352]

The Rose & Crown Inn, c1901-1911.
It was acquired by the People's Refreshment House Association in 1899. From the Culpin collection of Thorney postcards and photographs.

The band was commended for their 'excellent music [which] contributed in no small measure to the success of the proceedings'. At dusk, torches were lit, and an effigy of Kruger, a South African politician, crackled on the bonfire on the green next to the ancient Abbey. I like to think that fifteen-year-old Walter was not one of the many 'who broke into ringing and long continued cheers' as the likeness, known affectionately in his homeland as 'Uncle Paul', went up in flames.[353] Come the evening, fairy-lamps lit the inn's bunting, two portraits

Theophilus Parker, South Africa, 1901.

Taken in the year of the Bubonic plague. From the collection of Sue Oldroyd née Parker. During the Anglo-Boer (South African War) of 1899–1902, about 28,000 Boers died in concentration camps set up by the British, predominantly of measles, respiratory diseases, and typhoid. Some 79 per cent of the dead were children. In addition, at least 15,000 Africans perished in their own racially segregated camps. These deaths were... the consequence of inadequate accommodation, poor nutrition, and epidemic disease in a pre-antibiotic era following on the scrambled internment of civilians for military ends. Reference Laband, J., 2015. Elizabeth van Heyningen. The Concentration Camps of the Anglo-Boer War: A Social History. The American Historical Review, 120(2), pp.760-760.

of Her Majesty were illuminated, and Chinese lanterns lit the roads. I expect Stephen let off a 'nice display of fireworks'.[354] In keeping with an ancient custom for public celebrations, the end of the day was marked by the burning of tar barrels, the smell of which clung to the clothes of those nearby. The 26 May 1900 edition of the *Peterborough Standard* announced that 'Altogether it was a memorable occasion' which raised £12-5s [£1,592] for the starving women and children of besieged Mafeking.[355]

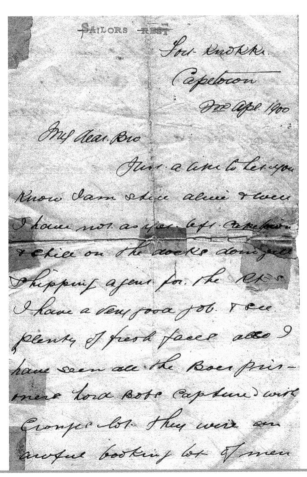

Letter written by Theophilus Parker in 1900 while billeted
at The Sailor's Rest, Cape Town, and sent to his brother Joel. p. 1.
In the keeping of Sue Oldroyd, Theophilus Parker's grandniece.

> no uniform what ever old &
> young from 16 to 70 they.
> Came down in bullock waggons
> & the stench of them was
> horrible Some had not.
> Changed their Shirts for
> 4 months & had not left.
> train for 4 days they
> were put on transport &
> I believe now are in the
> Island of St Helena I wonder
> how much longer. we shall be
> out here. I expect the boers
> will fight until the last.
> as they have all to loose &

Letter to Joel from Theo 1900, p. 2.

It was a time of mixed emotions for Walter and his family. Walter's older cousin Theophilus Parker (known as Theo and later as Thop) had been recalled to army service on 9 October 1899 and was serving as a corporal sapper in the Royal Engineers (38th Company). A week before the siege was broken, Walter's cousin Joel received a heart-breaking letter from his older brother Theo, aged twenty-nine, billeted at The Sailor's Rest, Cape Town.

Letter to Joel from Theo 1900, p. 3.

An extract reads:

> It is a very painful sight to see the poor fellows going home. Some with legs off & arms some looking as if they cannot live long. Close to where I am living there is a large hospital & near by [sic] is a military cemetery & they are being buried at the rate of 5 per day but we soldiers must not grieve. We only say so & so has snuffed it.[356]

Letter to Joel from Theo 1900, p. 4.

The apparent detachment with which Theo writes suggests a form of dissociation known as depersonalisation disorder. At the turn of the twentieth century, such minimising may have been seen as an admirable masculine trait or even a life skill, rather than a way of coping with overwhelming trauma.

Although Stephen may have tried to shield fifteen-year-old Walter from the contents of the family letter, the newspaper coverage probably 'gave the game away'. I expect Walter attended a crowded lecture, with lantern slides, about the Transvaal War.[357] No doubt the Parkers followed news of the siege, and they might have read a lengthy interview with a local man who drove an armoured train outside Mafeking:

'What about food. Did you get fat on your rations?' was my next question.

'No,' was the reply with a smile. 'During the siege of Mafeking we were very badly off, subsisting on biscuits and bully beef, with a little fresh meat occasionally, but after the siege was raised, we fared much better.'

'No doubt you were glad to get back to the town again?'

'You bet we were, although we had to re-lay the rails before we could get into Mafeking.'[358]

The Thorney annual feast

The same year as the Mafeking fundraiser was held, the village held its centuries-old Thorney annual feast on Whit-Monday (3 June) and Tuesday (4 June). Its religious roots were lost in the past. It had become a much-anticipated steam fair that attracted people from all generations. An influx of people went along for the thrill of riding Clarke's steam gallopers. Other attractions included the steam-powered swings, roundabouts, a dancing booth, coconut shies, Punch and Judy shows, hot savoury treats and a range of stalls. One table sold fancy ribbons, beads, gloves, combs, and hatpins. Another stall carried sweets, gingerbread, liquorice root and, perhaps, candyfloss; the new, sweet-smelling

Clarke's steam-driven gallopers.
With the kind permission of Preston Services.

spun sugar treat presented on a stick. Wooden toys and glass marbles could cover another trestle table, with stone bottles of ginger beer and lemonade set up nearby to refresh the dancers.[359]

The church garden fete

Of all the events in Thorney's social calendar, the one that stands out the most for me was the annual church garden fete. It was an essential fundraising event for the upkeep of the Abbey and reminded me of the church fetes of my childhood. Another whole-village affair, it was held for many years on the lawns of Thorneycroft, close to the Tank Yard. Sideshows included 'bowling for a pig', darts (to win a leg of ham), 'clock golf' and 'find the treasure' hidden in a crate of sweet-smelling sawdust. Ladies served scrumptious cream teas.

Thorneycroft House – the Steward's House.
Dated 2018. From the Culpin collection of Thorney postcards and photographs.

Before the Covid-19 pandemic we still had traditional fetes with stalls selling bottled fruit, pickles, cakes, and plants. But Walter's sisters also sewed, crocheted, and knitted for months at school, making shirts, embroidered tablecloths, rag rugs, knitted socks, scarves, gloves, and underwear to sell. Women made pale-green and pink peppermint creams, toffee, and pink-and-white-striped coconut-ices, to be sold in twists of paper. As is still prevalent, the pink colouring was achieved by using crushed cochineal insects. Walter could have mucked in with the sweet making. He certainly made delectable, mouth-watering treacle toffee in his later years. I am sure Walter's pa, Stephen, lent a practical hand, making sure it all passed 'without a hitch'.

Another Thorneyite tradition was the flower show and its accompanying musical fete. In July 1894, like every year, Walter's school was closed. It was the annual exhibition of the Thorney Horticultural Society and the highlight of their year. The show

Championship Shield, Thorney Flower Show, 1907.
From the Thorney Heritage Museum.

was an opportunity for individuals to show off their flowers and produce in the many classes held in two large marquees on Mr Topham's land. The fete was held in the paddock. It took a great deal of planning and the society's progress was reported on in the *Peterborough Standard* in the run-up to the day. As one of the committee members, Walter's pa Stephen got as much done as possible the night before: moving the piano, putting up trestle tables and setting up the tents. Smith Bros. (the company where Walter would later serve his apprenticeship) were paid to help prepare and clear the ground and Ethel's future father-in-law lent a hand. The children were let out of school, and the event was attended by the villagers and visitors from local areas and as far away as Peterborough, Eye and Wisbech. The Midland and Great Northern Joint Railway agreed to provide discounted rail tickets as an inducement to visit the event. A late-night train, leaving at 10.15 p.m., was arranged so that people could make

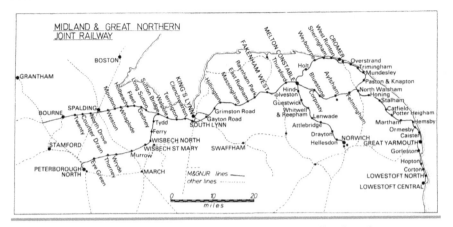

System map of the eastern part of the Midland and Great Northern Joint Railway.

the most of their day. I like to think Walter's uncle James and his family took advantage of such a ticket, and took the tram from Upwell to Wisbech, and caught the train into Thorney.

On the day of the fete, Stephen often sold admission tickets to the 'lawn'. Such jobs were delegated to Walter as he got older. At the flower show in 1898, the repertoire performed in the Abbey included award-winning violinist Charles Greenhead and talented Abbey organist Mr Arthur Thacker. They played a contemporary piece by the, then, well-known German-Swiss composer Joseph Raff, Bach's haunting *Air on a G String* and *Concerto in A Minor*, the lyrical *Romanze* by Schubert, and Handel's *Sonata No. 3 in F Major*. *Angels Ever Bright and Fair* ended the programme.[360]

No event was complete without the vibrancy and thrill of a big brass marching band. At the 1894 flower show, the Nottingham Six Tuba Band escorted people from the station to the showground.[361] More music was provided at the afternoon concert held on the terrace of Abbey House, where a platform was erected for the piano and orchestra. The programme

Thorney Methodist School Parade in front of Co-op c1900.
Photograph from the Peterborough Images Archive: www.peterboroughimages.co.uk.

included 'Admiral's Broom', a song by ballad composer Frederick Bevan published in 1891; a *Mendelssohn* hymn, 'I Would that My Love'; and the eighteenth-century hymn 'Oh Happy Day'.

Awaiting the visitors were abundant displays of freshly baked bread, butter sculptures, bowls of eggs, baskets of flowers, flower arrangements, fruits, and vegetables. There were three produce categories: Class A was for the cottagers and artisans, Class B was for amateurs, cottagers and artisans, and anyone could enter Class C.[362] Judging was taken seriously. Local lads had the job of barring entrance to the stuffy tents, allowing judges the privacy to discuss the various merits of the entries. Prizes for the best-decorated sunshade, bicycle and mail cart were awarded in 1894. The adjudicators were often from local estates, such as a gardener from Woburn Abbey who judged many classes in 1906. One judge of horticultural products had been a neighbour of the Parker family, Mr Alfred Elworthy, the son of William, a paralysed builder and contractor of Upwell.[363] Horse and pony races and donkey rides for the children were also a draw. For men, there was a fiercely fought tug-of-war. Some villagers opened their gardens to visitors hoping to win 'Best Kept Garden'.

The Thorney Foresters Society fete and gala

This was another important annual event. Before the National Insurance Act of 1911 and the establishment of the welfare state in 1945, friendly societies insured workers against loss of work through foul weather, ill health, accident, or death. The Foresters were such a society, providing sickness, travelling and funeral benefits. Members' widows and orphans were provided for if the wage earner had paid into the scheme. In this way, those who could afford it did their utmost to keep their families out of the workhouse should they, as breadwinner, become incapacitated or die.[364]

I understand from Cousin Mary that Stephen was a 'Foresters man'. As parents were urged to allow their offspring to join, at age nine Walter could already have been a member of their Buds of Progress Juvenile Society, which provided medical benefits for children.[365] On the day of the fete and gala, school was dismissed so that the children could go.[366] The caring culture of the

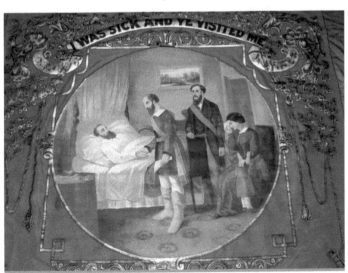

Forrester's Court No. 3095 Banner - reverse.
Photograph from the Foresters Heritage Trust.

Foresters is reflected on the reverse side of the Court 'Rubens' banner. The central image depicts a sick member of the Ancient Order of Foresters being visited by 'the Woodward', undertaking one of his primary duties. The Foresters Heritage Trust explains:

> *The purpose was twofold. On the one hand there was the financial aspect, with the Woodward passing over the sick pay entitlement. On the other was [the] fraternal aspect, the sharing of experience that made the Foresters, and other friendly societies, such a valuable part of a hard, and otherwise indifferent, world.*[367]

Ancient Order of Foresters sashes.
Three sashes worn by the Ancient Order of Foresters. Each length of silk was part of the Forester's regalia and was worn in their court. The first is pre-1892. The second is post-1892, after which women were allowed to join. This black-backed version would have been worn by Foresters attending the funeral of a fellow member. The third sash (date unknown) has the letters 'HM' embroidered on it, as this one belonged to an honorary member. The growing international reach of the Foresters is shown by the globe and flags on the successive sashes.

Even if Stephen were not part of the 'church parade, headed by the Peterborough Borough Band and the banner of the Court', Walter would surely have watched the adult male members pass by, wearing their full regalia including their striking green silk sashes.[368] I cannot imagine shy, independent Walter longing to be among their ranks. It is difficult to imagine what Walter's three sisters

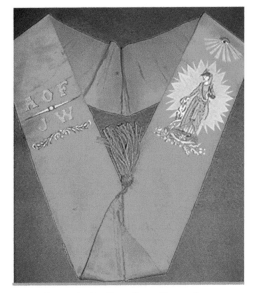

Forrester's Female collar, 1894.
The collar cost 5s [£32.71] each.
Photograph from the Foresters Heritage Trust.

and their mother, Ann, made of the spectacle, particularly after the annual High Court Meeting delegates admitted female benefit members from 1892.[369]

As was usual, the Reverend William Symons preached a sermon in the packed Abbey, after which the procession regrouped and paraded through the village, with the band playing lively airs. The *Peterborough Advertiser* reported that the 'Abbey-rooms provided an excellent sit-down dinner for about 140 people', probably all men. At the 1898 event, there was a lengthy toast list that included the 'Queen and Royal Family, Army and Navy, The House of Russell, Bishop and Clergy, The Doctor, The Foresters Society, The Secretary and The Visitors'.[370] The Buds of Progress Juvenile Section ate in the adjoining room. A public tea was provided in the afternoon for, I suspect, a good number of women.

A heavy shower in the early evening of the 1894 event did not prevent people assembling to watch the sports in the Abbey grounds followed by a fireworks display. Walter may have competed in the boys' under-twelve 100-yard flat race, or attended the pole jump, stone-picking event, and the tug-of-war. It is a shame he did not tell me the aim of 'Riding the Blind Horse' and the 'Muddle Race'. I hope Ann allowed the children to watch the fireworks light up the evening sky.

Children's school treats and outings

The newspapers and school logs tell us that the children had regular treats. These also took place on a school day and were eagerly awaited.[371] To add to the sense of occasion, the King's Dyke Brass Band met the children at the school and marched to Mr Topham's park grounds.[372] Weather permitting, the church and chapel treats included boisterous games, before a four o'clock high tea starting with a hot entrée and vegetables, followed by baked goods and tea.[373] The meal was laid out for the mothers and children in the Abbey Room, which seated 200 people. After the children had eaten, they stood to sing a 'collection of hymns for the entertainment of the adults and the pleasure of the children'.[374] The day ended at nine o'clock with the children 'sent home with a "bun"'.[375] Fortunately, living in the Tank Yard meant Walter and his sisters did not have far to go.

An afternoon meal being an event might seem old-fashioned now, but Thorney's women were likely inspired by the high tea taken by Anna, the 7th Duchess of Bedford, in 1840. The Duchess had been one of Queen Victoria's Ladies of the Bedchamber and a lifelong friend. A story has it that Anna was too hungry to wait for dinner, served as late as 9.30 p.m. in the summer. She had the servants bring to her dressing room buttered bread, biscuits, and cakes, to enjoy with a customary cup of Darjeeling tea. The young Queen Victoria heard of it and added to her day a 4 p.m. tea of 'light cake with buttercream and fresh raspberries – later known as Victoria Sponge Cake'.[376] By the 1880s, this pause for tea had become a fashionable national social occasion. As Thorney was part of the Bedford estates, I can imagine the ladies of the village vying with each other to provide the best refreshments.

Many such social occasions populated Thorney's annual calendar. However, children most looked forward to the annual Sunday school seaside outing as a reward for good attendance. According to the school log:

> *29 July 1892: Average lowered on Friday on account of the Sunday school treat, only 25 present.*

For many, it was the only time they travelled by train or saw the sea. Cousin Mary gave me an unnamed, undated type-written account, of one such trip. After getting up early:

> *The younger children marched to the boys' school with the girls and, after roll-call, the children trooped down to the station to wait for the train. The platform was crowded from end to end. As soon as the crossing gates opened, a ripple of excitement went through the crowd. Then the great moment came – the train arrived. The eager children dashed here and there trying to decide where and with whom to sit until, at last, everybody was seated and finally they were off.*

Music, dance, and entertainments

Like the rest of Victorian England, Thorney had an abundant musical life. There were organs in the chapel and the Abbey, and a piano in the Abbey Room. Villagers, including Ethel, sang in the choir and played in the orchestra. Brass bands visited regularly. New song sheets were sold weekly for people to sing at the piano at home, and in the Abbey Rooms. Whatever their age or taste in music, people knew the same songs and hymns. Cousin Mary told me: 'We were surrounded by music. All generations sang everywhere – out walking, with friends, in the taproom, in the street and at the kitchen sink. We danced whenever and wherever we could, indoors and out, on the carpet, stone kitchen floors, and wooden platforms laid to protect the grass. It's just what everyone did'.

Annual shows were also a feature of the village calendar. The Thorney Amateur Dramatic Society put on several entertainments throughout the year in Thorney and Peterborough.[377] In 1902 the Peterborough Co-operative Society Annual Entertainment was held in the Abbey Room. The operetta *Agatha* was performed, with a rendition of 'The Sailor's Hornpipe' that apparently 'brought the house down'.[378] In 1894 Stephen may have attended the Smoking Concert held at the Mutual Improvement Society.[379] These were regular events with a seated audience of fifty people. On this occasion, the programme opened with a piano recital, starting with the piece *Christmas Bells*. The Reverend Ferris recited Thomas Hood's poem 'The Dream of Eugene Aram', which told the tale of an educated murderer who was hanged in 1759.[380] If Stephen was present, I wonder if he felt uncomfortable listening to the rendition of the raucous, ancient drinking song 'Down

Among the Dead Men', thinking of his whisky-swigging wife at home. The song, thick with innuendo, was first published in 1728. 'Dead men' is an archaic term for empty bottles, and the expression to 'lie down among the dead men' meant to get so drunk as to end up on the floor among the empties. As was usual after an entertainment, 'God Save the Queen' was sung by everyone at the end of the evening.[381]

Although Thorney did not have a music hall, the Abbey Room was used as a venue for musical amusements. The Crowland Boy Minstrels gave an 'entertainment in the Abbey-room... before an appreciative audience'.[382] The visiting Eye Black and White Minstrels performed plantation songs such as 'We Are Getting It by Degrees'.[383] It is painful to recognise that these family entertainments with racist caricaturing, performed by troupes of white men 'blacked up' to depict people of African origin, were not recognised as abhorrent by the white audience.[384]

The chapel was not all about religion. The hall was used for lectures and concerts. It was a thriving part of the community. As the *Peterborough Advertiser* reported on 5 March 1898:

> *A lecture, entitled 'Life and Times of John Bunyan', was delivered by the Reverend J. Scruby in the Primitive Methodist Chapel Friday evening last week. Mr. Snowden, of Peterborough, presided.*[385]

26 March 1889 the *Lincolnshire Free Press* reported:

> *Concert. – On Wednesday evening last, a concert was given by the Temperance Society, of Hope, and Master Louie Armit, of Eye, in the Primitive Methodist Chapel...*

We are pleased to state that the whole programme was one of unalloyed enjoyment, praise being due to those who took part in the entertainment.[386]

Thorney held many musical fundraisers. For example, a dramatic entertainment, at the Estate Works, included *Good for*

Nothing: A Comic Drama in One Act by playwright John Baldwin Buckstone, with the Choral Class String Band. It raised money for the Cricket Club.[387] On another occasion The Thorney Minstrel Troupe sold tickets for the 'betterment' of the

Rose & Crown Hotel Hall.
Photograph taken from the Peterborough Images Archive: www.peterboroughimages.co.uk.

allotment society.[388] Walter's sisters – Ethel, Lily and Lucy – were said by Cousin Mary to have eagerly awaited the weekly dances, which culminated in the New Year Dance held in the hall at the back of the Rose & Crown Inn.[389] I can see them dragging along their shy brother to partner them, while Walter aimed to join his friends watching the girls lined up at one end of the hall, waiting to be asked to dance. The bustle, sights, sounds, and smells of these regular village events punctuated Walter's life. Although quiet by nature, I believe Walter welcomed the chance to mingle with unfamiliar people.

Lifelong learning

Village events did not only include 'jollies'. The Victorian working-class understood the benefits of practical lifelong

learning.[390] Academic instruction, talks and debates were provided in Thorney by the new working men's clubs, institutes, and a wide variety of friendly societies. With little state welfare, families relied on the head of their household to support them, so gaining new skills and knowledge was prized. First aid was one subject Thorneyites had the opportunity to learn. In January 1894, a doctor from Peterborough came to give a course on 'ambulance work'.[391] Such skills could have been lifesaving, as the nearest hospital was ten miles away, in Peterborough.

Thorneyites were outward looking and brought eminent speakers to the village. Edmund Garwood, an explorer, geologist, and photographer, gave a lecture on 'Explorations in Spit[s]bergen During the Summers of 1896–97'.[392] (*Spitsbergen* is a Norwegian island in the Arctic.) The address was similar to one that was reported in the *Geographical Journal* of 1899.[393] Might Stephen have seen Garwood's exceptional photographic plates lit by limelight? The Thorney Causeway Society arranged a lecture given by pacifist Miss Priscilla Peckover, a member of the Quaker family living in Peckover House, Wisbech. Miss Peckover was nominated for the Nobel Peace Prize four times, in 1903, 1905, 1911 and 1913.[394] A Parker, believed to be male, was noted as a member and part of the large audience.[395] I suspect the course of Cambridge University lectures held over the Michaelmas term on 'The World's Great Explorers' might have been out of Walter's reach.[396] However, it was attended by Miss Evelyn Egar, who is the only one mentioned to have passed an examination at the end of the course.[397] In another course females outnumbered the males in an exam:

> *Technical Education. – The following students have successfully passed the examination on the subject*

> *of 'Injurious Insects,' after a course of lectures by*
> *Mr. C. Wharburton, M.A., of Christ's College, Cambridge:*
> *Luke Bailey, Samuel M. Egan, Caroline Foreman,*
> *Mary C. Foreman [thirty-one- and thirty-two-year-old*
> *spinsters], Stephen R. Foreman, Ernest E. Law, John*
> *Irons, Margaret Horrell [aged eighteen], Lillian Miles,*
> *Margaret Morris [twenty-six-year-old spinster], and*
> *Ellen Provost [forty-two-year-old spinster].[398]*

While I was delighted to learn of this local opportunity for some women, it could be argued they only appear open to unmarried daughters of farmers, of a higher social class than Walter's sisters.

The women's interest may have been encouraged by the work of Miss Eleanor Ormerod and her annual *Report of Observations of Injurious Insects and Common Farm Pests.* Eleanor, a respected economic entomologist, produced an annual report from 1877 to 1898. From 1882 to 1892 she was a consulting entomologist to the Royal Agricultural Society of England. An article in the *Peterborough Advertiser* drew the attention of the reader to gall-mites and commented that 'systematic experiments are underway at the Duke of Bedford's experimental fruit farm at Woburn'.[399]

Other women's group activities are conspicuous by their absence. A debate of 1898 in the Mutual Improvement Society entitled 'Should Women Be Admitted to Have Equal Social Standing with Men?' concluded that women should not.[400] The local newspapers appear only to have encouraged 'ladies' in plain cooking, household management and looking after their family's health – all hard, time-consuming, solitary responsibilities that left them trapped at home.[401]

The horse and foal show

As in many places, Thorney held a horse and foal show. Horsepower was vital to moving goods and people, and the carrier, the 'man with a van' of Walter's time, collected villagers' purchases by post and acted as a taxi and removal company. Although steam-driven farming machines were being introduced, motor transport for the working person was not yet in reach.

More repairs.

A courting couple kissing in a car, posted 1905.
Postcard From Ethel Parker's postcard collection (now in the author's keeping).

Walter's pa, Stephen, served on the committee of the horse and foal show, and in 1892 he attended its 'luncheon in the Abbey Rooms'.[402] The show was no insignificant country affair. According to the *Peterborough Standard* of 30 July 1895, the surrounding areas were home to 'some of the best and most widely experienced [horse] breeders in the country'.[403] The author of the article commented that the Thorney show 'had 40 animals paraded in the ring at one time, which cannot be said for any other show in England'.[404]

The year 1900 saw Thorneyites hosting 122 entries in thirteen classes.[405] The villagers lined the roads to watch the horse-keepers walk the majestic animals through the village to the event, some drawing newly painted carts that gleamed in the sunshine. It must have been quite a sight to see 'gentlemen in their horse-drawn traps, overflowing with people, hoping their farm's horses would bag a prize'.[406] In 1902 the eleventh show by the Thorney Shire Foal Society took place in Mr Topham's 'roomy and well-wooded Park' known as Park Field.[407] Many subscribers funded it. The annual flower show added a sixth of its gate takings to the Thorney Shire Foal Society's kitty, and others paid between 5 shillings [£30] and £3 [£363]. The Duke of Bedford was the principal contributor and paid £25 [£3,023] a year. Those who wished to enter a class paid a small fee. The income covered the show's expenses. These included the secretary's salary, judges' fees, judges' lunches, stationery, stamps, billposting, press advertising, catalogue printing, ground preparation, live music, cup engraving, the coveted rosettes, and the prizes themselves. The prize money awarded in 1912 was £139-10s [£16,217] from an annual income of £182-10s-2d [£21,206]. Youths were paid a shilling [£6] to help with the preparations, or two shillings to sell catalogues on the day. I expect Walter and his friends were in the thick of it.

Local newspapers reported that breeders, like Messrs Gee of Thorney, well-known to the Parkers, took their horses to many shows. In 1905 Messrs Gee won '£88 3 shillings in cash [£10,543], £10 10s [£1,256] in gold medal, £5 [£598] in silver plate and £1 1s [£126] in silver medal' in Upwell, Thorney and Cambridge. That year they took a further ten first prizes, five-second prizes, three third prizes and two fourth-place prizes, as well as two highly commended and three commended awards.[408]

Agricultural sales and exhibitions also allowed Walter and his friends to observe specialised breeders and trainers of horseflesh. These were all experiences which would be valuable to Walter in the coming years. There were other significant fairs and shows held in nearby villages and towns. For example, Peterborough had the Bridge Fair, held on the first Tuesday, Wednesday and Thursday in October, in the fields on the south side of the river. Its purpose was the sale of wool, sheep, horses, breeding stock and general goods.

Bridge Fair Crowd, Town Bridge, Peterborough,
on their way to the annual Bridge Fair.
Bridge Fair Crowd, Town Bridge, Peterborough, on their way to the annual Bridge Fair.

Thorneyites also attended the Peterborough Agricultural Society Annual Show, held in July. Parents sometimes took their children. However, when they returned to the schoolroom, the boys were separated from their peers as punishment for having been 'absent without leave'.[409] We know from a postcard sent by Walter's sister Ethel that she travelled to Peterborough. So, it seems inevitable that Walter also visited this local ancient city.

Hospital Sunday

Until the National Health Service Act of 1946, hospitals were significantly funded by ordinary people raising money. Peterborough Infirmary was Thorney's local hospital. The villagers went all out to raise money for it on the annual Hospital Sunday.[410] All the village organisations gathered to parade through Thorney, headed by a brass band, such as the March Silver Band or the Salvation Army Band. Following the musicians were the friendly societies, each bearing a magnificent banner. The men wore the coloured sash of his organisation; the width of the material depicted his rank. The parade ended at the Abbey, where everyone attended a service and donated a traditional penny to the Sunday Hospital Fund.[411] The band were given lunch. Once refreshed, they gave a concert on the village green. Thorneyites had particular reason to value the Peterborough Infirmary as in 1896 it was the first hospital outside of London to have an X-ray machine.[412]

Politics and unions

On the afternoon of Tuesday 22 May 1894, a Liberal Unionist Association was formed in the sizeable room at the estate works.[413] Seventy people were present. I believe Stephen – who, according to his granddaughter Mary, had a keen interest in local affairs – was at this meeting. The *Peterborough and Huntingdonshire Standard* mention that an 'S. Parker' proposed a motion related to the local government changes at a vestry meeting held in the Abbey-rooms on 16 June 1894 to discuss the separation of Thorney from Peterborough.[414] The proposal was successful, and Thorney became a rural district and would remain so until 1974. The Liberal Unionist Association's elections were held each January in the Abbey Room, where, as expected, the Duke of Bedford was re-elected as president.

Holidays

In 1871 Sir John Lubbock introduced the Bank Holidays Act. For the first time, four holidays with pay were defined in England. These were Easter Monday, the first Monday in August, 26 December (Boxing Day) and Whit Monday. This free time allowed working families to spend time together in a new way. The railways meant people could venture out of their immediate area to experience previously unimaginable sights.

English town and cities are never more than about seventy miles from the coast, and day-trippers made the most of their new freedom. The first widespread, large-scale expansion of English and Welsh seaside resorts had arrived, and a new, aspirational, secular idea of the 'holiday', as opposed to *'holy*

Paddling at Great Yarmouth by Martin Paul, 1892.
Photographer Martin Paul. With permission from the Victoria & Albert Museum.

Marine Parade, Great Yarmouth, c1910.
In the background is the Revolving Observation Tower, opened on 19 July 1897. The cage originally revolved around the central tower as it ascended. Postcard from the author's collection.

The interior of the Winter Gardens, Great Yarmouth, c1904.
From the Broadland Memories Archive.

Boating Pond, Great Yarmouth, Norfolk, England.
Postcard from the author's collection.

BEACH G⁺ YARMOUTH.

Crowded beach, Great Yarmouth, Norfolk, c1900-1910s.
Postcard from the author's collection.

days', was born. By the 1890s many working-class people used cheap rail excursions, often organised by Sunday schools, employers or temperance societies, to unwind from the stress of everyday life and spend time with family.[415] For example, the *Peterborough Advertiser* announced a special price for a trip to Yarmouth offered by the Great Eastern Railway on 25 July 1900. Later in the year the *Peterborough Advertiser* reported:

> *A large crowd of excursionists from Peterborough visited Skegness on Thursday. An excursion to London will leave Peterborough on September 27th, and on Friday, September 28th, a cheap excursion will leave Peterborough for Scotland.*[416]

The nearest beach was forty miles from Thorney. The purpose-built Victorian seaside resort of Hunstanton was made fashionable by King Edward VII, who drove there from Sandringham. In the words of John A. Glover-Kind's music hall song of 1907, 'Oh, I do love to be beside the seaside'.

Excursions.

GREAT EASTERN RAILWAY.
WHITSUNTIDE HOLIDAYS.
ON Whit-Monday, May 30th, 1898, Excursion Tickets will be issued to HUNSTANTON as under:—

From	By Trains at a.m.	a.m.	Fare for the Double Journey. Third Class.
Peterborough....	..	8 30	
Whittlesey	..	8 45	2s. 3d.
March	7 50	9 5	

Available for return from Hunstanton at 4·35, 6·45, or 7·10 p.m the same day.
WILLIAM BIRT,
General Manager.
London, May, 1898.

Excursions from the Peterborough Advertiser,
Saturday. 28 May 1898.

Hunstanton Railway Station, early 1900s.
Photograph by M. Bone; in the public domain via Wikimedia Commons.

Hunstanton, 1910.
Postcard taken from the author's collection.

Cliff and Beach, Hunstanton North.

Hunstanton Beach & Cliff, 1911.
Postcard from the author's collection.

So began the tradition of family trips to the sea. Children played with their buckets and spades, building sandcastles alongside their parents, who sat fully clothed, in penny deckchairs shaded from the sun. Entrepreneurs offered donkey rides, roundabouts, and boat trips. There were stuntmen, ventriloquists, mimics, clowns, actors, acrobats, and jugglers to watch, along with 'freak' shows. Punch, and Judy entertained both adults and children.[417] It would not surprise me if Walter and his siblings were taken to the first amusement arcade, opened in 1897 in Yarmouth, or to see Cooke's Circus in 1903.[418] Near the beach Victorian cheap seaside staples – fish and chips, cockles, whelks, ice cream and candyfloss – were eaten on the move.[419]

Given Stephen's outward-looking nature and income, I cannot imagine him depriving his family of such outings. The trips could have given Walter a taste for life away from judging, prying eyes. Was he itching to get away?

Christmas

From the late 1890s a Christmas scene as we might recognise it was just becoming a reality for Walter and his sisters. There had already been a long tradition of bringing in natural greenery, but the Christmas tree is a North European custom.

The 1848 engraving of Queen Victoria & the royal family decorating a tree.
Anonymous illustration; in the public domain via Wikimedia Commons.

It is unclear when it was introduced, but some sources claim that the first 'Christmas trees' were yew trees, brought into the palace by Queen Charlotte, Queen Victoria's mother.[420] However, it was not until an 1848 drawing of Queen Victoria, Prince Albert and their children at Windsor Castle, surrounding a tree decorated with glass baubles and festive candles, that the Christmas tree became an iconic image.[421] The picture was published in newspapers throughout the world and embedded a new Christmas aspiration for the well-off.[422]

Charles Dickens penned many Christmas stories using his childhood experiences of the 'cold decade', a mini-ice age caused by two volcanic eruptions in 1809 and 1815.[423] But he was also a social commentator keen to expose social and moral injustices through fiction.[424] In *A Christmas Carol*, he portrays a humble family alive with kindness, compassion and a generous spirit, headed by Bob Cratchit. Cratchit is mistreated by his employer, Scrooge, who comes to discover the price of greed. Given *A Christmas Carol*'s moralising overtones, reputation, and popularity, it seems reasonable to suppose it was on the shelf of the reading room in Thorney.

'Marley's Ghost' illustration by John Leech, Charles Dickens' A Christmas Carol, 1843.
From the original publication of Charles Dickens' A Christmas Carol. In the public domain via Wikimedia Commons.

By the 1880s the sending of cards was popular, creating a lucrative industry that produced 11.5 million cards in 1880 alone. I can picture Walter and his sisters being encouraged to colour pre-printed Christmas postcards to send to family, taking advantage of the half-penny postage stamp.

On the last day of the Michaelmas term, Walter received an orange as a gift and attended a large Christmas tea given by the Abbey Sunday school. The local newspapers often reflected Christmas traditions:

I think the suspended stocking is an admirable institution. It requires so much pleasant and amusing scheming to get that stocking filled unseen by the intended recipient, and very often a great deal of temporary deafness and blindness must be simulated, such deception being entirely praiseworthy. For days and often for weeks before Christmas one is constantly stumbling upon something that is not then intended for sight or for hearing; and what loving friend or parent forgets to show the utmost astonishment when the day comes for the bestowal of the gift? The time (Christmas Day) is one full of pleasant surprises; indeed, half the happiness of the season depends on carefully planned surprises.[425]

From around 1880 some parents placed an apple, an orange, a few nuts, a sugar mouse, and a big, shiny bronze penny into a stocking. For others, threaded popcorn and gifts of fruit, nuts, sweets, or small handmade trinkets were hung on the Christmas tree. As presents became bigger, hand-knitted gloves, scarves and socks and handcrafted wooden toys appeared underneath its branches.

By the end of the 1890s, Walter feasted on a Norfolk turkey for his Christmas meal, rather than the cheaper beef joint.[426] It amused me to discover last-minute Christmas shopping is not new, as shown from this 1898 newspaper extract:

Here is an experience of one of the Peterborough poulterers. [sic] At half-past 11 o'clock on Christmas eve a gentleman called at the shop and asked the price of a turkey. He said he would have it but requested that it might be plucked and he would call for it in half-an-hour! That would bring it [to] midnight. 'But will you call for it,' asked the poulterer [sic] with a dash of the incredulous in his voice? 'Well, here's half-a-crown to be going on with,' he replied. Thereupon the turkey was plucked, and just as the

> *clock struck midnight, the belated customer called and paid for his turkey!*[427]

Crackers which snapped when pulled, revealing small gifts and paper hats, were in vogue with the middle class by the end of the Victorian period.[428] Singing and charades were a feature of family gatherings as well as party games:

> *A very old idea (and we do not seem to improve on some of these ancient Christmas sports) is to appoint a "Master of Revels," or "Lord of Misrule," as the old books call him. The "Lord of Misrule" (who may be one of the youngest children) is king of the festivities. He chooses the games, and his orders are absolute. A forfeit is paid by anyone who disobeys him or opposes any of his caprices. He may issue the wildest and queerest of commands, and the more fun and novelty he can introduce the more complete success is this little temporary monarch.*[429]

Church and chapel

Although Walter and his family could stay away from church services, the parish church was still an embedded part of life that 'bound communities together'.[430] Services in the ancient Abbey, or chapel, were an essential part of Christmas week for many.[431] Although no longer a legal requirement, the milestones of life, birth, marriage and death, were associated with baptism, wedding and funeral services in the parish church. Regardless of religious belief, the church still had an important role as a place for people to gather, support each other, socialise, and exchange information so it cannot be underestimated. Along with the changing seasons, the church calendar provided a structure for people's lives through its Sunday school, choir practice, fetes, outings, socials, bazaars, flower festival, fundraisers, and youth club. While some people may have attended because they felt a pressure to conform, the church was also a place that offered guidance, and was somewhere to reflect and find wisdom, shared values to live by and, perhaps, discover a lifelong mate.

Walter's family, like countless others, kept a foot in more than one place of worship. The Parkers attended special services in the recently refurbished Abbey, owned by the 11th Duke of Bedford, with its oak benches that seated 370 people.[432] In this Anglican church, a defined hierarchy continued. Pews were rented to the congregation to cover the costs of running the building. As was the case in other churches the most expensive seats were at the front, nearest the minister, lower-cost pews were

Interior of St. Mary & St. Botolph's nave, Thorney, previously part of Thorney Abbey.
Richard Croft / St.Mary & St.Botolph's nave / CC BY-SA 2.0.

in the middle, and there were eighty-four free seats at the back.[433] Even though this practice was being questioned (for example, by the vicar of nearby Oundle), it was unimaginable to any working-class family to have sat in a rented pew near the front, even when the seats were empty.[434]

By attending services Stephen could enjoy a break from home life and learn what was happening in the village – useful to the cottage inspector. But according to Cousin Mary he was a Methodist at heart, and the family regularly attended the modern 130-seat Primitive Methodist Chapel, which opened in 1886 and was updated in 1898.[435] Ethel played the organ here in her early teens. There were compelling reasons for working people (particularly agricultural workers, servants, and small farmers) to belong to the chapel. The Primitive Methodists were democratic. Everyone was equal; even children were taken seriously and encouraged to be active members. Most decisions and day-to-day policy were decided at the local chapel.[436]

The empowerment built into the way the Primitive Methodists worshipped and behaved must have been a thrilling experience compared to the messages sent from some Anglican pulpits that stressed people's place in the grand order of things. It was heady stuff, particularly for a working-class person ineligible to vote. The Anglican Church had aligned itself with the landed gentry and this, alongside their grip on schools and teacher training, went against a growing working-class ethos of self-reliance, self-improvement, and self-governance, personified by Walter's pa. Many Primitive Methodists liked the clarity of the Christian message they heard, which often concentrated on saints and sinners, salvation, and damnation. Its style was direct, often spontaneous, and passionate. The meetings also provided a chance to bond with neighbours and community, easing isolation and loneliness. The Primitive Methodist Church gave comfort and consolation. Its firm stance on temperance might have particularly appealed to Walter.

Did Walter's ma, Ann, hear on Citizen Sunday in 1898 one of the 'five thousand sermons on the evils of drink which were broadcast from Primitive Methodist pulpits'?[437] Author Richard Brown suggests that working-class women were more involved than their men in church and chapel and had a considerable influence on if, where and when the family attended.[438] But given Ann's alcoholism, I find it difficult to picture her sitting comfortably in the chapel or the Abbey on Citizen Sunday.

Wherever Walter was seated, he heard a sermon lasting a minimum of thirty minutes; its purpose was to instruct or give a moral lesson. The effectiveness of the sermon was a popular topic of conversation for Victorians. Some thought the pulpit had lost its influence. However, in 1883 H.H.M.Herbert wrote, 'There is no sign that the modern world...can dispense with the art of the preacher', and a critic writing in the *Saturday Review* asserted that the 'preaching of Christianity has not lost its power on society'.[439] So, we can hope Walter was inspired. Popular preachers had their sermons published. Walter kept two printed sermons until his death, one from 1877 and the other from 1889. Given their dates, I believe he inherited them from his ma, Ann.

No doubt Ann sent her children to Sunday school, either at the chapel schoolroom or the Abbey Sunday school based at the girls' school. This exposure meant many Thorneyites grew up with a basic knowledge of the Bible, Christian stories, and hymns alongside Christian teaching. I wonder how Thorney Abbey's vicar, the Reverend William Symons, and his colleague from the Primitive Methodist Chapel presented the scriptures to Walter when they visited his school.[440] The Reverend Symons earned a *Bachelor of Arts* (second-class degree) in 1874 in the Natural Sciences from Trinity College, Cambridge.[441] He became a priest in 1875. We know the Duke of Bedford, as patron and impropriator of Thorney, had appointed Symons with a living of £230 [about £28,150 in 2020], excluding baptism, marriage and funeral fees.[442] The Duke's choice may have been influenced by a shared interest in the natural world by a Duke who was passionate about evidence-based scientific agriculture.[443] Symons might have appreciated the Duke's developing the social housing his ancestor had built and his political activities.[444] It is intriguing to think Walter and the Parker family may have listened to a thoroughly contemporary vicar, the face of conventional morality reinventing itself for this modern age.

Family tree

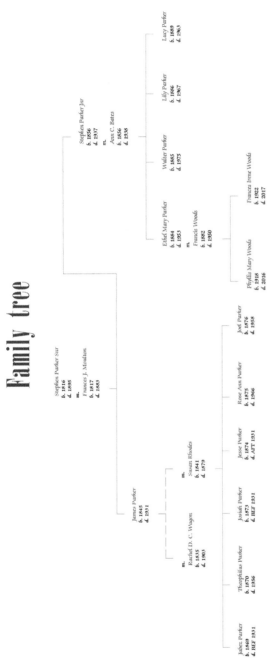

Stephen Parker Snr
b. 1816
d. 1895
m.
Frances J. Moulton
b. 1817
d. 1883

James Parker
b. 1845
d. 1931
m.
Susan Rhodes
b. 1841
d. 1879

Rachel D. C. Wapm
b. 1835
d. 1903

Jabez Parker
b. 1869
d. BEF 1931

Theophilus Parker
b. 1870
d. 1956

Josiah Parker
b. 1873
d. BEF 1931

Jesse Parker
b. 1874
d. AFT 1931

Rose Ann Parker
b. 1875
d. 1966

Joel Parker
b. 1876
d. 1958

Stephen Parker Jnr
b. 1856
d. 1937
m.
Ann C. Bates
b. 1856
d. 1938

Ethel Mary Parker
b. 1884
d. 1953
m.
Francis Woods
b. 1882
d. 1950

Walter Parker
b. 1885
d. 1975

Lily Parker
b. 1886
d. 1967

Lucy Parker
b. 1889
d. 1963

Phyllis Mary Woods
b. 1918
d. 2016

Frances Irene Woods
b. 1922
d. 2017

Health

In a world without antibiotics, it is not surprising that the Victorians were concerned with health above all other issues.[445] At the beginning of every year, the local newspaper would publish a health report about their area. Here is an example, from 1898:

The Health of the District *The following report has been handed to the Council of the Rural District of Thorney – during 1897 42 births were registered and 19 deaths, as follows:- Under 1 year, 6... over 10 under 20, 1; over 20 and under 30, 1; over 30 and under 40, 0; over 40 and under 50, 1; over 50 and under 70, 3; over 70, 6; total 19....The cases of infectious diseases notified during the year were 12, namely, 3 of erysipelas, all slight cases [Erysipelas is a superficial infection, affecting the upper layers of the skin]; eight of scarlet fever, two families being attacked, all doing well; and one case of diphtheria. Inspected the various houses and premises, and found them all in good sanitary condition.[446]*

Yet, Walter and his siblings were not necessarily confident of their survival. Their second cousin, Isaac Parker of Upwell, born the autumn before Walter, died of Friedreich's ataxia when Walter was fourteen years old.[447] According to the National Institute of Neurological Disorders and Stroke:

> *[Friedreich's is] a rare, incurable, inherited disease that causes nervous system damage and movement problems. It begins between ages ten and fifteen years old and leads to impaired muscle coordination that worsens over time.[448]*

The head of the boys' school also lost two children, including his daughter Ethel May Law, aged 17 years, when Walter was aged ten.[449]

In my mind, I have conjured up an image of Walter's ma doing all she could to keep her children healthy. However, during the Victorian period concepts of waterborne and airborne infections were not yet accepted. Disease was primarily understood to result from inherited susceptibility, lifestyle, or noxious exhalations.[450] Treatment consisted of cod liver oil, rest, fresh air, a bland diet, and opium-based drugs 'doled out' at home without medical supervision. Adults and children were often prescribed meat, milk, eggs, and alcohol.

By the end of the nineteenth century, the health of the poor and many of the working-class was recognised as deficient. This was reflected in their shorter stature and higher death rates at all ages.[451] The situation was highlighted by the poor physical condition of the male army volunteers during the Boer War 1899–1902; two-fifths of those volunteering were rejected as unfit for active service.[452] However, in 1902 Dr Carter of Liverpool reported a marked fall in mortality; the overall figures were not as dire as we might suppose:

> *Deaths from starvation had fallen from eighteen to twelve per 1,000,000; deaths from scurvy, 1 in 1,000,000 have remained stationary; but deaths from intemperance have risen from forty-five per 1,000,000 of those living in the year 1878 to seventy-seven per 1,000,000 in 1897.[453]*

The period saw many scientific breakthroughs. In Germany, in 1878, microbiologist Robert Koch found the bacteria that caused septicaemia. He went on to identify the tuberculosis and cholera bacteria (1882 and 1883). The bacteria for typhoid, pneumonia and the plague were also identified in the 1880s. In France, in 1884, Charles Chamberland discovered that viruses also cause disease. But the basic understanding that bacteria and viruses cause illness was not yet common knowledge among those caring for the sick in the community. As a result, misinformation abounded, and the useful nuggets reported in newspapers rarely explained to the housewife what she could do to help her family. For example, a local newspaper said it had been:

> *...conclusively demonstrated...that summer diarrhoea is primarily due to the increased temperature of the earth, whereby certain micro-organisms are set free in the air, these causing certain chemical changes in the food, manufacturing an irritant poison.*[454]

Doctors regularly offered home nursing tips for common ailments. This treatment for burns appeared in numerous newspapers:

> *Free use of soft soap upon a fresh burn will remove the fire from the flesh in less time than it takes to write these words. If the burn be severe, after relief from the pain, use linseed oil, and then sift upon it wheat flour. When this is dried hard, repeat the oil and flour until a complete covering is obtained. Let this dry until it falls off, and a new skin will be formed without a scar. This treatment leaves nothing more to be desired.*[455]

There were campaigns to educate people. For instance, James Sawyer, a well-known physician from Birmingham, specified

nineteen secrets to longevity in the *Peterborough Advertiser* in 1898: 'Keep the following nineteen commandments, and Sir James sees no reason why you should not live to be one hundred'.[456]

1. *Eight hours' sleep.*

2. *Sleep on your right side.*

3. *Keep your bedroom window open all night.*

4. *Have a mat to your bedroom door.*

5. *Do not have your bedstead against the wall.*

6. *No cold tub in the morning, but a bath at the temperature of the body.*

7. *Exercise before breakfast.*

8. *Eat little meat and see that is well-cooked.*

9. *(For adults) Drink no milk.*

10. *Eat plenty of fat to feed the cells which destroy disease germs.*

11. *Avoid intoxicants [alcohol and drugs], which destroy these cells.*

12. *Daily exercise in the open air.*

13. *Allow no pet animals in your living rooms. They are apt to carry disease germs.*

14. *Live in the country if you can.*

15. *Watch the three Ds – drinking water, damp, and drains.*

16. *Have change[s] of occupation.*

17. *Take frequent and short holidays.*

18. *Limit your ambition.*

19. *Keep your temper.*[457]

Most of Ann's information about health and well-being probably came from a handbook, such as *Cassell's Family Doctor by a Medical Man*, published from 1897 in fortnightly parts costing a few pence each. Compendiums like this offered reassurance and enabling, practical advice for common conditions such as scabies and ringworm as well as sudden illness or accident.

Common illnesses

During Walter's youth, the most common reason for absence from school was ill health – in the pupil, among their siblings or 'at home'. 'Attendance... exceedingly poor' was a common entry in the school log, as was two girls 'home the same day as there was a case of measles in the house'.[458] Infectious diseases killed. The most dangerous illnesses in terms of the number of children who died following infection were tuberculosis, diarrhoea and dysentery, whooping cough, measles, scarlet fever, typhoid, diphtheria, and smallpox.[459] I hope Walter and his siblings were not given a fried mouse to eat, an East Anglian 'remedy' for whooping cough.[460]

The school logs detail a cycle of typhus and typhoid, cholera, smallpox, measles, whooping cough, and scarlet fever. These epidemics were as much part of the yearly calendar as Garland Day and the Peterborough Fair. With few effective treatments, the schools were regularly closed hoping to reduce the number of people infected, for example, 17 July 1893, six cases of scarlet fever. Winter brought diphtheria, alongside the usual colds. The school closing for five weeks was not uncommon.[461] And 'January 14th School medical officer examined children's throats, 2 children sent home, throats infected with diphtheria bacilli, next day another child sent home. 17th another child sent home'.[462]

Influenza, scarlet fever, and consumption made children seriously ill, sometimes for months at a time. The influenza epidemic of 1903 affected a significant proportion of people in the district. Although diarrhoea was a common complaint, it was poorly understood and 'the severest form of dehydration caused by explosive, bloody diarrhoea was often, disastrously, treated with opium with wine or water added'. (The need for specific oral rehydration therapy, which replaced the lost salt, glucose and other essential minerals, was not well known until 1920.[463]) While most children were nursed at home, sometimes to aid recovery they were sent to a convalescence home for children or one with a children's wing.[464] These provided people a place to recuperate. They were commonly near the sea or in the countryside and provided a 'change' of air thought vital for a return to health.[465] The Duke of Bedford was Patron to Okehampton Convalescent home in Devon. Here working-class patients could be admitted 'for a weekly rate of 12s 6d if the case is recommended by a 'clergyman or medical man'.[466]

Convalescent Home, Hunstanton, early 1900s.
From the author's collection.

Historian Eli Anders, Visiting Assistant Professor of Writing and Writing Fellow at Haverford College states that 'convalescent homes, with spaces like sitting rooms, individual bedrooms, libraries, and game rooms [sic], sought to emulate the peaceful conditions of the home, rather than the depressing environment of the hospital'.[467] Here the individual could best move from being an invalid to someone in an active state of recovery. According to a school log, Emily Goodwin, of Thorney, was sent away, in March 1893, 'absent since Christmas, is delicate, has gone to Whittlesea for a change'.[468]

We do not know what health crisis caused Walter's sister Lily to be withdrawn from school in March 1893, aged six, and again in July 1893. The second absence lasted seven months. The death rate from the notorious respiratory tuberculosis, a disease of the lungs, was finally declining in Victorian Britain. However, many still contracted it, including Walter's youngest sister Lucy. We can imagine Ann's fear when she learnt her youngest daughter had consumption. Not only had it killed Ann's mother when Ann was four years old, but Ann's first-born had died from one of its complications. Cousin Mary told me that Ann took 'no chances' and Lucy 'grew up in the garden', as an abundance of fresh air was the principal treatment. Lily and Lucy were not alone in being absent from school for months at a time. A school log records:

> *1892, August 12th, Elisa Cousins has been absent for the past 15 weeks; October 7th Amy Cousins returned to school after 15 weeks.*[469]

The loss of education was something that would affect Lucy keenly when, as a widow, she struggled to support herself and her son.[470]

The medical officer

The medical officer was a common sight at school. He checked the children for signs of disease to prevent widespread outbreaks, and also looked for scabies, head lice and ringworm. Following an illness, the medical officer might, like the doctor, permit children to attend school for reduced hours, often starting later in the day. The sanitary inspector or medical officer regularly ordered that the equipment the Duke provided to the school be burned and replaced to reduce infection. For example, 'lead pencils have been received in place of those destroyed by order of the medical officer'.[471] To prevent further outbreaks of disease, the school was scrubbed from floor to ceiling, and the walls freshened with distemper.

Pulmonary and bovine tuberculosis

Despite the poor health of the working and pauper classes, by the early 1900s better nutrition for some (from a greater quantity of food, because of higher incomes, the fall in family size and sanitary reform) had led to better health overall.[472] However, one chronic infection caused significant numbers of disability and deaths. In 1882, Robert Koch stated that one-seventh of the human population was killed by tuberculosis.[473] By 1892, 85 per cent of English medical officers believed that tuberculosis was communicable via raw milk and undercooked meat.[474] Yet the possibility that bovine tuberculosis could be transferred from cows to humans was hotly disputed. Theobald Smith subsequently published his findings on human and bovine tubercle in 1898 when he demonstrated the causative bacteria to be two different

organisms that are now known as *Mycobacterium* tuberculosis (M. tuberculosis) and *Mycobacterium bovis (M. bovis)*.[475] *M. bovis* was found to be principally responsible for non-pulmonary forms of tuberculosis.[476] Although *M. tuberculosis* was apparently in decline 'tuberculosis was the single highest cause of death and disability in nineteenth-century Britain. People in their 30s and 40s had a depressingly high chance of dying from it'.[477]

Meanwhile, *M. bovis* was on the rise.[478] For Walter's generation, drinking milk was akin to Russian roulette. Although those with a compromised immune system were more vulnerable, it was impossible to know which children would become infected by bovine tuberculosis until it was too late. Elsewhere in Europe, milk producers boiled their milk to kill the bacteria before it reached the customer. The understanding that bringing infected milk to boiling point, 'absolutely freed [it] from all poisonous germs' was ignored in England.[479] Meanwhile, in Scotland

A Co-op milkman, Peterborough Co-operative Society.
A horse-drawn milkman working for the Peterborough Co-operative Society (location unknown).
Photograph taken from the Peterborough Images Archive: www.peterboroughimages.co.uk.

insurance was available to compensate butchers who bought infected meat.[480] Change took place in England at a glacial pace, despite cows supplying Birmingham's milk being the first to be tested on a large scale, and from 1907 to 1927 no less than 40.4 per cent were found to be infected.[481] Shockingly, the British government did not impose a workable system through which bovine TB could be eradicated until the 1950s. It was a preventable tragedy that infected cows would pass the infection to generations of English children well into the middle of the twentieth century.

It has been conservatively estimated that a minimum of 500,000 (and possibly 800,000 or more) preventable human deaths in the period 1850–1950 were attributable to bovine TB, especially among young children, who were the main milk drinkers.[482] The treatments of clean air, quality nutrition and bed rest often caused a stay in an isolation hospital or sanatorium. For each person who died of bovine TB, seven to ten people lived with the lifelong emotional scars of sudden, repeated separation from their families and the physical consequences of the infection in their bones and joints.[483]

However, the most disabling factor was that most of these 'crippled' children were excluded from education and their community. Many parents were pressured into the view that their disabled child would be better cared for in an institution. Little thought was given to the appropriateness of a child with a limp spending all their time with another without speech, or a much lower developmental age. Few children with a disability, however mild, were educated except, latterly, those with a hearing or sight impairment. Survivors of bovine TB, whose joint damage led to mobility issues, would be largely prevented from earning a living.[484]

Family tree

Isaac Parker
b. 1773
d. 1845
m.

Jacob Parker
b. 1807
d. 1889

Stephen Parker Snr
b. 1816
d. 1895

James Bates
b. 1819
d. 1875
m.

Ann Rands
b. 1818
d. 1860

Stephen Parker Jnr
b. 1856
d. 1937
m.

Ann C. Bates
b. 1856
d. 1938

Stephen Parker
b. 1845
d. 1915

Isaac Parker
b. 1884
d. 1900

Lily Ann Parker
b. 1882
d. 1883

Ethel Mary Parker
b. 1884
d. 1953

Walter Parker
b. 1885
d. 1975

Lily Parker
b. 1886
d. 1967

Lucy Parker
b. 1889
d. 1963

CHAPTER 9

A Farm Labourer

When I reflect on Walter's life, I am struck by how work and the activities of his pre-teen years gave him an industry and competence some would now see as unusual. Children of this era knew they were contributing something significant to their home life. They were not talking or playing a game about living; they were experiencing it. If, as research shows, a child's concept of their worth relates to their being good at something they consider worthwhile, we can suppose Walter's learning of everyday life skills had a powerful impact on how he saw himself.[485] Given the extent that people's levels of self-esteem influences the quality of their social relationships, I believe that village life nurtured Walter's self-esteem, mitigating, perhaps, some of the difficulties of his relationship with his mother.[486]

According to the Erikson developmental model, pubescent teens need to build their identity and focus on social relationships.[487] Older children start to question the things they have previously learnt and gradually separate from the family by becoming more independent. If this stage is positively completed, it is thought adolescents will gain a committed identity. It is during this life stage that, Cousin Mary told me, Walter refused

to doff his cap in respect. Walter showed a firm sense of self, with values to live by, despite his mother's addiction.

In the 'intimacy versus isolation' stage, Erikson argued young adults focus on establishing intimate relationships (not necessarily sexual ones) and have the chance to share their identity. If this stage is resolved, individuals can gain satisfaction, love, and affiliation. If not, they can become isolated. It would be understandable if this and his mother's misuse of alcohol left Walter feeling lonely.

Unlike many of his contemporaries, Walter did not need to earn to help feed the family. Instead, he finished the education open to him. Elsewhere, young children were sent away to work for a pittance. They received board and lodgings, and their absence reduced the financial strain on the remaining family. One young agricultural labourer, Richard Hillyer, described his early working life in his autobiography, *Country Boy*:

> *Every night I dropped asleep over my supper, and then woke up just enough to crawl upstairs and fall into bed. A black depression spread over me. 'This is what it is going to be from now on,' I thought, 'Lifting, haling, shoving, trudging about from day to day, nothing else through all the years... It was like settling down into a deep bed of mud, cold, gluey, isolating...*[488]

Although Walter's earnings were not necessary, I believe his first experience of agricultural work was before he left school at the end of May 1898, aged thirteen. This would be in keeping with his father's work ethic, the family's experience, and the expectations of his peers. Choice of occupation was a luxury, and Walter understood from an early age that he had to earn his keep. We know from the 1901 census that, like generations of Parkers before him, Walter was working the land by the time he was fifteen years old. He was one of the millions of people at the bottom of the agricultural hierarchy dependent on a wage affected by variable harvests, the price of the crops and the English weather. Walter was not alone. In 1891, 8.3 per cent of the male English labour-force worked as agricultural labourers or farm labourers.[489] In comparison, in the same year, 2.7 per cent were used in cotton textile production.[490]

The Duke of Bedford had many tenant farmers. According to a map of 'Thorney Town' held by the Cambridgeshire Archives, there were at least three farms a leisurely stroll from Walter's home. So, it is not surprising he is recorded in the 1901 census working as an agricultural labourer, but living with his family in Station Road at the Tank Yard address.

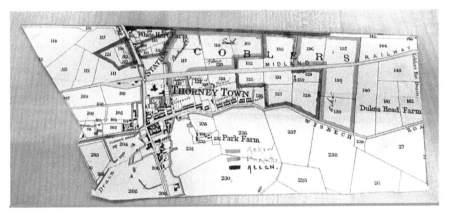

Thorney Town Map from the Cambridgeshire Archive.

The working day

Walter was expected to work six days a week, Monday to Saturday. If he was lucky, his employer gave him Plough Monday off, generally the first Monday after Twelfth Day (6 January), in addition to the four bank holidays enjoyed by most workers. If Walter was walking to one of the local farms, he might have been able to have a lie-in until a quarter past five. However, if he had responsibility for getting the horses ready for the day ahead, or worked with the cowman getting milk to the early city train, he had to rise much earlier. The working-class breakfast was often 'two large hunks of [stale] bread put into a basin and sprinkled with salt over which boiling water was poured – referred to as kettle broth'.[491] However, in Walter's more affluent home, he enjoyed porridge with milk.

Joining the other workers in the farm's courtyard, Walter would be told what tasks he was to do that day. For most of the year, he worked for eight to ten hours with a brief break for 'dinner'. A typical midday meal was wheaten bread and cheese with a pickled onion. Alternatively, he could have had a Bedfordshire 'clanger', introduced by workers from the Bedford estates. Made from Sunday leftovers, this was an elongated steamed suet-crust dumpling, similar to a pasty. It had a savoury filling at one end and a sweet one at the other; the savoury piece was scored to show which end to eat first. The savoury filling was a little meat with spiced, diced potatoes and vegetables. The sweet end was flavoured with jam, apple, or another seasonal fruit.[492] Walter took sweet tea in an earthenware pot to drink cold with his dinner. It was expected that the housewife would prepare the labourer's dinner when she got breakfast ready. Was Walter's ma sober enough to do this, or was a sister expected to step into the breach?

What Walter wore

By the early 1900s, a typical farm labourer's clothes comprised a warm, waterproof jacket made of a hard-wearing blend of cotton and flax that was serviceable and cheap, a cotton shirt, corduroy

trousers, and a cap, as seen in the illustration. In Suffolk, the wearing of cords by working men was ubiquitous, and a farmworker not doing so was 'considered to be getting above his station'.[493] (I remember Walter still wearing this 'uniform' in the 1960s and 1970s.) In his youth, Walter wore hand-made boots made from leather, with steel-capped toes and hobnailed soles. The leather would initially be hard and cause blisters.

Nineteenth century agricultural labourers.
This photograph represents labourers' wear throughout the century. The oldest worker (in the centre) wearing breeches is dressed in the style of the early 19th century. The smocks worn by three of the men were typical by the middle of the century, and the corduroy trousers and jacket worn by the man on the left are more typical of the latter part of the century. The different styles may reflect the different ages of the men. The women are wearing generic domestic servant clothes.
From http://www.heardfamilyhistory.org.uk/uniforms.

Boots cost 14 shillings (£85), so each day Walter cleaned them thoroughly when he finished work.[494] He regularly worked dubbing wax into the leather to soften it and to expel water. In hot or wet weather, he stuffed his boots with grass to soak up the moisture and reduce the chances of chafing or a fungal infection taking hold.

Farming culture on the Bedford Estates

Although it may appear that Walter was embarking on lowly work, he was doing it in one of the most forward-thinking evidence-based farming communities in Britain. The 1875 Agricultural Holdings (England) Act gave tenant farmers the right to receive consistent levels of compensation for the value of their improvements to the soil. The Council of the Royal Agricultural Society (RAS) looked to turn opinion into substantial scientific evidence before it reluctantly decided that the cost of setting up an experimental station could not be justified.[495] Francis Charles Hastings Russell, 9th Duke of Bedford and vice-president of the RAS, was a pioneer of modern agriculture. He had a fierce interest in scientific practice (to the point of ruinous spending), and he stepped in, offering Mill Farm, in the parish of Husborne Crawley. The 9th Duke of Bedford, known as Hastings, assumed the entire long-term cost of the undertaking.

By 1876 Hastings had set up the innovative Woburn Experimental Farm, the first of its kind. It included Stackyard Field, which the Duke leased from his tenant at Birchmore Farm. He started a longitudinal study on the value of different animal manure on diverse types of soil.[496] The experiments, directed by the Chemical Committee of the Royal Agricultural Society, aimed to find out the merits of different types of manure on the growth of wheat and barley, the role of fertiliser in clover sickness and the value of laying down permanent pastures. The Woburn Continuous Wheat and Barley Experiments ran from 1876–1990.[497]

From 1895, the experimental fruit farm rigorously examined any matters connected with fruit growing, whether of practical or purely scientific interest.[498] The 1896 trials on fertiliser looked at the feeding of bullocks and sheep, and how nitrogen was introduced. In addition, the 11th Duke funded the council to establish a farm school for twenty scholars on the Woburn estate. It aimed to provide 'instruction in the principles upon which the best farm practice is founded'. It 'combine[d] theory with daily practical work on the farm, including the care of stock, dairy work and poultry, reaping, bee-keeping, land measuring, ploughing, hedging and ditching, stacking and thatching, and the care and use of machinery'.[499]

The 11th Duke's endeavours were crucial because, as Howard Edwin Bracey pointed out, 'Until the end of the nineteenth century... there was virtually no organised agricultural education or instruction' in Britain.[500] In his book, the Duke declared that the mass of information would be made available as practical leaflets.[501] He passionately believed in sharing the knowledge gained, not just with his tenant farmers but also with the cottagers on all his estates and the county council farm school.

Another part of the dissemination of new knowledge was through lectures given 'for the benefit of all who may care to attend'.[502] The 11th Duke was interested in other pioneering work, and in November 1900 he invited a representative from Garton's experimental farm, which concentrated on new techniques in plant breeding, to lecture on the growth of cereals and grasses.[503] The Duke's steward presided, encouraging a large attendance from the Thorney community. The local newspaper favourably commented on the Duke's promotion of scientific agriculture in their article about the Thorney Foal Show in 1900.[504] Information was shared between the estates, and I expect Walter soaked up as much as he could, squirrelling away the knowledge in the way of many young men, until it might be of use.

Farm work

Agricultural work is often portrayed as low-skilled work for the 'dull-witted', which says less about the work itself and more about the ignorance of an urban population that has become disconnected from the harsh demands of the land. The Royal Commission on Labour of 1893 acknowledged the gradations of skill, some substantial, required for various types of farm work:

> *The general impression respecting the ordinary agricultural labourer is that of a man engaged in work which requires little intelligence, skill, or training, but in reality there are few duties which he has to perform which do not call for a certain amount of judgment, dexterity, and practice; and the training and management of horses, the art of ploughing, mowing, or sowing, the use of spade or fork must be learned, and the labourer who had not learned to economise his forces and attack his work at the point of least resistance would be worn out very quickly.[505]*

My grandfather had a favourite saying, 'If you want to find a fool in the country, you had better take him with you'.[506] Much of Walter's knowledge was learnt from the previous generation. He paid close attention to the way the older men worked. I remember his seemingly effortless walk. My father told me he thought Walter's movements were slow and plodding until he worked alongside him and found they were sure, economic, and effective. As Walter said, you should not throw away your energy at the beginning of the day, but work at a pace that would last as long as the light.

If Walter had proved his worth the year after he left school, he became a 'half-man'; that is, he received half a man's wages. According to a resource on Cambridgeshire history, he did 'light jobs...taking the loaded wagons to the stack yard; or (drag-work), and leading a horse with the drag-rake'. 'The horses he handled would be the staid old jobbing horses that had lost all their sprightliness after long years of hard ploughing'.[507]

Walter undertook a wide variety of tasks. Exceptional skill was involved in some, such as ploughing, animal husbandry, the slaughter and disposal of animals, draining and levelling land,

and mending and putting up field fences and gates. Innovative technologies could have been used for other tasks, like sowing and planting crops, threshing, and rolling land, alongside the traditional jobs of reaping and staking cereal crops, lifting root crops, and preparing them for storage, and hedging. Labourers were also expected to chop and stack wood, thatch, create hedges and ditches, and keep a close watch on the horses. English rural labourers were mostly fuelled by a diet of bread and potatoes, with meat consumption varying from season to season, and area to area. Men were often better fed than the rest of the family to help them stay fit enough to work. Walter, still living with his parents, had a much more varied diet. For the labourers outside the closed villages of grand estates, the effect of rural poverty could be seen in malnutrition, associated ill-health, and workhouse admissions.[508]

One of the most valued of the farmworkers was the horseman. A lot depended on him. He was responsible for the care and management of the horses, which provided transport and much of the power in farming until around

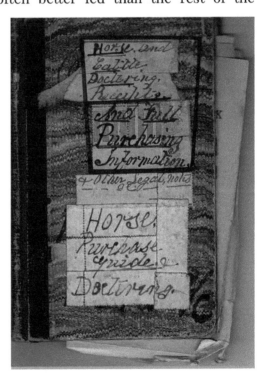

Joel Parker, notebook cover.
Horse and Cattle Doctoring, purchasing information and other legal notes. Also includes The Horse keeper's "Effective" Receipt Book containing the Arabian Horse Tamers' Secret, How to make a horse follow you like a dog, and others on the art of horse taming by Rupert Graham. Kept by Walter's cousin Joel Parker (1876-1958) in Upwell. In the keeping of Cousin Sue Oldroyd née Parker

The following.
Pages 1 — 19 inclusive
are extracts copied,
from A Treatise
So
His Royal Highness,
The Duke of York.

Qualities, & Defects.
To be taken into
account, before
Purchasing A Horse.
" On the Foot.
Ought to be Round,
rather than long, and
of proportion, to size of
the Horse, with a
good high, or deep hoof.
gradually narrowing by
the black part, or heel.
But this must not be
out of proportion deep.
he Frog, & bars should
e hard; and free from
e appearance of disease,
d black, or very dark.

Joel Parker, notebook, pp. 12 & 13.

1945. The horseman was in charge of the welfare, grooming, feeding and medical care of the animals. His skill for field work such as ploughing, drilling, and cultivating was vital to the success of his employer.[509] Horsemen often jotted down what they had learnt in a notebook, like the example shown in the following illustration kept by Walter's cousin Joel Parker in Upwell. Walter became a skilled horseman.

Agricultural pay

Agricultural workers in Cambridgeshire, not tied to an estate, were historically some of the lowest paid in the country.[510] On 19 September 1900, the *Peterborough Advertiser* reported that potato

pickers were paid an average of 2s-6d (£15.79) a day, not enough to pay the families weekly tea and sugar bill.[511] But despite the great agricultural depression in the closing years of the nineteenth century, tenants on many country estates enjoyed 'a degree of affluence, leisure and conviviality'.[512] The 11th Duke prided himself on never evicting a farm tenant. However, between 1879 and 1895, to ensure the farmers could continue to employ labourers and work the land, the Duke was forced to reduce their rent seventeen times.

While the Duke's support enabled employment for youths like Walter, all was not rosy. By 1898 Thorney had a co-operative, part of the Peterborough Co-operative Society, which baked bread and sold groceries at reasonable prices.[513] The customers were paid an annual dividend, and a manager was paid a salary and derived no benefit for selling inferior goods.[514] Not all setups were this ethical, though. Casual farmworkers could be 'paid' in farm tokens, sometimes known as 'strawberry money'.[515] These only had value on the farm itself, where they would be exchanged for produce; off-site, they were worthless.

Hickman's Farm tokens, Thorney, 1950s.
These tokens were used to pay workers on Hickman's farm in Thorney in the 1950s and were often called 'strawberry money'. (Hickman & Co. was based at what is now Pigeons Farm and the Fen Farming Company was at Bank Farm.) They were issued by local farms to people on piecework picking crops and were exchanged for 'proper' currency at the end of the day. Photograph by Paul Young; taken from the Peterborough Images Archive: www.peterboroughimages.co.uk.

If Walter was still working on the farm at age sixteen or seventeen, as was likely, he was paid three-quarters of the wages a full-man received. By 1902, he could have been earning nine shillings [£54] a week.[516]

Harvest

Agricultural labourers,
Wisbech area, c1900.
From the Facebook group:
Wisbech and Surrounding Villages Old Photos

Agricultural labourer, Norfolk harvest, c1900.
A man carrying tied sheaf. Norfolk harvest, c1900.
With the kind permission of News from the
North folk and South folk. https://icenipost.com/.

At haymaking and harvest time, everyone in the labouring class had to pull their weight. Men, women, and children worked from dawn to dusk for as long as the weather held. It took eighteen to twenty days of gruelling work to bring in a cereal harvest. Traditionally, thirty-four men mowed the wheat or oats. To lay it evenly, their scythes were fitted with cradles made of iron rods. Each man was followed by two women and a boy or girl, called gavellers, whose job was to rake the mown cereal into rows, ready for tying into sheaves. Eight teams of men followed on to shock or stack the sheaves. Ten sheaves were placed in a shock. The grain-heads were kept off the ground while still in the field, before threshing. A female gaveller worked behind each wagon, feeding the sheaves to two men, one on each side of the wagon who did the pitching. This handling of the sheaves from the ground onto the wagon was the heaviest job of all. As a three-quarter man, Walter could be found on top of the load, with another, more experienced man working alongside him. They received the wheat and arranged it evenly.

A loaded cart, Norfolk harvest, 1900.
With the kind permission of News from the North folk and South folk. https://icenipost.com/.

After the grain was cut, it had to be threshed, flailed, and winnowed. Once threshed, the grain was separated from the lighter chaff. Hopefully, all the Duke's tenant farmers were no longer separating the grain

Haystack with cart Norfolk harvest, c1900.
With the kind permission of News from the North folk and South folk. https://icenipost.com/.

from the ear by hand using a flail but working with a steam-driven thresher. A successful harvest meant workers often earned enough money to pay their annual rent, or collected enough coins for a replacement set of clothes and boots. As a bachelor living with his parents, Walter was expected to pass his wages over to his mother towards his keep. I hope his ma did not drink his earnings.

Once the harvest was in, the farmer's wife provided the workers with a celebration on a Saturday evening. Everyone would gather in the farmyard (or in a barn, if the weather was wet or windy) and sit down to a roast dinner with the farm's home-brewed beer or cider. It was an important social event, and a relief after the long, hard, and uncertain hours in the fields, when a change in weather could still bring disaster.

One such celebration was a harvest supper given by Mr D. Gibbs:

> *Afterwards songs were sung by the men and visitors. Then the men all stood up and sang, 'For he's a jolly good fellow,' and 'For she's a jolly good Lady,' and gave three cheers for the master and mistress... As the clock struck twelve the company rose and sang, 'God save the Queen' [and] sang, 'Praise God from whom all blessings flow.' Everything passed off wonderfully well.*[517]

After the meal, the men would smoke. It may be that Walter already smoked the clay pipe common to his class. (He was a pipe-smoker throughout the time his son-in-law Harry knew him.) Although it could be the early hours of the morning before the labourers went to bed, all were expected to be in church or chapel for the harvest thanksgiving service the following morning.[518]

While Walter managed to steer clear of accidents, his fellow Thorneyite, John Marshall, died of his injuries in 1898 when he fell off a stack at harvest time. Walter was in an occupation that had a lower death rate than any other manual work, apart from engine drivers and gardeners. Overall, life expectancy was rising.[519] By 1900 conditions for farmworkers had improved, although fewer were needed because of the introduction of modern steam machinery. If Walter was paid in cash, he earned around ten shillings (£63) a week.

By contrast, outside the estates there were year-long and multi-year contracts for farm servants and skilled workers. Casual day labour was often made up of women, children and young adults contracted out temporarily by gangmasters to whichever farmer needed their services.[520] There was a marked difference in conditions between the day labourers and those workers who lived at the farm where they worked. The casual day labourer who lived in his rented cottage had the freedom to starve. He might receive his wage as a mix of cash, beer, or tokens. He would be laid off when the weather was too bad to work outside or when the specific job he had been hired to do was finished. Inevitably, there were periods when he was reliant on charity or poor relief, the shame of which was felt keenly. No wonder Walter looked to leave the land and better himself as his father had done before.

CHAPTER 10:

All Change

Stephen Parker reached the pinnacle of working-class opportunity in Thorney by becoming the estate and cottage foreman and inspector of cottages to the Duke of Bedford. He stepped into the shoes of a Scot, John Irons, who moved out of Thorney in March 1900.[521] Stephen's new role included managing the estate cottages and paying the estate workers.[522] The 11th Duke described the role of cottage foreman in his book 'In considering the staff of a great estate; it is not easy to overrate the importance of the cottage foreman'. He states the role demanded an 'intricate knowledge of the other tenants' circumstances' and he refers to the inspector of cottages' 'difficult and delicate duties' necessitating a man of 'special qualities'. The Duke adds that 'the management of the cottages is a cause of constant care and anxiety' and that 'unless the cottage foreman is carefully chosen as a man of tact and good feeling, friction and discontent are inevitable'.[523]

The Duke's carefully worded portrait, written a few years after the Parkers took up residence in the Tank Yard, tallies with Cousin Mary's detailed description of my great-grandfather. What the Duke was unlikely to know was that Stephen had a subversive side. When I was eleven years old, Walter confused me by proudly showing me his father's signature, *S. Parker*, scratched onto a windowpane of the water tower, etched with

a borrowed diamond ring. Walter's niece Mary still appeared to be shocked when she told me of the numerous windows in the village which had been similarly vandalised. This rebellious act risked his reputation. Moreover, if Stephen were convicted, each incident could incur a fine of up to 'five pounds' [£632].[524] If a child absorbs their first lessons in behaviour suitable for their place in society from their family, particularly from the parent of the same sex, I wonder what Walter took from his father's nonconformist actions.[525]

The Duke supported the elderly on his estates. One of Stephen's unenviable tasks was to convince widows to downsize to smaller or shared accommodation to free up housing for working families. One woman, believed a danger to herself, gave the foreman short shrift: 'I want the house to myself and do not want to be messed about'.[526]

Guiding the next generation

Settled into his new role, it would be understandable if Stephen reflected on his social mobility. His working life started as an insecure casual agricultural labourer with low pay. Through education and honing his skills, he reinvented himself as a bricklayer, carpenter, and builder. These stepping-stones gave Stephen experience that was useful to the Duke of Bedford's estate when he became the manager of the water and sewage works.

Stephen became estate foreman, aged forty-four years, and according to Erikson's theory of identity and *psychosocial development*, his gaze would shift to guiding the next generation. If people do indeed experience a need to create or nurture things that will outlast them, it would be natural for Stephen to look at how he might influence his only son's future. By now Walter had a thorough grounding in farm work, but agriculture was seemingly in crisis, and the future was unclear.[527] No doubt Stephen believed Walter would have more opportunities if he learnt a trade.

Walter's apprenticeship – 1902

By 1902 Walter was an experienced land worker, but he wanted more. He was among many young men opting to leave farm work. By 1901 one-fifth of men engaged in agriculture were over fifty-five and the aggregate number of rural workers had dropped by a third in thirty years.[528] Walter aspired to be his own man and earn enough to support a family, but how was he to accomplish this? The importation of cheap wheat from the USA and Canada was disastrous to many growing wheat crops in England. In a long and widely reported speech in Thorney in 1896, the pensive Duke said he was all for free trade, but there was a good case for the readjustment of taxation on the land to enable the continuation of rural work.[529] If the Duke was finding it difficult to run his estate at Thorney at a profit, perhaps Walter thought it prudent to look elsewhere for his living.

The front of Walter's apprenticeship document.
In the author's collection.

On 22 August 1902 Walter, aged seventeen, signed his name to become apprenticed for four years to Robert Thomas Smith and Edward William

Smith, trading as the Smith Bros. They were the main contractor for the Duke of Bedford on the Thorney estate.[530] Walter was following his father, Stephen, and his uncle James into the building trade. Like his cousins Theophilus and Joel, Walter's apprenticeship was as a carpenter and joiner. Had Walter reviewed his options working up the agricultural hierarchy and found them wanting? The age-appropriate vacancies in the local newspapers did not fill him with enthusiasm.

> *Harness Maker – Wanted, respectable young Man. Country Trade. Constant employment. – Ross and Son, King's Lynn.*[531]

Whatever his motivation, seventeen-year-old Walter was fortunate that his father could support him through his training. Stephen's responsibilities were laid out in the apprentice document (see Appendix D):

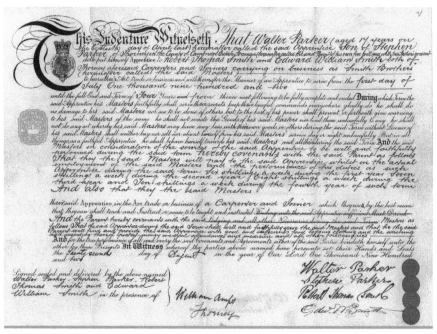

Walter's full apprenticeship document.
From the author's collection.

> *[The said parent] will find and provide the said Apprentice with good and sufficient food, lodging, clothing and the washing and mending thereof, pocket-money, medical attendance and medicine and all other necessities.*[532]

The six shillings a week that Walter received in 1902 would be the equivalent of £36.27 in 2019. This may not seem much, but his skill as a carpenter and joiner would supplement his future income when living on the Canadian prairies and help him find work during the Great Depression of the 1930s, and beyond.

Walter Parker (standing at the centre) as an apprentice working for the Smith Brothers of Thorney, c1902.
From the author's collection.

During his apprenticeship, Walter was part of a team that built houses and carried out repairs on the Bedford estate. As he was coming to the end of his contract, his employers were contracted to restore the nave roof of Thorney Abbey.[533] When Walter finished his training in March 1907, he was given, as was typical, a pocket version of the New Testament by his employer. As indicated by his pencil marking, whatever his religious beliefs, he returned to Mark, Chapter 8, verse 36:

> *For what shall it profit a man, if he shall gain the whole world, and lose his own soul?*

Walter kept the gift for his lifetime.

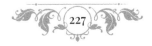

Walter Parker (Last row of two, left-hand) as an apprentice working for the Smith Brothers of Thorney, c1902.
From the author's collection.

Walter Parker's co-workers, Smith Brothers of Thorney.

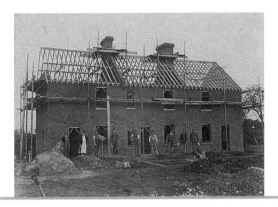

House building, Smith Brothers.
Believed to be Walter's co-workers at Smith Brothers of Thorney.
From the author's collection.

Thrown out of the Tank Yard

According to a family tale, in the early 1900s, it was Stephen's turn to do what he believed was right. He refused to allow his daughter Lucy to work as a domestic for one of the Duke's senior men with the excuse 'No child of mine will go into service'. (Conveniently ignoring that his daughter Lily was already settled with a family.) Coming after Walter's shocking behaviour when he failed to doff his cap in respect, the Duke's man declared, 'I'll have you out, Parker.'[534] Stephen lost his job and the family home.

Cousin Mary told me that, Stephen, sure of the Duke's ear, wrote an appeal explaining the man's character. In response to his plea, the Duke 'pardoned' him and arranged for Stephen and his family to move into 28 Wisbech Road, an end cottage with three bedrooms, two downstairs rooms, wash-house and earth closet, pigsty and enough land at the bottom of the garden to provide the family with fruit and vegetables.[535] Presumably, the

No. 28 Wisbech Road, Thorney.
From the author's collection.

Duke recognised Stephen's status by offering him an end house, as these were grander-looking, taller abodes with slightly larger front rooms, upstairs and down.[536] Stephen returned to work as a bricklayer and carpenter, where his skill with his hands and his relaxed, comfortable way with people allowed him to support his family.

This explanation of how the Parker family came to leave the Tank Yard cottage is an engaging story, and there may even be a kernel of truth to it. Regretfully, though, the timing is off. Postcards sent to Ethel for her collection by her sister Lucy were addressed to the Tank Yard in Station Road, rather than Wisbech Road, as late as January 1907.[537]

Duke of Bedford Cottages on Wisbech Road, 2014.
Photograph supplied with the kind permission of John Clark,
Chris Lane and the Thorney Society.

Stephen Parker – A man of property

With the loss of a comfortable income, Stephen and Ann were surely thankful for the ongoing rent from Stephen's property in Upwell. Its existence was a surprise to me and Walter's niece Mary. Knowledge of it came from the 1903 Taxation Survey.

Valuation record created under the 1910 Finance (Land Values Duties) Act VD schedule book.

Stephen & James Parker property Town Street, Upwell, Norfolk recorded on the valuation record created under the 1910 Finance (Land Values Duties) Act VD schedule book (Ref.470/O136) c1911. From the Cambridgeshire Archive

It showed that Stephen owned the grandly named Shrewness Villa, built by his older brother James. A family document written by James's second wife, Rachel, states that James incorporated a prayer for her into a hollow brick on 24 June 1897, St John the Baptist Day, behind the name and date plaque between the front windows of the original house. The Taxation Survey for Upwell and the written records associated with it show that Stephen and his brother James owned adjacent properties on

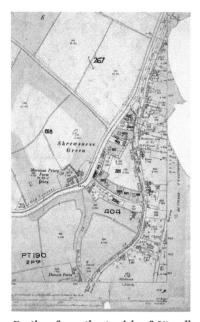

Portion from the parish of Upwell Isle, 2nd edition 1903 Taxation Survey, Upwell XIII.15.13.

Stephen & James Parker property Town Street, Upwell, Norfolk from a portion of the parish of Upwell Isle, 2nd edition 1903 Taxation Survey, Upwell XIII.15.13. From the Cambridgeshire Archives.

Town Street. Only Shrewness Villa, the property owned by Stephen, remains. It stands on what is now a large plot of land by town standards. At the time of writing, two horses help keep the grass short. Two homes have since replaced James's property.

The Land Value Duties Schedule shows that Stephen was not eligible to vote, as his property was worth less than £10 a year [£1,209]. But as homeowners, Stephen, and James were liable to pay the Poor Rate. This tax helped the destitute who had been forced into the workhouse. As long as her husband owned property, did Ann feel they were safe from the workhouse?[538]

Walter's sisters

While Walter was making plans for his future, a selection of picture postcards collected by Ethel (and fortuitously purchased by me, from an antiques dealer in Thorney) reveals close links between Walter's sisters. This slice of life, much like the way we text brief messages, allows me to speculate that Ethel, Cousin Mary's mother, a talented tailoress and a draper's assistant in Thorney in 1901, undertook her apprenticeship in Northampton.

Shrewsness Villa (Upwell)

+ In the name of the Father, and
of the Son and the Holy Ghost
Except the Lord build the house
their labour is but lost that
build it.
I lay this Brick with a prayer
that God's blessing of Peace
may rest upon this house &
upon all who may dwell in it.
"Keep far our Foes, give Peace
at Home" Where Thou art
Guide no ill can come
The Lord preserve our
goings out & our comings in
from this time forth for
Evermore Amen.
Our Father which art in
heaven &c

Prayer written by James Parker.

Prayer 'I lay this Brick with a prayer that God's blessing of peace may rest upon this house & upon all who may dwell in it'. It was installed behind the '1897' plaque. A copy is the keeping of Cousin Sue Oldroyd née Parker.

Romance blossomed because in 1904 'Will' sent an impersonal card c/o a Miss Savage at 57 Bentinck Road, Nottingham (sixty miles from Thorney), breaking off his relationship with Ethel.

Note written by Rachel Parker, 1897.

Note written by Rachel Parker about the prayer written by her second husband James. In the keeping of Cousin Sue Oldroyd née Parker.

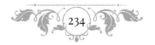

Shrewness Villa, including its extension, 2017.

Photograph from the author's collection.

Rear of Shrewness Villa, 2017.
Photograph from the author's collection.

The daughter at the Nottingham address nearest in age to Ethel was Lydia. Perhaps it was this Lydia from whom Ethel received postcards. It seems possible that Ethel boarded with the Savage family. According to the 1901 census, Lydia's father was a lace-

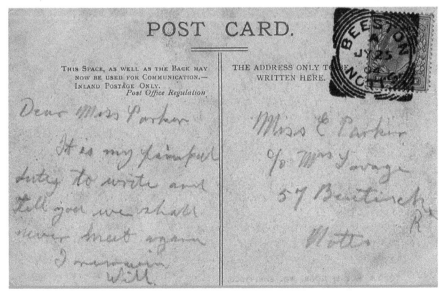

Dear 'John' postcard to Ethel from 'Will', 1904.
From Ethel Parker's postcard collection.

maker, Lydia was a 'tailoress, trousers' and her younger sister also worked in the clothing trade. From the postcard collection, we know that Ethel visited London before Walter left the village.

Postcard to Ethel Parker from Lydia, 1905.
From Ethel Parker's postcard collection.

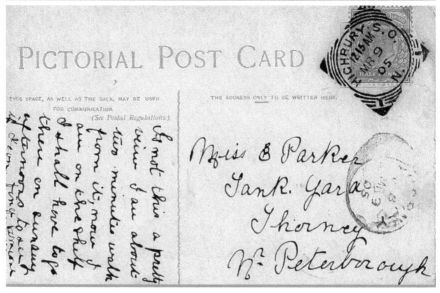

Reverse of a postcard to Ethel Parker from Lydia, 1905.
From Ethel Parker's postcard collection.

Other cards from female friends were posted from Christchurch, Stamford, Finsbury Park (London), Empingham (East Midlands) and Leicester. Presumably, these were friends Ethel met through her apprenticeship, challenging the view that working-class English women did not travel for work. In a 1905 picture postcard, Lydia refers to herself as being 'on the shelf' at age twenty.

Lily Parker, aged 20, studio photo, 1906.
From the author's collection.

Walter's sister Lily, known as Lil, was a maid in service in Whittlesea, and later a housemaid in the parsonage in Chelford, Macclesfield. One postcard reveals she was not always released by her Whittlesea employers to return to Thorney, especially if the weather was poor. But she wrote frequent letters and was visited by Ethel. The youngest Parker daughter, Lucy, travelled locally, though any record of what she was doing has not survived.

The picture postcards selected by Walter's sisters often featured Edwardian couples with romance in mind. One thanks Ma, Ann, for a treat, and another lets Ann know a daughter had arrived home safely. Some cards are more mysterious, such as

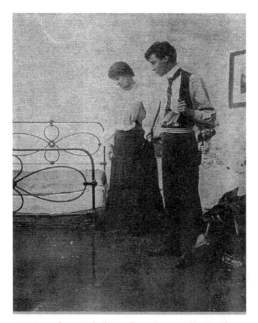

the one potentially related to a gift for Stephen's or Ethel's upcoming birthday. Intriguingly, Ethel sometimes received postcards in mirror writing, keeping what was said private from prying eyes.

Postcard to Ethel Parker from Lily Parker, 1905.
From Ethel Parker's postcard collection.

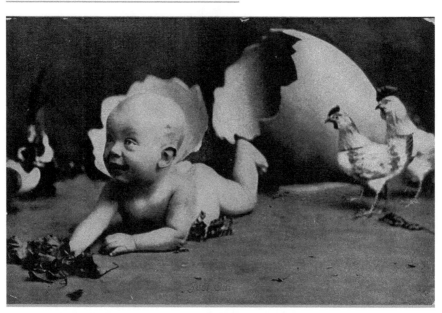

Postcard 'Just Out' sent to Ethel Parker from Lucy Parker, 1907.
From Ethel Parker's postcard collection.

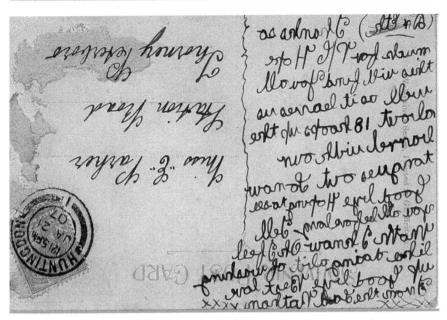

Reverse of a postcard 'Just Out' to Ethel Parker from Lucy Parker, 1907.
Lucy writes to Ethel using mirror writing. From Ethel Parker's postcard collection.

Postcard to Ethel Parker from Lily Parker, 1905.
From Ethel Parker's postcard collection.

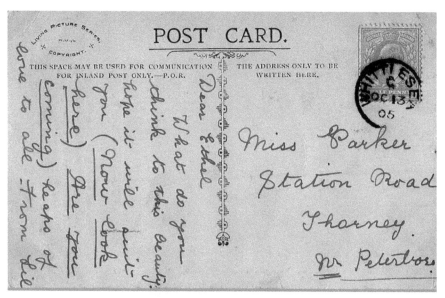

Reverse of a postcard from Lily Parker to Edith Parker, 1905.

From Ethel Parker's postcard collection.

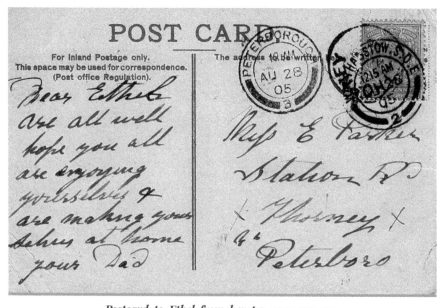

Postcard to Ethel from her pa, 1905 reverse.

Sent to the Tank Yard on Station Road, from her father, Stephen.

Postcard to Ethel, 1907, unsigned.
From Ethel Parker's postcard collection.

It nice
to be like
this
by moon light

Miss E Parker
Tank Yard
Local Thorney

Reverse of a postcard to Ethel, 1907, unsigned.
From Ethel Parker's postcard collection.

Postcard 'Cupid's Darts' to Lucy Parker from Ethel Parker, 1905.
From Ethel Parker's postcard collection.

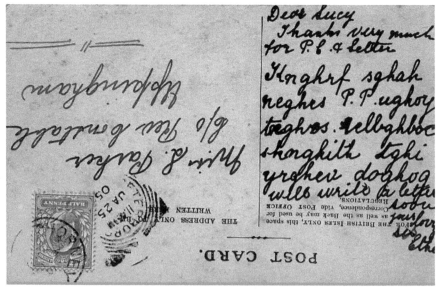

Reverse of the postcard 'Cupid's Darts' to Lucy Parker (in mirror writing)
from Ethel Parker, 1905.
Reverse To Lucy from Ethel, 1905.
From Ethel Parker's postcard collection (now in the author's keeping).

Emigration

His apprenticeship completed; twenty-one-year-old Walter had to decide his future. Although he now had a trade, there were three more experienced carpenter/joiners in the village, as well as his father. 'Chippies' often worked long hours and commonly were not hired in foul weather.[539] Even if Walter had wanted to stay, he believed that his treating one of the Duke's men with gross disrespect (and perhaps his pa's refusal to allow a daughter to work for the man) severely diminished his local work opportunities as an adult.

We can imagine how living in the strongly hierarchical structure of a 'closed' parish might feel to a young man eager to make his mark. It would be understandable if Walter found Edwardian village life at best gave 'a paralysing conventionality' and at worst an 'interminable sequence of petty bickering'.[540] Living in a small population does not suit everyone, although for some the security of being known and recognised in a small community outweighs any downside. I suspect Walter felt impelled to disentangle himself from the village and his family, not knowing that our unresolved conflicts, and the external expectations and internalised obligations we absorb, travel with us and can store up issues for ourselves and any descendants.[541]

Whatever his motivation, by 1907 Walter had lost interest in local job prospects. Walter had done his time working for a boss; now he was galvanised by the notion of being his own man. His trade and work in agriculture gave him exciting options and he had managed to obtain positive references from the clerk of works and the Duke's steward. Great Britain was at the head of a vast empire. The British Industrial Revolution had led to an explosion

SITUATIONS VACANT.

DRESSMAKING.—Apprentices and Improvers wanted at once.—A. W. MAY, Market Place [7502

EDWIN B. BELLARS requires YOUNG LADIES as Apprentices for the Show Room, Millinery, and Dressmaking Departments; also a well-educated YOUTH as an Apprentice for the Drapery. [7343

GOOD BODICE HANDS; Apprentices for Dressmaking at once. —LEADER AND REED, Crescent. [7647

WANTED, at once, APPRENTICES to the Millinery and Dressmaking.—A. and S. DIGBY, Church-terrace. Wisbech.

WANTED, Young LADY to assist in Shop.—Apply, Mrs. CROSS, 13, Market Place. [7685

YOUND LADY Wanted by the Mignon Studio, Market Street.—Apply, Friday, at 10 a.m. [7655

WANTED, good GENERAL SERVANT, not under 20; two in family.—Miss BATTERHAM, 34, North Brink. [7597

WANTED, strong GENERAL SERVANT. —Apply, Mrs. BRITLIFF, Crown Tavern, Wisbech. [7680

A VACANCY for an intelligent Youth as APPRENTICE to the Electrical Engineering; small premium required. — Apply by Letter, the Wisbech ELECTRICAL Co., South Brink, Wisbech. [7674

BLACKSMITH.—Constant work for young man; single preferred. — Apply, G. HORN, Outwell. [7407

WANTED, a respectable Youth as an APPRENTICE for the Electrical Trade; premium required.—MCALPIN & Co., 5a, Nene Quay, Wisbech. [7673

WHEELWRIGHT.—Good all round, used to light and heavy, constant; also good COACH PAINTER; have Vacancy for Apprentice.—Apply, JAS. FOSTER, Wisbech St. Mary. [7654

Situations vacant notice from the Wisbech Constitutional Gazette and Isle of Ely Standard, February 1907.

of technology, including trains and steamships. Wilbur Wright had piloted the Flyer III for 24 miles over the Huffman Prairie; the original Ford Model A had gone into production, home gramophones and amateur photography had become accessible, zeppelins reached the skies and radio broadcasters took to the airwaves.[542]

Where to go?

We know that Walter's cousin Theo, a joiner, became a soldier and settled in South Africa after the Anglo-Boer War of 1899–1902. A cousin, another Stephen, left the land to join the Suffolk Regiment, 12th Foot, and served in India. The army was not to be Walter's choice. Although access to information was limited, Walter's school had had a world map on the wall, and he likely extracted value from all the printed material he could access.[543] Richard Jefferies, a Victorian author and naturalist, who grew up

BEDFORD OFFICE.
THORNEY.
PETERBOROUGH.

CLERK OF WORKS:
H. WILLIAMS.

26ᵗʰ Oct : 1907

I have been acquainted with the bearer, Walter Parker, for the past 4 years, he: having served his apprenticeship, as a carpenter & joiner, with the firm of Messrs Smith Bros: Contractors, who do the principal part of the building work, upon this Estate, for His Grace, the Duke of Bedford K.G.

I have always found him, quiet, steady & industrious, and an attentive & competent workman, and I can thoroughly recommend him to anyone, desirous of employing, a carpenter or joiner, on any ordinary building work.

I may also state, that his father, has occupied the post of, Estate Foreman here, for the past 15 years.

I shall be pleased to answer, any further questions, concerning him, should such, at any time be needed.

Hugh Williams

Walter Parker's reference from the Clerk of Works, 1907.

From Hugh Williams Clerk of Works page 1. Taken from the author's collection.

BEDFORD OFFICE,
THORNEY,
PETERBOROUGH.

March : 5ᵗʰ : 1907.

I have known Walter Parker since he was a boy and I have pleasure in stating that I consider him reliable and respectable and of industrious habits, he has been in the employ of a firm of contractors in this village with whom he has served his apprenticeship as a joiner.

His father holds a position under myself as Estate foreman and has lived upon this Estate for many years, his parents are most respectable people.

I shall have pleasure in speaking in his favour at any future time

Walter Parker's reference from The Duke's agent, 1907.

Letter of reference, Arthur Forest, Agent to the Duke of Bedford, page 1.
From the author's collection.

and I wish him every
success in the future.
Signed
Arthur V. Forrest.
(Agent to His Grace the
Duke of Bedford. K.G).

Walter's reference from The Duke's agent, page 2.
Letter of reference, 1907, Arthur Forest, Agent to the Duke of Bedford, page 2

on a small farm in Wiltshire, was noted for his depiction of rural life. In 1884 he wrote:

> *Cottagers...read every scrap of printed paper which drifts across their way... All information in our day filters through the newspaper...London newspapers come now to the village and hamlet in all sort[s] of ways. Some by post, others by milk cart, by carrier and by traveller; for country people travel now and invariably bring back papers bought at the railway bookstalls. After these have been read by the farmers and upper sort of people, the fragments get out through innumerable channels to the cottagers.*[544]

During the early twentieth century, emigration from Britain reached unprecedented levels, with 3.15 million people leaving between 1903 and 1913.[545] The most popular destination was Canada, the nearest British colony. The local newspapers of

Walter's youth carried world news, and he grew up reading advertisements for workers and free land for homesteaders offered to the adventurers willing to sail to Canada, Australia, or New Zealand. Agents were paid to sign people up to farm in Canada, on the strength of propaganda leaflets. Walter could read the regular shipping notices and letters from Canadian farmers, some of whom had the newspapers from where they had lived in England sent to them for ten shillings [£60] a year.[546]

Hardship and Happiness

The papers said, 'Go west, young man, go west,
Your fortune you will make
A land of opportunity awaits you
Who knows what will be your fate.'
Yes, I read that newspaper clipping
I heeded that call without sleeping
I arrived in Winnipeg in 1908
To find that the west was a great
Wide wonderful place and I
Was just one of the large human race.[547]

Canadian propaganda

Canada campaigned to attract the 'right sort' of immigrants to populate the prairies, namely 'Germans, Icelanders, Scotchmen, Englishmen, Americans, Frenchmen, Scandinavians, Belgians, Russians, Australians, and Irishmen'.[548] Supported by the British government keen to reduce its population, between 1897 and 1911, 723,424 Brits left for Canada.[549] To attract them the Canadian government spent $2m CAD in the same period on advertising (based on the year 1914 figures this amounted to approximately $55m CAD in 2020).[550] According to the 1915 book by Canadian journalist, historian, and social worker, Agnes Laut, immigration officials had reckoned that each colonist was worth, as a producer, $1,500 ($33,625 CAD–1914 figure).[551] Following the Immigration Act of 1906, the amount steamship (and railway) agents were paid increased to £1 per head (£120) for farmers, farm labourers and domestic staff. To promote Canada, agents visited fairs in England (and Scotland) with samples of Canadian goods like wheat and maple syrup. Leaflets showing what they hoped would be an appealing way of life were handed out at events on many high streets.[552]

It was not just the Canadian government, the railway companies or the landowners who were promoting the Canadian prairies. Those who had already taken the plunge often sent glowing letters back home. To further spread the word, lectures were held:

> *A lecture on Canada, illustrated with lantern views, was given on Saturday evening at St Margaret's Hall to an interested audience. Advice for intending emigrants was given during the evening, and several took advantage of an offer made to have a chat with the lecturer, Mr Walter Stark, president of the British Emigration, Tourist and Colonisation Society of Liverpool.[553]*

In another lecture:

> *The director of the British Emigration Tourist and Colonisation Society informed the audience that young men willing to work hard could save as much in Canada as they could earn at home.[554]*

The most significant information Walter had about Canada could have come from his sister Lucy. In 1900 a Canadian competition was launched, aimed at British school children. Each child who entered an essay received a specially produced textbook and atlas, which included: 'Statistics about each of the Canadian provinces accompanied by maps, including information about population, agriculture, climate and landscape, and, when applicable, minerals, railways, fisheries and livestock'.[555] The names and addresses of Canadian agents were printed inside the cover of the atlas.[556] The first prize for the competition was £5 [£632], the amount each would-be emigrant needed in their pocket to be allowed entry into Canada. Walter only needed to take a few steps to visit his nearest agent, Billy Amps, at the grocery store opposite the Rose & Crown.

Walter Parker's refusal to take off his hat in respect to one of the most important men in his village showed his ability to think for himself and act with integrity. Now, aged twenty-one, he planned another bold move. He decided to swap the suffocation of village life and an alcoholic mother for homesteading on the Canadian Prairie. If trauma freezes us to a spot in history and causes inherited patterns of behaviour, so too positive action might inspire a different path with experiences that provide a reset button.[557] In Canada, Walter had a chance to live by his own values and define his own path, rather than wrestle with other people's expectations and demands.[558]

Walter Parker, aged 21 years, studio photograph, c1906.
From the author's collection.

The Allan Line's RMS Ionian and SS Commonwealth at the landing stage, Liverpool. Original postcard printed c1902.

With distance, he could re-frame his early life with a different storyline.[559]

Bolstered by the confidence of youth, competence in a trade and practical farming knowledge, Walter Parker left England on the steamship SS *Ionian* in March 1907. He travelled with his neighbour and chum; a young plumber named Ernest Kitchen. They were bound for Canada, which, in the ten

Ernest Kitchen, 1925.
Photograph provided by his relative, Sharon Attewell.

years between 1906 and 1916, welcomed two million new residents during its biggest population explosion.[560] In escaping, Walter may not have considered the disruption of his geographical, cultural and family attachments that researchers have found so fascinating.[561] It would be understandable if Walter thought he could leave the guilt of escaping obligations behind.

Adventure beckoned, and another world waited to be explored. Could Walter find a fresh start thousands of miles away from all he knew?

Walter's refusal to doff his cap

Whatever the factual truth of this family tale, there seems little doubt that as a youth Walter chose not to doff his cap to one of the Duke's men. The causal relationship with his departure is muddled, but we can be sure that the event set off a series of repercussions which would, in time, take Walter halfway around the world. The story I inherited about Walter leaving Thorney to safeguard his family perhaps says more about his emotional state than strictly what happened. This would be in keeping with how our understanding of ourselves and those we love changes over time, with distance, experience, and reflection. It is a poignant thought, but from a practical point of view, Walter had more options if he left the village.

I find it hard to accept that I know nothing of what Walter's pa, Stephen, felt about his son's maverick behaviour. Did he believe Walter acted according to his moral compass, one that reflected Stephen's view? It is possible that Stephen blamed himself for his son's disrespectful manner, or, understanding it, forgave him. If Walter had truly disgraced the family, I would have expected there to be a family anecdote that tells of Stephen, a Victorian father, banishing Walter to family in Upwell or Yorkshire.

In his refusal to take off his cap, I like to think Walter acted truthfully, in a way the adults felt unable to do. But we cannot know if Cousin Mary accurately remembered what she was told by her mother, Walter's sister Ethel–or if she was told the facts as they were known at the time. (Mary had not been born when the incident happened.) Whatever the truth, it feels as if Walter's principled stance created an ethical inheritance whereby people were encouraged 'to do the right thing' whatever the cost.

We might be tempted to take the story of a man's predilections at face value. After all, the appalling abuse and exploitation of children is as old as humanity. But we have no evidence to support it. I have deliberately kept the accused man's role vague, as it cannot be right to cast aspersions based on such flimsy hearsay without even a concrete timeline. Nor can we overlay current mainstream values and understanding on a Victorian culture that raised the age of heterosexual consent for girls from thirteen to sixteen years in 1885, and where society's responsibility for safeguarding vulnerable people was seen in a different light to the 'Me Too' campaign.[562]

If Walter knew of someone in a position of power who had been harming people in Thorney, I do not believe he would have spoken of such a toxic and horrific aspect of life to anyone, particularly his daughter. Walter's future wife, Hilda, may have learnt of it during her time living and working in the village. Yet she lived by, 'If you can't say anything nice, say nothing at all', so it seems farfetched that Hilda told her daughter Cousin Mary's version of the story. It is also possible my mother knew of such whisperings, and true to her values, chose not to speak of it.

It is sobering to remember that, despite Sigmund Freud detailing the pervasive, injurious effect of childhood sexual abuse in the 1890s, evidence of widespread public awareness did not start to appear until after Walter died in 1975.[563] Indeed Walter's perception, if that can be said at all, would naturally have been dissociative, mirroring the patterns of individual and cultural dissociation of the age. Looking back, I realise that to bring this project to fruition, I unconsciously harnessed the compulsion of my eight-year-old self to make sense of my grandfather, Walter Parker. But I also realised I was looking for answers to questions my mother did not overtly pose before her early death in 2002. I appreciate that, as author Scott Phillips has suggested, I have not simply been 'doing' family history or genealogy, but geneatherapy, driven by a need to understand my ancestors; to grasp why they took certain paths, or forged their own.[564] To consider what impact his mother's loss, mental health, trauma and alcoholism had on Walter's youth, I inevitably shone a spotlight on myself. I considered the impact this part of the family has had on my identity. The story I have woven has helped me to better understand myself and explain who I am to others.

As I write this postscript seven years after I stumbled into the Thorney Museum, housed in the building where Walter grew up, I find myself pondering my legacy. I believe we need to be kind to the depths of our being when we recognise that we, too, have written unresolved issues into our neurology and psychology. We can only do the best we can at the time and learn the lessons life presents to us according to the limits of our skills, energy, and resources. We will get stuck, walk another's road, miss our path in the dark and sometimes feel overwhelmed. All any of us can do is move forward from now and trust that those who come after us will continue the journey towards a wholly healthy legacy.

In his book on behavioural epigenetics, David Moore writes:

> *We are all profoundly influenced by the contexts in which we develop, and we have some control over those contexts; therefore, it is our responsibility to do what we can to help ourselves and others grow into compassionate, enlightened and fulfilled individuals... Do not assume you are trapped by your biology. Strive. Nurture... children with care. Choose and construct your environment thoughtfully, and live your life in a way that fosters ongoing health and development, because what you do matters.*[565]

As I pause my journey, I remember the words: 'life must be remembered backwards but lived forward'.[566] Sometimes, it would appear, we look forward but live with the unexamined archaic narrative scripts inherited from our ancestors.[567] As James Hollis writes:

> *The past is not gone, it is not even past; and it is the task of this moment to uncover and challenge the ghosts of the past so we can live a life that has meaning for us.*[568]

To learn more, I need to follow Walter to his chosen life in Canada; to uncover who he was and what he experienced four thousand miles from home, what he returned to England with, and what effect becoming a parent and World War Two would have on this Victorian man.

Take care,

Helen

Helen Parker-Drabble
Proud granddaughter of Walter Parker
Swindon, Wiltshire
October 2020

APPENDIX A
Wisbech Division Petty Sessions 1887

Saturday, March 24th — Before Colonel Reed (Chairman), and H. Sharpe, Esq. Henry Utteridge, labourer, of Upwell, brought up in custody, charged by Robert Falkner, Relieving Officer, with deserting his wife and family and leaving them chargeable to the common fund of the Wisbech Union.

—Utteridge, who went away, with a fellow labourer's wife in February, pleaded guilty to the charge.

—The Clerk: Then what have you to say in mitigation of punishment, not in justification of the offence for no man is justified in running away from his wife and family.

—Utteridge said he was enticed away.

—Colonel Reed: By a woman.

—Utteridge: Yea.

—Colonel Reed: That is a mean thing to say.

—The Clerk, in reply to the Bench, said the accused was liable to three months' imprisonment with hard labour. He (the Clerk) understood that the relief granted to [the] accused's family amounted to about £5 [£651.99].

—Utteridge said he was willing to pay it.

—Colonel Reed: That's not it; we must mark our sense of such conduct as you have been guilty of.

— Utteridge said it should never occur again.

—Colonel Reed: No, we can't let you off without punishment; we have decided to send you to prison for one month with hard labour.

—Utteridge: I beg your pardon; I hope you'll forgive me this time.

—Colonel Reed: No, can't do that.

—Utteridge was then removed. His wife was in court and cried bitterly when she heard the decision of the Magistrates.

Games & Pastimes

What's the time, Mr Wolf?

Choose one player to be Mr Wolf. They stand with their back to the rest of the players lined up at the opposite end of the play area.

The players call out, '*What's the time, Mr Wolf?*'

Mr Wolf shouts out a time between 1 & 12 o'clock.

The number he shouts is the number of steps the players take toward him (for 9 o'clock take 9 steps).

Once the players get close to Mr Wolf, he shouts *Lunch time!* and chases them back to the start.

If a player is caught by Mr Wolf, that player becomes Mr Wolf, and the game starts again.

Bulldog

One or two players are chosen to be bulldogs.

The bulldogs stand in the middle of the play area. The remaining players stand at one end of the area (home). The aim of the game is to run from one end of the field of play to the other, without being caught by the bulldogs. When a player is caught, they become a bulldog themselves.

The winner is the last player or players 'free'.

Pick up Sticks

Pick-up Sticks is a game in which a bundle of 'sticks', between 8 and 20 centimetres long, are dropped onto a flat surface. Each player in turn tries to remove a stick from the pile without disturbing any of the others. If any other stick moves, their turn ends, and they lose a turn. A player keeps removing sticks until they cause a secondary stick to move, ending their turn. The player with the most sticks wins.

Blind Man's Buff

In this game one player is blindfolded and spun around several times. The other players, who are not blindfolded, call out to the 'blind man' and dodge away from 'him' to avoid being caught. The 'blind man' must guess the identity of 'his' captive before the blindfold is removed (if the guess is wrong, the captive is released, and the game continues). If the 'blind man' guesses correctly 'he' takes off the blindfold and uses it to cover the eyes of the person 'he' caught and named.

Pin the tail on the donkey

This is a game played by a group. A picture of a donkey with a missing tail is tacked to a wall within easy reach of the players. One at a time, each person is blindfolded and handed a paper 'tail' with a tack poked through it. The blindfolded person is then spun around until they are disoriented. The person tries to pin the tail on the donkey. The player who pins their tail closest to the target, the donkey's rear, wins.

Letter from Cousin Theo, 1900

Sailor's Rest
Fort Knokks
Capetown
2 April 1900

My dear Bro,

Just a line to let you know I am still alive & well. I have not as yet left Capetown & chill on the docks [donigill?] shipping agent for the [?]RES [Royal Engineer Sappers?]. I have a very good job & see plenty of fresh faces. Also I have seen all the Boer prisoners Lord Robs [Roberts] captured with Cronjes lot. They were an awful looking lot of men. No uniform whatsoever, old & young from 16-70, they came down in bullock waggons & the stench of them was horrible. Some had not changed their shirts for a month & had not left [c]hain for 4 days & they were put on transport & I believe now are in the island of St Helena. I wonder how much longer we shall be out here. I expect the Boer will fight until the last as they have all to lose & nothing to gain for we shall not give them their independence. Some think there will be a great siege at Pretoria, but others don't. But

anyhow we shall not be back much before Xmas. The yeomanry and militia will be first to go back.

It is a very painful sight to see the poor fellows going home, some with legs off and arms, some looking as if they cannot live long. Close to where I am living there is a large hospital & near by is a military cemetery & they are being buried at the rate of 5 per day but we soldier's must not grieve. We only say so and so has snuffed it. I got the pouch & bacca & I can assure I prized it very much. I will send you something from here that you will like. Give my best love to father and mother & all at home. With best love to you, hoping to see you soon.

From your loving Bro,
Theo

[Original spelling has been maintained, with some punctuation added.]

Apprenticeship Indenture

[The spelling and punctuation have been left unaltered]

The said Apprentice...his Masters faithfully shall serve their secrets keep their lawful commands everywhere gladly do he shall do no damage to his said Masters nor see to be done of others but to the best of his power shall prevent or forthwith give warning to his said Masters of the same he shall not waste the Goods of his said Masters nor lend them unlawfully to any he shall not do any act whereby his said Masters may have any loss with their own goods or others during the said term without License of his said Masters shall neither buy nor sell nor absent himself from his said Masters' service day or night unlawfully But in all things as a faithful Apprentice he shall behave himself towards his said Masters and all theirs during the said Term.

And the said Masters in consideration of the services of the said Apprentice to be well and faithfully performed during the said term hereby covenants with the said Parent as follows that they the said Masters will pay to the said Apprentice whilst in the actual employment of the said Masters and the performance of

his duties as such Apprentice during the said term Six shillings a week during the first year Seven shillings a week during the second year Eight shillings a week during the third year and Ten shillings a week during the fourth year of such term.

And also that they the said Masters their said Apprentice in the Art trade or business of a Carpenter and Joiner which they use by the best means that they can shall teach and Instruct, or cause to be taught and instructed.

And the Parent hereby covenants with the said Masters as follows that the said Apprentice during the said Term shall well and faithfully serve the said Masters and that he the said Parent will find and provide the said Apprentice with good and sufficient food lodging clothing and the washing and mending thereof pocket money medical attendance and medicine and all other necessities.

And for the true performance of all and every the said Covenants and Agreements either of the said Parties bindeth himself unto the other by these Presents.

In Witness whereof the parties above named have hereunto set their Hands and Seals the twenty second day of August in the year of Our Lord One Thousand Nine Hundred and Two.

Signed, sealed and delivered by the above named

Walter Parker, Stephen Parker, Robert Thomas Smith and Edward William Smith in the presence of William Amps, Thorney. [Shopkeeper]

Walter's journey continues
in *A Victorian Migrates* and *A Victorian's Legacy*

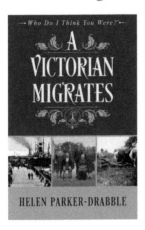
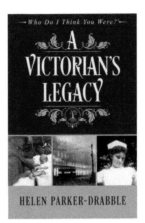

If you would like exclusive content sent to your inbox, visit the website www.helenparkerdrabble.com and click the 'Exclusive Content' button. (You can opt out at any time.) You will get:

1. An occasional update, images, or exclusive appetisers from the series *Who Do I Think You Were?*®

2. I will tell you when books from the series *Who Do I Think You Were?*® are released.

3. I will email occasional free resources for family historians.

4. I will enter you into any free giveaways I run to win a personalised colour hardback edition from the series *Who Do I Think You Were?*®

Thank you for your interest. It means a lot to me.

Take care,

Helen

Helen Parker-Drabble is a proud author member of the Alliance of Independent Authors. ALLi is an ethical non-profit membership organisation for those who want to control their intellectual property and publish independently. ALLi provides trusted advice, supportive guidance, and a range of resources, within a welcoming and dynamic community of independent authors and advisors.

If you would like to know more about the Alliance of Independent Authors, please follow my affiliate link: https://tinyurl.com/y59zrgsh or visit www.allianceindependentauthors.org/.

Acknowledgements

Most importantly, I would like to acknowledge the irreplaceable contribution of family members: Phyllis Mary Skells née Woods (1918–2016), Frances Irene ('Rene) Pell née Woods (1922–2017) and Alan Pell, who knew my grandfather Walter and furthered my understanding of him. Also, Amanda Pell, Susan and Richard Oldroyd, and John Malyon, who lent me much appreciated support.

Walter was a proud Thorneyite and Thorneyites were integral to my research, especially Thorney Society members Dorothy Halfhide (also curator of the Thorney Museum), Margaret Fletcher (a founding member), and Jeremy Culpin; John Walter Culpin, carpenter, painter, and decorator who provided insight into working life in the village; Eric Rayner of the *Thorney Post*; Sam Falco, BA (Hons), MSt (Cantab), MPlan; Jeremy Mold, Organist and Choirmaster at the Abbey Church of St Mary and St Botolph, also referred to as Thorney Abbey.

I would like to thank the dedicated staff and volunteers of museums and archives who helped me with my research: The Thorney Museum; Peterborough Images Archive – Paul Young; Peterborough Archive Services; Peterborough Museum and Art Gallery; Cambridgeshire Archives; Huntingdonshire Archives; Blackie Collection, University of Glasgow Library, Research Annexe; Wisbech and Fenland Museum; The Broadland Memories Archive and the Archives of Manitoba.

I found social media networks invaluable. Members of the following Facebook groups provided detailed information or

support: Thorney Community Forum; Writing Family History – Study and Support Group; Family History Writing Studio; Norfolk Ancestors; Norfolk Family History Society; Cambridgeshire Family History Society; Wisbech and Surrounding Villages Old Photos; Fenland Family History Society; Norfolk Dialect Preservation Society and the Huntingdonshire Local History Society.

Ancestry.com enabled me to reach out to the family of Ernest Kitchen, Walter's neighbour, and life-long friend, in Thorney and on the Canadian prairies. Robert Scales generously facilitated my posting an album of lost photographs to Sharon Attewell. Sharon kindly provided a photograph of 'Ernie'.

A great many people have encouraged me, asked me interesting questions, and cheered me on: Harry Drabble; Lyn Goodwill; Stephen, Karen, Amy, Louise, and Cara Parker Drabble; Iain Hamilton; Suzie Simmons; Vrinda Pendred, coach and editor; Gill Blanchard, tutor and mentor; Dr George Regkoukos, consultant historian; Eastcott Writers, especially Kevin Worrall, Alice Morton, and Judith Hawkins; Lynn Serafinn, Trentino Genealogy; Darryl Moody, Local Studies Librarian, Swindon Central Library; Nicola Stevenette; Keith Lewis; Angela Atkinson; Andy Binks, Swindon Heritage and The Swindon Society; Alan Lillis; Karen Angel; Karen Moffat; Ann Ward; Karen Harris; Stephen Grosvenor; Daphne Hardwick; Caroline Pitt; Debanjali Biswas, photographer and proofreader, and Helen Baggott, proofreader.

Finally, I want to express my gratitude to photo restorers Simon Barraclough (www.fix-your-pix.co.uk) and Claudia D'Souza (www.thephotoalchemist.biz), whose meticulous photographic restoration work should preserve old family photographs for another century.

About the author

I'm a lifelong explorer of social history, a weaver of factual family tales, and hold a Diploma in counselling. Fascinated by psychological theory and the stories we develop to make sense of ourselves and our family, my original quest was to understand my Victorian grandfather, Walter Parker, born in 1885 in the English village of Upwell on the Norfolk/Cambridgeshire border.

I believe family history doesn't survive unless it's in print, so I pondered how to share what I had learnt. Inspired by a few trailblazers, I set out to write an engaging and accessible book that would not only explore working-class life in an English village, but could encourage other family historians struggling to pass on what they have painstakingly discovered.

During my research, a transgenerational legacy of loss, trauma, anxiety, and depression unravelled. It revealed repeated patterns of behaviour that I too had unwittingly passed on. This discovery helped me understand my work's focus. As a geneatherapist my mission is to use historical and current understanding of mental health, psychology, and neuroscience to deepen our understanding of our ancestors and benefit present and future generations.

It is through acknowledging and exploring these patterns that we can develop a deeper understanding of those who came before us, and pass on a healthier legacy to the next generation.

The best thing about publishing a book is connecting with readers who share my passion for family history, psychology, or mental health. So, I would be delighted if you sent me an email to say, 'Hi', or to share something you've discovered about your family. Alternatively, why not let me know of any interesting research you come across? My email address is helen@helenparkerdrabble.com. I hope to hear from you.

Thank you for reading. If you enjoyed Who Do I Think You Were?® *A Victorian's Inheritance*, please consider leaving an honest review at your favo[u]rite store. Reader reviews are one of the few ways independent authors can be discovered. For someone at the beginning of their publishing journey, having reviews means I can submit for advertising, which helps readers find my books. The more I sell, the quicker the second book in the series will be published. Enough said!

Take care,

Helen

About the
history consultant

George Regkoukos is a historian with a PhD from King's College London, currently engaged by the University of Oxford. He specialises in the Modern History of Russia and Social Network Analysis, and runs a podcast about masterpieces of Russian art.

George is also a professional editor providing services for family historians and self-published authors of histories or historical fiction. He runs an e-book publishing and software development company. For those who wish to publish digitally, his 'planning to publishing' package is an excellent value-for-money set of services which is unique in the e-publishing market.

As a history consultant for my series, Who Do I think You Were?®, George advised me on research methods, sources, formatting, and language. He gave me historical perspective, suggested alternative approaches to write my research and helped me optimise my materials and output. His consultancy gave me the confidence to launch my book A Victorian's Inheritance world-wide.

Helen Parker-Drabble

To find out more about George and his services, or to request a free sample, you can visit www.georgeregkoukos.com. You can also find him on LinkedIn, Academia, and SoundCloud.

Endnotes

The author has used the following online inflation calculators to indicate the nineteenth and early twentieth-century currency equivalence in 2019/2020:

- Pre 1900 sterling inflation calculator: In2013dollars.com. *(2019)*. 2000 pounds in 2019 | UK Inflation Calculator.
- Historic inflation calculator: how the value of money has changed since 1900 (sterling) Browning, R. (2020). *Historic inflation calculator: how value of money changed since 1900*. This is Money — https://www.thisismoney.co.uk/money/bills/article-1633409/Historic-inflation-calculator-value-money-changed-1900.html [Accessed January 2020].
- Inflationcalculator.ca. (n.d.). *Inflation Calculator | Keep Track of Canadian CPI and Inflation*. (Canadian dollars 1914 onward)

1   Population of Thorney as advised by Thorney Museum curator, Dorothy Halfhide, in an email dated February 17, 2020.

2   The village of Thorney is seven miles east of Peterborough and fifty miles north of Cambridge.

3   Legislation.gov.uk. (2020). *Vagrancy Act 1824*. http://www.legislation.gov.uk/ukpga/Geo4/5/83 [February 2021].

4   Ibid.; Fowler, S. (2008). *The people, the places, the life behind doors*. Barnsley, UK: Pen & Sword Books Ltd. pp. 160–61.

5   Further reading: Brennan, J. and Houde, K. (2017). *History and systems of psychology*. 7th ed. Cambridge University Press.

6   Marchiano, L. (2017). *Our Children's Psychological Inheritance*. blogs.psychcentral.com.

7   Hollis, J. (2013). *Hauntings – Dispelling the Ghosts Who Run Our Lives*. Asheville, NC: Chiron Publications, Preface; p. 1.

8   Cooley, C. (1902). *Human Nature and the Social Order*. New York: Charles Scribner's Sons; or 'You can't be a self by yourself.' In Barret, L., (2020). *How Emotions are made: The Secret Life of the Brain*. [S.l.]: Picador, p. 191.

9   Bretherton, I. (1992). "The origins of attachment theory: John Bowlby and Mary Ainsworth". *Developmental Psychology*, 28(5), pp. 759–775.

10   Veale, L. and Endfield, G., (2016). "Situating 1816, the 'year without summer', in the UK". *The Geographical Journal*, 182(4), pp. 318-330.

11   *Norfolk Chronicle and Norwich Gazette*, Saturday 07 September 1816. p. 2, column 4.

12   Flatman, C., (2020). *The Origins of The Riots in Littleport And Ely In May 1816 and The Reaction of The Establishment to the Disturbances*. Unpublished MA Thesis. The Open University.

13   Cambridge Chronicle and Journal, *Friday, 27 December 1816*.

14   Mealing, B. (2013). *Life in a Victorian School*. Cheltenham: The History Press.

15   Griffin, E. (2014). *Liberty's Dawn: A People's History of the Industrial Revolution*. 1st edition. New Haven and London: Yale University Press, p. 116.

16   Ibid.

17   Moore, D. (2017). *The Developing Genome: An Introduction to Behavioral Epigenetics*. Oxford: Oxford University Press, p. 182.

18   Berridge, V. & Edwards, G. (1982). "Opium and the people: opiate use in nineteenth-century". *Medical Journey*, 26(4), pp. 458–62.

19   Smith, W. P. (2012). *Discovering Upwell*. Illustrated edition. England: Carrillson Publications, p. 184.

20   Gerritsen, J. W. (2000). *The Control of Fuddle and Flash: A Sociological History of the Regulation of Alcohol and Opiates*. Brill Academic Publishers.

21   Anonymous. (1867). "A Question for Dr. Hawkins" *The British Medical Journal*, 1(338), p. 759.

22   Ibid.

23   Saunders, N. J. (2014). *The Poppy: A History of Conflict, Loss, Remembrance, and Redemption*. London: Oneworld Publications.

24   Anonymous. (2000). England 12 | *IDEA: International Dialects of English Archive*. https://www.dialectsarchive.com/england-12 [Accessed February 2021]; Morris, C., n.d. *Docky Bag*. University of Cambridge. https://www.cam.ac.uk/museums-and-collections/collaborative-projects/my-museum-favourite/docky-bag [Accessed February 2021].

25   If we are inclined to condemn, perhaps we should reflect that the ever-faithful gripe water, the panacea for wind and all ills, was still being sold in 1989 even though historically it contained between 3.6 and 8 per cent alcohol. 'Calpol's packaging says it is for the relief of pain and fever, but we give it for distress, and the brand has always encouraged this in its marketing'. Kleeman, J., 2019. "Why parents are addicted to Calpol". *The Guardian*, https://www.theguardian.com/lifeandstyle/2019/jun/04/why-parents-are-addicted-to-calpol [Accessed February 2021].

26   Goodman, R. (2013). How to be a Victorian: A Dawn-to-Dusk Guide to Victorian Life. New York: Liveright Publishing Corporation, p. 243.

27   *Norfolk Chronicle and Norwich Gazette*, Saturday 6 December 1845,

Supplement, column 8.

28   Pappas, S. (2020). *Opioid Crisis Has Frightening Parallels to Drug Epidemic of Late 1800s*. www.livescience.com. [Accessed February 2021].

29   Anderson, I. (1993). *The decline of mortality in the nineteenth century: with special reference to three English towns*. Unpublished MA Thesis. University of Durham, p. 25.

30   This moved morphine, cocaine, opium, and derivatives containing more than 1 per cent morphine into part one of the poisons schedule. Drug policy in the UK: from the 19th century to the present day. In: (2013). *Drugs of dependence: the role of medical professionals*. British Medical Association Board of Science, p. 87. https://www.bma.org.uk/media/2103/drugsofdepend_roleofmedprof_jan2013.pdf [Accessed February 2021].

31   Carey, N. (2013). *The Epigenetics Revolution: How Modern Biology Is Rewriting Our Understanding of Genetics, Disease and Inheritance*. New York: Columbia University Press, p. 259.

32   Griffin, E. (2014). *Liberty's Dawn: A People's History of the Industrial Revolution*. New Haven and London: Yale University Press, pp. 109–33.

33   de Pennington, J. (2017). *British History in depth: Beneath the Surface: A Country of Two Nations*. bbc.co.uk. http://www.bbc.co.uk/history/british/victorians/bsurface_01.shtml [Accessed August 2020]; Hamlin, C. (1995). "Could you starve to death in England in 1839? The ChadwickFarr controversy and the loss of the "social" in public health". *American Journal of Public Health*, 85(6), 856-866.

34   Heijmans, B., et.al (2008). "Persistent epigenetic differences associated with prenatal exposure to famine in humans". *Proceedings of the National Academy of Sciences*, 105(44), pp. 17046–17049; Lavebratt, C., Almgren, M. & Ekström, T. (2011). "Epigenetic regulation in obesity". *International Journal of Obesity*, 36(6), pp. 757–765; Remely, M. et. al (2015). "Obesity: epigenetic regulation – recent observations". *Biomolecular Concepts*, 6(3), pp. 163-75.

35   Department of Clinical Epidemiology, Biostatistics and Bioinformatics, Academic Medical Centre, University of Amsterdam, Amsterdam, the Netherlands; Veenendaal, M., et.al (2013). "Transgenerational effects of prenatal exposure to the 1944–45 Dutch famine". BJOG: An *International Journal of Obstetrics & Gynaecology*, 120(5), pp. 548–554.

36   Further workhouse admissions for the family: 10 September 1873, 31 March 1874, 30 April 1874, 25 August 1874, and 9 October 1874; from a report by the Historical Research Service, Huntingdonshire Archives.

37   According to her death certificate Susannah Parker died in the presence of her sister Ann. Nothing more is known about this sister.

38   Goose, N. (2006). "Farm service, seasonal unemployment and casual labour in mid nineteenth-century England". *Agricultural History Review*, 54(2), pp. 274–303; Waller, I. H. (2008). *My Ancestor Was an Agricultural Labourer*. London: Society of Genealogists Enterprises Ltd p. 20.

39 Clayton, P. & Rowbotham, J. (2009). "How the mid-Victorians worked, ate and died". International Journal of Environmental Research and Public Health, 6(3), pp. 1235–1253.

40 Gillard, D. (2018). *The History of Education in England – Introduction, Contents, Preface*. Educationengland.org.uk. http://www.educationengland. org.uk/history/ [Accessed February 2021].

41 Sotero, M. (2006). "A Conceptual Model of Historical Trauma: Implications for Public Health Practice and Research", *Journal of Health Disparities Research and Practice*, 1(1), pp. 93–108; ScienceDaily. (2020). *Experiencing Childhood Trauma Makes Body and Brain Age Faster: Findings Could Help Explain Why Children Who Suffer Trauma Often Face Poor Health Later in Life*. https://www.sciencedaily.com/releases/2020/08/200803092120.htm [Accessed February 2021].

42 Worden, J. & Silverman, P. (1996). "Parental death and the adjustment of school-age children". *OMEGA – Journal of Death and Dying*, 33(2), pp. 91–102.

43 Holmes, V. (2017). *In Bed with the Victorians: The Life-Cycle of Working-Class Marriage*. London: Palgrave Macmillan, p. 88.

44 Carey, N. (2012). 'The epigenetics revolution: how modern biology is rewriting our understanding of genetics, disease, and inheritance'. *Choice Reviews Online*, 49(12), pp. 49-6870.

45 Moore, D. (2017). *The Developing Genome: An Introduction to Behavioral Epigenetics*. Oxford: Oxford University Press, p. 222.

46 Escher, J. (2015). *David Moore Q&A*. Germline Exposures. http://www. germlineexposures.org/david-moore-qa.html [Accessed February 2021].

47 Anon. (2016). *Not only trauma but also the reversal of trauma is inherited*. https://www.sciencedaily.com/releases/2016/06/160623120307.htm [Accessed February 2021]. Further information: Moore, D. (2017). *The Developing Genome: An Introduction to Behavioral Epigenetics*. Oxford: Oxford University Press.

48 McEwen, B., Gray, J. and Nasca, C., (2015). "Recognizing resilience: Learning from the effects of stress on the brain". *Neurobiology of Stress*, 1, pp. 1–11.

49 Yeazell, R. B. (2013). "Marriage". Victorian Review, 39(2), pp. 208–215.

50 A practice that Cousin Sue Oldroyd's parents told her had continued to their generation.

51 Griffin, E. (2014). *Liberty's Dawn: A People's History of the Industrial Revolution*. 1st edition. New Haven and London: Yale University Press. pp 109–133.

52 Lambert, T. (2019). *Life in the 19th Century*. Localhistories.org. http://www. localhistories.org/19thcent.html [Accessed February 2021].

53 While the work of psychologist Justin Sokol, Dr Oliver Robinson and others, build on Erikson's work, bringing it into the 21st century, they studied young adults who live in a very different social milieu to the one

which Walter and his siblings inhabited. I therefore chose the Erikson model for deepening my understanding of Walter. Sokol, Justin T. (2009) "Identity Development Throughout the Lifetime: An Examination of Eriksonian Theory," *Graduate Journal of Counseling Psychology*: 1(2), Article 14. pp 1-11; Robinson, O.C. (2015). "Emerging adulthood, early adulthood and quarter-life crisis: Updating Erikson for the twenty-first century". In: R. Žukauskiene (ed.) *Emerging adulthood in a European context*. New York: Routledge, pp. 17–30.

54 Seymour S.C. (2013) "'It Takes a Village to Raise a Child': Attachment Theory and Multiple Child Care in Alor, Indonesia, and in North India". In: Quinn N., Mageo J.M. (eds) *Attachment Reconsidered. Culture, Mind, and Society*. New York: Palgrave Macmillan, pp. 115-139.

55 Fleming, J. (2004). *Erikson's Psychosocial Developmental Stages*. https://www.semanticscholar.org/paper/Erikson-and-Personal-Identity%3A-a-Biographical-Fleming-Erikson/ab44d6a2d3178e4e159108ab5333504d23cc9508 [Accessed February 2021].

56 Borough Council of King's Lynn and West Norfolk (1977; last revised 2010). *Upwell Conservation Area Character Statement*. p. 3.

57 The wall stretches from Bowness on Solway, Cumbria in the east to Wallsend, Newcastle in the west. English Heritage. *Hadrian's Wall | English Heritage*. More information: https://www.english-heritage.org.uk/visit/places/hadrians-wall/ [Accessed February 2021].

58 Bradley, K. (2013). *The Town of Well: Some Glimpses of the Early History of Upwell and the Surrounding Countryside.* Upwell: Published by Keith Bradley.

59 Lner.info (2019). "Wisbech and Upwell Railway: route". LNER Encyclopedia. https://www.lner.info/co/GER/wisbech/route.php [Accessed February 2021].

60 Oldroyd, R. (2015). *Growing Up in Upwell*. Handwritten pages in the author's possession.

61 Kelly's Directories (1904). *Kelly's Directory of Cambridgeshire*. London: Kelly's Directories Ltd, p. 215.

62 Bretherton, I. (1992). "The origins of attachment theory: John Bowlby and Mary Ainsworth". Developmental Psychology, 28(5), pp. 759–775.

63 Feldman, R., (2017). The Neurobiology of Human Attachments. *Trends in Cognitive Sciences*, 21(2), pp. 80-99.

64 Lester, B., et. Al. (2018). "Epigenetic Programming by Maternal Behavior in the Human Infant". *Pediatrics*, 42(4), p.e20171890. https://www.ncbi.nlm.nih.gov/pmc/articles/PMC6192679/ [Accessed February 2021].

65 Chamberlain, G. (2006). "British maternal mortality in the nineteenth and early twentieth centuries". *Journal of the Royal Society of Medicine*, 99(11), pp. 559-63; This compares with 9.8 women per 100,000 who died during pregnancy or up to six weeks after childbirth or the end of pregnancy in the UK 2014-16. Knight M, Bunch K, Tuffnell D, Jayakody H, Shakespeare J, Kotnis R, Kenyon S, Kurinczuk JJ (2018). (Eds.) on behalf

of MBRRACE-UK. *Saving Lives, Improving Mothers' Care – Lessons learned to inform maternity care from the UK and Ireland Confidential Enquiries into Maternal Deaths and Morbidity 2014–16*. Oxford: National Perinatal Epidemiology Unit, University of Oxford.

66   Atkinson, P., Francis, B., Gregory, I. & Porter, C. (2017). "Spatial modelling of rural infant mortality and occupation in nineteenth-century Britain". *Demographic Research*, 36, pp. 1337-1360.

67   Forbes, T. (1971). "The Regulation of English Midwives in The Eighteenth and Nineteenth Centuries". *Medical History*, 15(4), pp. 352-362. Also: Shelton, D. (2012). "Man-midwifery history: 1730– 1930". *Journal of Obstetrics and Gynaecology*, 32(8), pp. 718–723; Loudon, I. (1992). *Death in childbirth: An International Study of Maternal Care and Maternal Mortality 1800– 1950*. Oxford: Clarendon Press.

68   In comparison, there has been a reduction in the rate of extended perinatal mortality in the UK in 2017: 5.40 per 1,000 total births for babies born at 24+0 weeks gestational age or later compared with 5.64 in 2016. This represents a 12% reduction in extended perinatal mortality since 2013, equivalent to nearly 500 fewer deaths in 2017. 2. The stillbirth rate for the UK in 2017 has reduced to 3.74 per 1,000 total births from 4.20 in 2013, which represents 350 fewer stillbirths. 3. The rate of neonatal mortality for babies born at 24 weeks gestational age or later in the UK continues to show a steady decline over the period 2013 to 2017 from 1.84 to 1.67 deaths per 1,000 live births. This represents a 10% reduction in neonatal mortality over the last five years. Draper ES, Gallimore ID, Smith LK, Kurinczuk JJ, Smith PW, Boby T, Fenton AC, Manktelow BN. (2019), on behalf of the MBRRACE-UK Collaboration. *Perinatal Mortality Surveillance Report, UK Perinatal Deaths for Births from January to December 2017*. Leicester: The Infant Mortality and Morbidity Studies, Department of Health Sciences, University of Leicester.

69   *Thetford & Watton Times and People's Weekly Journal,* Saturday 26 February 1881, p. 5, column 3.

70   *Cambridge Independent Press*, Saturday 02 April 1887, p. 7, column 4.

71   Jaadla, H. & Reid, A. (2017). "The geography of early childhood mortality in England and Wales, 1881–1911". *Demographic Research*, 37, p. 1871.

72   Atkinson, P., et.al (2017). "Patterns of infant mortality in rural England and Wales, 1850-1910". *The Economic History Review*, 70(4), pp. 1268-1290.

73   Stevens, E., Patrick, T. & Pickler, R. (2009). "A History of Infant Feeding". *Journal of Perinatal Education*, 18(2), pp. 32–39. More information: Dwork, D., (1987). "The milk option. An aspect of the history of the infant welfare movement in England 1898–1908". *Medical History*, 31(1), pp.51-69; Atkins, P.J., (2003). "Mother's milk and infant death in Britain, circa 1900-1940". *Anthropology of food*. Vol:2. https://doi.org/10.4000/aof.310 [Accessed February 2021] ; Morabia, A., Rubenstein, B. and Victora, C., (2013). "Epidemiology and Public Health in 1906 England: Arthur Newsholme's

Methodological Innovation to Study Breastfeeding and Fatal Diarrhea". *American Journal of Public Health*, 103(7), pp. e17-e22 ; Newsholme, A., (1899). *The Elements of Vital Statistics.* London: S. Sonnenschein & Co.

74 (1877). *Cassell's household guide: being a complete Encyclopaedia of domestic and social economy, and forming a guide to every department of practical life.* London: Cassell, Petter, and Galpin, Ludgate Hill, E.C., p. 270.

75 Dyhouse, C., (1978). "Working-Class Mothers and Infant Mortality in England, 1895–1914". *Journal of Social History*, 12(2), p.255. Further information: Newsholme, A., (1899). *The Elements of Vital Statistics.* London: S. Sonnenschein & Co.

76 Stevens, E., Patrick, T. & Pickler, R. (2009). "A History of Infant Feeding". *Journal of Perinatal Education*, 18(2), pp. 32–39. https://www.ncbi.nlm.nih.gov/pmc/articles/PMC2684040/ [Accessed February 2021].

77 Millward, R. & Bell, F. (2001). "Infant Mortality in Victorian Britain: The Mother as Medium". *The Economic History Review,* 54(4), p. 727.

78 West, C. (1848). Lectures on the Diseases of Infancy and Childhood. London: Longman, Brown, Green, & Longmans.

79 Strange, J. (2006) "Dangerous Motherhood: Insanity and Childbirth in Victorian Britain by Hilary Marland". [Review article]. *History*, 91(303), p. 471.

80 Strange, J. (2010). Death, grief and poverty in Britain, 1870–1914. Cambridge: Cambridge University Press.

81 Tunaru, S., et. al (2012). "Castor oil induces laxation and uterus contraction via ricinoleic acid activating prostaglandin EP3 receptors". *Proceedings of the National Academy of Sciences of the United States of America*, 109(23), pp. 9179–9184.

82 Epsom salts, or rather magnesium sulphate, is on the World Health Organization's List of Essential Medicines, a list of the most important medication needed in a basic health system. The list can be accessed here: https://www.who.int/medicines/publications/essentialmedicines/en/ [Accessed February 2021]; Elbossaty, W. (2018). "Pharmaceutical influences of Epsom salts". *American Journal of Pharmacology and Pharmacotherapeutics,* 5(1:2), pp. 1–3 doi:10.21767/2393-8862.100011.

83 Zinc sulphate is on the World Health Organization's List of Essential Medicines. https://pubchem.ncbi.nlm.nih.gov/compound/24424 (Accessed February 2021).

84 We know that even small doses of codeine can be lethal, depending on one's genetic inheritance, turning them into large doses of morphine. Moalem, S. (2014). *Inheritance: How Our Genes Change Our Lives and Our Lives Change Our Genes.* London: Sceptre Books, p. 109.

85 No longer considered wives' tales; some vinegars are known to kill the flu virus and *Mycobacterium tuberculosis bacteria.* Johnston, C. & Gaas, C. (2006). "Vinegar: medicinal uses and antiglycemic effect". *Medscape General Medicine*, 8(2).

86 *Peterborough Advertiser*, 18 January 1899, p. 4, column 3.

87 The family recipe book was started in 1860 by Mary Hopkinson, Mrs Charles Aaron Allott, four years after her marriage in Sheffield. It is now cared for by Susan Oldroyd née Parker, Walter's first cousin (twice removed).

88 Sanu, A. & Eccles, R. (2008). "The effects of a hot drink on nasal airflow and symptoms of common cold and flu". *Rhinology*, 46 (4), pp. 271–5.

89 Flanders, J. (2003). *The Victorian House*. London: Harper Perennial p. 103.

90 'The making of rugs using old fabrics pulled through a backing fabric and knotted in place. The type of rug produced is known by various names, including 'rag', 'thrift', 'proddie', 'peggie', 'hooky', 'proggy', 'clippy' and 'bodgy' rug.' Carpenter, D., (2017). *Rag Rugging*. Heritage Crafts Association. https://heritagecrafts.org.uk/rag-rugging/ [Accessed February 2021].

91 Flanders, J. (2003). *The Victorian House*. London: Harper Perennial p. 104.

92 Philp, R.K. (1875). *The Lady's Every-Day Book: A Practical Guide in The Elegant Arts and Daily Difficulties of Domestic Life*. London: Bemrose & Sons, p. 13.

93 Flanders, J. (2003). *The Victorian House*. London: Harper Perennial p. 104.

94 Ibid., p 104.

95 Cousin Sue Oldroyd remembers getting water for her mother from an outside pump in the 1950s, as told to be me in 2013.

96 According to a notebook entry by Doreen Drabble née Parker, in the author's possession.

97 Kelly, E. (1892). *Kelly's Directory of Cambs, Norfolk & Suffolk [Part 1: Cambridgeshire]* London: Kelly & Co., p. 151.

98 Ibid., p. 50.

99 Duke of Bedford, "On Labourers Cottages", 3.R.A.S.E. vol.10, 1849. (Quoted in Buzzing, P. (1989). *Estate management at Goodwood in the mid-nineteenth century: A study in changing roles and relationships.* Unpublished PhD thesis. The Open University.)

100 Falco, S. (2016). *The Gradual Simplification of a Scheme: The Phase-by-Phase Documentary and Fabric Analysis of the Duke of Bedford's Model Cottage Provision at Thorney 1849–65.* Unpublished PhD Thesis. University of Cambridge.

101 Kelly, E. R. (ed.), (1883). *Kelly's Directory of Cambridgeshire, Norfolk and Suffolk*. 8th ed. London: London: Kelly & Co., p. 117.

102 Bevis, T. (2005). *Walking around Thorney: A Synopsis of a Unique Social Experiment*. March: T. Bevis, p. 4.

103 *Thetford & Watton Times and People's Weekly Journal*, Saturday 3 *December 1887*.

104 Strange, J. (2012). "Fatherhood, Providing, and Attachment in Late Victorian and Edwardian Working Class Families". *The Historical Journal*, 55(4), pp. 1007–1027.

105 Bevis, T. (2005). *Walking Around Thorney: A Synopsis of a Unique Social*

Experiment, p 3.   Published by the author: 28, St. Peter's Road, March, Cambs. PE15 9NA.

106   Bedford, H. A. R., 11th Duke of (1897). *A Great Agricultural Estate, Being the Story of the Origin and Administration of Woburn and Thorney.* London: Murray, p. 247.

107   Kelly, E. R. (ed.), (1883). *Kelly's Directory of Cambridgeshire.* 8th ed. London: Kelly & Co., p. 117.

108   Clayton, J. (n.d.). *A Study of Some Aspects of the Power and Influence of the Duke of Bedford in the Village of Thorney 1851–1919.*

109   Miller, S. & Skertchly, S. (1878). *The Fenland, Past and Present.* London: Longmans, Green, and Co; email to the author from Sam Falco, 29 July 2018. According to Kelly, E. R. (ed.), (1883). *Kelly's Directory of Cambridgeshire, Norfolk and Suffolk.* 8th ed. London: London: Kelly & Co., p. 117, all of Thorney cottages had gas and water by 1883.

110   Notes from a discussion on 20 July 2018 between Jeremy Culpin (b. 1965) and John W. Culpin (b. 1935) about some of John's recollections of Thorney.

111   Bedford, H. A. R., 11th Duke of (1897). *A Great Agricultural Estate, Being the Story of the Origin and Administration of Woburn and Thorney.* London: Murray, p. 92.

112   Friends of Thorney (2014). *Thorney in Focus – An Historic Village in the Fens.* Great Britain. Thorney Society, p. 162.

113   Ibid.

114   Bedford, H. A. R., 11th Duke of (1897). *A Great Agricultural Estate, Being the Story of the Origin and Administration of Woburn and Thorney.* London: Murray, pp. 87, 91.

115   Ibid., p. 90.

116   Ibid., p. 79.

117   Ibid., p. 51; George, R. (1843). *An Enquiry into the Principles of Human Happiness and Human Duty.* London: William Pickering, p. 107.

118   Bevis, T. (2005). *Walking around Thorney: A Synopsis of a Unique Social Experiment.* March: T. Bevis, p. 4.

119   Hickmott, A. (1899) *Houses for the people: a summary of the powers of local authorities under the Housing of the Working Classes Act, 1890, and the use which has been and can be made of them* (Revised 2nd ed). London: Fabian Society. Further reading: Reader, W. J. (1967). *Life in Victorian England.* London: B. T. Batsford Ltd.

120   Bedford, H. A. R., 11th Duke of (1897). *A Great Agricultural Estate, Being the Story of the Origin and Administration of Woburn and Thorney.* London: Murray, p. 50.

121   Ibid., p. 79.

122   The Rose and Crown Tap mentioned in newspaper article *Lincolnshire Free Press,* Tuesday 25 February 1896, p.8, column 5.

123   *Sheffield Evening Telegraph,* Thursday 06 April 1899, p. 8, column 2; *Peterborough Advertiser Wednesday,* 12 April 1899, p. 2, column 2.

124 "The Refreshment of the People". (1901). *The Spectator.* p. 8. http://archive.spectator.co.uk/article/23rd-february-1901/8/the-refreshment-of-the-people [Accessed August 2020]; Prestonpans Historical Society (n.d.). "British Gothenburg experiments: Chapter III: The People's Refreshment-House Association, Limited"; Manager of Rose & Crown Hotel, 1901 census.

125 Bedford, H. A. R., 11th Duke of (1897). *A Great Agricultural Estate, Being the Story of the Origin and Administration of Woburn and Thorney.* London: Murray, p. 111.

126 Prestonpans Historical Society (n.d.). "British Gothenburg experiments: Chapter III: The People's Refreshment-House Association, Limited".

127 Higginbotham, P. (2019). *Poor Law and Workhouse Administration and Staff.* Workhouses.org.uk. [Accessed February 2021].

128 The 'Abbey rooms', as opposed to 'Abbey room', appears in the *Kelly's Directory of Cambs, Norfolk & Suffolk, 1892.* [Part 1: Cambridgeshire], p. 152. I believe the area was split with a movable screen, or curtain. The Abbey room was the larger space.

129 From conversation with Phyllis Mary Skells, *née* Woods, known as Mary, 2015.

130 'The frequency of dramatic upward moves from the lower, manual ranks into the professional and white-collar classes was low'. Long, J. (2013). "The surprising social mobility of Victorian Britain". *European Review of Economic History*, 17(1), pp. 1–23.

131 Thompson, F. (1981). "Social Control in Victorian Britain". *The Economic History Review*, 34(2), pp. 189–208.

132 Kelly, E.R. (ed.) (1896). *Kelly's Directory of Cambridgeshire, Norfolk and Suffolk.* London: London: Kelly & Co., p. 168.

133 Erected in the village in 1886; https://www.british-history.ac.uk/vch/cambs/vol4/pp219-224#h2-0001. [Accessed February 2021]. My Primitive Methodists. (2019). *Thorney Primitive Methodist Chapel.* https://www.myprimitivemethodists.org.uk/content/category/chapels/cambridgeshire/p-t. [Accessed February 2021].

134 Waller, I. H. (2008). *My Ancestor Was an Agricultural Labourer.* London: Society of Genealogists Enterprises Ltd, p. 20.

135 Hopkins, E. (1974). "Working Conditions in Victorian Stourbridge". *International Review of Social History*, 19(3), pp. 401-425.

136 Beach, B. & Hanlon, W. (2016). "Coal smoke and mortality in an early industrial economy". *The Economic Journal,* 128(615), pp. 2652–75.

137 Mason, N. (2001). "The Sovereign People are in a Beastly State": The Beer Act of 1830 and Victorian Discourse on Working-class Drunkenness. *Victorian Literature and Culture*, 29(1), pp. 109–127.

138 Winskill, P.T. (1892). *The Temperance Movement and Its Workers, Volume 1; A Record of Social, Moral, Religious, and Political Progress.* London: Blackie and Son Limited, p. 18; Webb, S. & Webb, B. (1903) *History of Liquor*

Licensing in England Principally from 1700 to 1830. London: Longman, Green, & Co., pp. 115–116.

139   Ibid., p. 18.

140   Holdsworth, W. A. (1872). *The Licensing Act, 1872, with Explanatory Introduction and Notes; An Appendix containing the Unrepealed Clauses of Previous Licensing Acts and An Index.*, London: George Routledge and Sons pp. 42–67.

141   Cobbe, F. P. (1878). "Wife torture in England [wife beating]". *The Contemporary Review*, vol. 32, 1st edition, pp. 55–87.

142   Riemer, A. R., Gervais, S,J., Skorinko, J. L. M. et al. (2018). "She looks like she'd be an animal in bed: dehumanization of drinking women in social contexts". *Sex Roles*, 80(9–10), pp.617-629. Quoted here: WPI. (2019). *Study Finds Both Men and Women Take a Negative View of Women Who Drink.* https://www.wpi. edu/news/study-finds-both-men-and-women-take-negative-view-women-who-drink [Accessed February 2021].

143   As told to the author in 2013 by Ann's granddaughter Mary (informed by her mother, Walter's sister Ethel), and referred to in a memoir in the *Thorney Post*, unknown writer, and edition.

144   Vaillant, G. (2009). *Natural History of Alcoholism Revisited*. Cambridge: Harvard University Press.

145   Weissman, M. (2009). "Translating intergenerational research on depression into clinical practice". *JAMA Psychiatry*, 302(24), pp. 2695-2696. https://www.ncbi.nlm.nih.gov/pmc/articles/PMC2904067/ [Accessed February 2021]; Risks to Mental Health: An Overview of Vulnerabilities and Risk Factors – Background paper by WHO secretariat for the development of a comprehensive mental health action plan. (2012). World Health Organization. https://www.who.int/ [Accessed August 2020].

146   Loudon, I. (1988). "Puerperal insanity in the nineteenth century". *Journal of the Royal Society of Medicine*, 81(2), pp. 76–79.

147   Showalter, E. (1987). *The Female Malady: Women, Madness and English Culture, 1830–1980*. London: Virago.

148   Bushel, C., (2013). *The Hysteria Surrounding Hysteria: Moral Management and The Treatment of fe-male insanity in Bristol Lunatic Asylum.* Unpublished Undergraduate thesis. University of Bristol, *p. 8.*

149   Bushel, C., (2013). *The Hysteria Surrounding Hysteria: Moral Management and The Treatment of fe-male insanity in Bristol Lunatic Asylum.* Unpublished Undergraduate thesis. University of Bristol, *p. 14.*

150   Beveridge, A. and Renvoize, E., (1988). "Electricity: A History of its use in the Treatment of Mental Illness in Britain During the Second Half of the 19th Century". *British Journal of Psychiatry*, 153(2), pp. 157-162. Note: In the UK electric shock treatment is still used to treat severe depression, catatonia and mania that have not responded to other treatments. For more information: https://www.mind.org.uk/information-support/drugs-and-treatments/electroconvulsive-therapy-ect/about-ect/ [Accessed

February 2021]; Aftab, A., (2016). "Late Victorian Psychiatry as Depicted in Stonehearst Asylum". *American Journal of Psychiatry Residents' Journal*, 11(5), p.16; Renvoize, E. and Beveridge, A., (1989). "Mental illness and the late Victorians: A study of patients admitted to three asylums in York, 1880–1884". *Psychological Medicine*, 19(1), pp. 21-22.

151   Groneman, C., (1994). "Nymphomania: The Historical Construction of Female Sexuality". *Signs: Journal of Women in Culture and Society*, 19(2), pp. 337-367; Brown I. (1866). *On the Curability of Certain Forms of Insanity, Epilepsy, Catalepsy, and Hysteria in Females*. London: Robert Hardwicke; Scull, A. & Favreau, D. (1986). "The Clitoridectomy Craze". *Social Research*, 53(2), p. 75.

152   Brown I. (1866). *On the Curability of Certain Forms of Insanity, Epilepsy, Catalepsy, and Hysteria in Females*. London: Robert Hardwicke; Scull, A. & Favreau, D. (1986). "The Clitoridectomy Craze". *Social Research*, 53(2), p. 75.

153   Brown I. (1866). *On the Curability of Certain Forms of Insanity, Epilepsy, Catalepsy, and Hysteria in Females*. London: Robert Hardwicke; Scull, A. & Favreau, D. (1986). "The Clitoridectomy Craze". *Social Research*, 53(2), p. 75; Arnold-Forster, A. (2014). *Clitoridectomies: Female Genital Mutilation c. 1860– 2014*. Notches Blog. http://notchesblog.com/2014/11/18/ clitoridectomiesfemale-genital-mutilation-c-1860-2014/ [Accessed February 2021].

154   Wise, S., (2013). *Inconvenient People: Lunacy, Liberty and The Mad-Doctors in Victorian England*. Berkeley, CA: Counterpoint, p. 49.

155   Skelly, J. (2014). *Addiction and British visual culture, 1751–1919*. Farnham: Ashgate Publishing Limited, p. 28.

156   Hands, T. (2019). *Drinking in Victorian and Edwardian Britain*. [S.l.]: Palgrave Macmillan, p. 13.

157   Luddy, M. (2009). *Women and Philanthropy in Nineteenth-Century Ireland*. Cambridge, UK: Cambridge University Press, pp. 207-8, 248; Kerr, N. (1886). "Society for the study and cure of inebriety". *Inaugural address delivered in the Medical Society London Rooms*, 25 April 1884, London: H. K. Lewis and Co., Ltd; as reported in *The Lancet*, 127(3267), p. 695.

158   Skelly, J. (2008). "When seeing is believing: women, alcohol, and photography in Victorian England". *Queen's Journal of Visual & Material Culture*, no1, pp. 1–17.

159   Cobbe, F. P. (1878). "Wife torture in England [wife beating]". *The Contemporary Review*, vol. 32, 1st edition, pp. 55–87.

160   Ryckman, R. (2012). *Theories of Personality*. 10th ed. Belomont, CA: Wadsworth Publishing Co. Inc., p. 28.

161   Dana, C. (1909). *Alcoholism as a cause of insanity*. Philadelphia: American Academy of Political and Social Science, p. 81.

162   Showalter, E. (1987). *The Female Malady: Women, Madness and English Culture, 1830–1980*. London: Virago, p. 29.

163 Hands, T. (2019). *Drinking in Victorian and Edwardian Britain*. [S.l.]: Palgrave Macmillan, p. 46.

164 Ibid, p. 45.

165 Ibid, pp. 41; 45–46.

166 Ibid, p. 45.

167 Kerr, N. (1886). "Society for the study and cure of inebriety". *Inaugural address delivered in the Medical Society London Rooms*, 25 April 1884, London: H. K. Lewis and Co., Ltd, as reported in *The Lancet*, 127(3267), p. 695; Colich, N., Ho, T., Ellwood-Lowe, M. et al. (2017). "Like mother like daughter: putamen activation as a mechanism underlying intergenerational risk for depression". *Social Cognitive and Affective Neuroscience*, 12(9), pp. 1480–9.

168 Weiner, B. & White, W. (2007). "The Journal of Inebriety (1876–1914): history, topical analysis, and photographic images". *Addiction*, 102(1), pp. 15–23.

169 Skelly, J. (2008). "When seeing is believing: women, alcohol, and photography in Victorian England". *Queen's Journal of Visual & Material Culture*, no1, p. 4.

170 Griffin, E., (2020). *Bread Winner: An Intimate History of The Victorian Economy*. New Haven and London: Yale University Press, p. 248.

171 Griffin, E., (2020). *Bread Winner: An Intimate History of The Victorian Economy*. New Haven and London: Yale University Press, p. 248; Mearns, G. (2011). "'Long Trudges Through Whitechapel': The East End of Beatrice Webb's and Clara Collet's Social Investigations", *Interdisciplinary Studies in the Long Nineteenth Century*, 19(13). https://doi.org/10.16995/ntn.634, p.15. [Accessed February 2021]

172 Berridge, V. (2004). "Punishment or treatment? Inebriety, drink, and drugs, 1860–2004". *The Lancet*, 364, pp. 4–5.

173 Nicholls, J. (2009). *The Politics of Alcohol: A History of the Drink Question in England*. Oxford: Oxford University Press, pp. 59–72.

174 Mann, K., Hermann, D. & Heinz, A. (2000). "One hundred years of alcoholism: the twentieth century". *Alcohol and Alcoholism*, 35(1), pp. 10–15. https://academic.oup.com/alcalc/article/35/1/10/142396 [Accessed February 2021]; Wallis, J. (2018). "A Home or a Gaol? Scandal, Secrecy, and the St James's Inebriate Home for Women" *Social History of Medicine*, 31(4), pp.774–795 https://doi.org/10.1093/shm/hky020. [Accesses February 2021]

175 Hands, T. (2019). *Drinking in Victorian and Edwardian Britain*. [S.l.]: Palgrave Macmillan, p. 27.

176 Berridge, B. (2011). "House on the hill: Victorian style". *Druglink*, 26(2), p. 14; Anonymous. (1903). "Inebriate reformatories". *The British Medical Journal*, 2(2243), pp. 1653–4.

177 Paine, W. (1899). "The Law of Inebriate Reformatories and Retreats, comprising the Inebriates Acts, 1879 to 1898." *Journal of Mental Science*, 46(195), pp. xxxvii p.226.

178 Beckingham, D. (2010). "An historical geography of liberty: Lancashire and the Inebriates Acts". *Journal of Historical Geography*, 36(4), pp. 388–401; Hunt G., Mellor J., Turner J. (1990) "Women and the Inebriate Reformatories". In Jamieson L., Corr H. (eds) *State, Private Life and Political Change. Explorations in Sociology*. Palgrave Macmillan, London. pp. 163-185 https://doi.org/10.1007/978-1-349-20707-7_9, p. 775. [Accessed February 2021]

179 Wallis (2018), p. 778.

180 As told to the author by Ann's granddaughter Phyllis Mary Skells née Woods. (2014).

181 *Cambridge Chronicle and Journal*, Friday 2 September 1892, p. 6, column 6.

182 Saphire-Bernstein, S., Way, B., Kim, H., Sherman, D. & Taylor, S. (2011). "Oxytocin receptor gene (OXTR) is related to psychological resources". *Proceedings of the National Academy of Sciences*, 108(37), pp. 15118–15122.

183 McEwen, B. and Akil, H., (2020). "Revisiting the Stress Concept: Implications for Affective Disorders". *The Journal of Neuroscience*, 40(1), pp. 12-21. https://www.jneurosci.org/content/40/1/12#T2 [Accessed February 2021].

184 Biglan, A., Flay, B., Embry, D. & Sandler, I. (2012). "The critical role of nurturing environments for promoting human well-being". *American Psychologist*, 67(4), pp. 257–271.

185 Sacchet, M., Levy, B., Hamilton, J. et al. (2016). "Cognitive and neural consequences of memory suppression in major depressive disorder". *Cognitive, Affective, & Behavioral Neuroscience*, 17(1), pp. 77–93.

186 Gottschalk, S. (2003). "Reli(e)ving the Past: Emotion Work in the Holocaust's Second Generation". *Symbolic Interaction*, 26(3), p. 376; Kirmayer, L., Brass, G. & Tait, C. (2000). "The Mental Health of Aboriginal Peoples: Transformations of Identity and Community". *The Canadian Journal of Psychiatry*, 45(7), pp. 607–616.

187 Ibid.

188 The word, which translates as 'black humour' condition, as well as the association between sadness and a hypothesised 'imbalance of humours', dates back to Classical Greece.

189 Freud, S. (1917). "Mourning and melancholia". In *The Standard Edition of the Complete Psychological Works of Sigmund Freud, Volume XIV (1914–1916): On the History of the Psycho-Analytic Movement, Papers on Metapsychology and Other Works*, pp. 237–58.

190 Solomon, A. (2001). *The Noonday Demon: An Anatomy of Depression*. New York: Scribner, pp. 64-7.

191 Prescott, C. A., Aggen, S. H. & Kendler, K. S. (2000). "Sex-specific genetic influences on the comorbidity of alcoholism and major depression in a population-based sample of US twins". *Archives of General Psychiatry*, 57(8), pp. 803–11; Kessler, R., Crum, R. & Warner, L. (1997). "Lifetime co-occurrence of DSM-III-R alcohol abuse and dependence with other

psychiatric disorders in the National Comorbidity Survey". *Archives of General Psychiatry*, 54(4), pp. 313-321, p. 313; Kessler, R., Chiu, W., Demler, O. & Walters, E. (2005). "Prevalence, severity, and comorbidity of 12-month DSM-IV disorders in the National Comorbidity Survey replication". *Archives of General Psychiatry*, 62(6), p. 617-627; Turner, S., Mota, N., Bolton, J. & Sareen, J. (2018). "Self-medication with alcohol or drugs for mood and anxiety disorders: A narrative review of the epidemiological literature". *Depression and Anxiety*, 35(9), pp. 851–860.

192   Levinson, D. (2006). "The genetics of depression: a review". *Biological Psychiatry*, 60(2), pp. 84–92; Shih, R., Belmonte, P. & Zandi, P. (2004). "A review of the evidence from family, twin and adoption studies for a genetic contribution to adult psychiatric disorders". *International Review of Psychiatry*, 16(4), pp. 260–83.

193   Kendler, K. S., Kessler, R. C., Walters, E. E. et al. (1995). "Stressful life events, genetic liability, and onset of an episode of major depression in women". *American Journal of Psychiatry*, 152(6), pp. 833–42; Moore, D. (2017). *The Developing Genome: An Introduction to Behavioral Epigenetics*. Oxford: Oxford University Press, p. 205.

194   Sullivan, P., Neale, M. & Kendler, K. (2000). "Genetic epidemiology of major depression: review and meta-analysis". *American Journal of Psychiatry*, 157(10), pp. 1552–62.

195   Kertz, S., Koran, J., Stevens, K. & Björgvinsson, T. (2015). "Repetitive negative thinking predicts depression and anxiety symptom improvement during brief cognitive behavioral therapy". *Behaviour Research and Therapy*, 68, pp. 54–63.

196   Kim, S., Fonagy, P., Allen, J. & Strathearn, L. (2014). "'Mothers' unresolved trauma blunts amygdala response to infant distress'". *Social Neuroscience*, 9(4), pp. 352–363; Iyengar, U., Rajhans, P., Fonagy, P., Strathearn, L. & Kim, S. (2019). "Unresolved Trauma and Reorganization in Mothers: Attachment and Neuroscience Perspectives". Frontiers in Psychology, 10. https://doi.org/10.3389/fpsyg.2019.00110 [Accessed February 2021].

197   Kirmayer, L., Brass, G. & Tait, C. (2000). "The Mental Health of Aboriginal Peoples: Transformations of Identity and Community". *The Canadian Journal of Psychiatry*, 45(7), pp. 607–616.

198   Strathearn, L., et. al (2019). "Pathways Relating the Neurobiology of Attachment to Drug Addiction". *Frontiers in Psychiatry*, 10: 737 https://www.   frontiersin.org/articles/10.3389/fpsyt.2019.00737/full   [Accessed February 2021].

199   Barret, L., (2020). *How Emotions are made: The Secret Life of the Brain*. *[S.l.]: Picador, p. 174.*

200   Braun, S. R., Gregor, B. & Tran, U. S. (2013). "Comparing bona fide psychotherapies of depression in adults with two meta-analytical approaches". *PLoS ONE*, 8(6): e68135.; Hollon, S., DeRubeis, R., Shelton, R. et al. (2005). 'Prevention of relapse following cognitive therapy vs

medications in moderate to severe depression'. *Archives of General Psychiatry*, 62(4), pp. 417-422, p. 417.

201 Strange, J. (2006). "Dangerous Motherhood: Insanity and Childbirth in Victorian Britain by Hilary Marland". [Review article]. *History*, 91(303), p. 471.

202 Pratt, M., Zeev-Wolf, M., Goldstein, A. & Feldman, R. (2019). "Exposure to early and persistent maternal depression impairs the neural basis of attachment in preadolescence". *Progress in Neuro-Psychopharmacology and Biological Psychiatry*, 93, pp. 21-30.

203 Thompson, R., Mata, M., Gershon, A. & Gotlib, I. (2017). "Adaptive coping mediates the relation between mothers' and daughters' depressive symptoms: A moderated mediation study". *Journal of Social and Clinical Psychology*, 36(3), pp. 171-195.

204 Costa, D., Yetter, N. & DeSomer, H. (2018). "Intergenerational transmission of paternal trauma among US Civil War ex-POWs". *Proceedings of the National Academy of Sciences*, 115(44), pp. 11215–11220.

205 In 1920, an Army Order authorised the issue of an oak leaf emblem decoration to be pinned or sewn diagonally on to the 'Victory' medal ribbon. This signifies that C E Malyon had been 'Mentioned in Despatches'. Gazette Info: Gazette issue 30570. Mentioned in Despatches by Lieutenant-General Sir Stanley Maude, K.C.B.; For distinguished and gallant services and devotion to duty. Deserving of special mention. Gazette Date: 08/03/1918 Gazette Page: 3117 Duty Location: Mesopotamian Expeditionary Force Service: British Army Regiment: Royal Army Medical Corps.

206 The National Archives; Kew, London, England: WO 392 POW Lists 1943-1945; Reference Number: WO 392/25 The National Archives; Kew, London, England; WO 392 POW Lists 1943-1945; Reference Number: WO 392/25. 5.

207 You can find out more about this side of the family and Frederick Charles Malyon in the second and third book in this series.

208 Freud, S. (1896). *The aetiology of hysteria*, pp. 207–214. I have kept the punctuation of the original.

209 Costello, V. (2012). *A Lethal Inheritance*. New York: Prometheus Books, p. 149; Weissman, M. (2009). "Translating intergenerational research on depression into clinical practice". *JAMA Psychiatry*, 302(24), pp. 2695-2696.

210 Costello, V. (2012). *A Lethal Inheritance*. New York: Prometheus Books, p. 156.

211 Schutzenberger, A. (2014). *The Ancestor Syndrome: Transgenerational Psychotherapy and the Hidden Links in the Family Tree*. Hoboken: Taylor & Francis, p. 61.

212 King University Online. (2015). Defining the Traits of Dysfunctional Families| King University Online. https://online.king.edu/ [Accessed February 2021].

213 Wyrzykowska, E., Głogowska, K. & Mickiewicz, K. (2014). "Attachment

relationships among alcohol dependent persons". *Alcoholism and Drug Addiction*. 27(2), pp. 145–61.

214 El-Guebaly, N., West, M., Maticka-Tyndale, E. & Pool, M. (1993). "Attachment among adult children of alcoholics". *Addiction*, 88(10), pp. 1405–1411.

215 Saleem, S., Asghar, A., Subhan, S. & Mahmood, Z. (2014). "Parental Rejection and Mental Health Problems in College Students: Mediating Role of Interpersonal Difficulties". *Pakistan Journal of Psychological Research*, 34(3), pp.639-653; Burns, R. (2010) "The effects of parental alcoholism on child development" *Graduate Research Papers*. 151. https://scholarworks.uni.edu/grp/151 [Accessed August 2020]; Perez, E. (2015). *Family Roles: Towards a systematic application of the role method.* Unpublished Graduate Paper, Concordia university.

216 Bowlby, J. (2006). *Attachment and loss*. 2nd ed. New York, N.Y.: Basic Books, p. 345.

217 Fearon, P. (2004). "Comments on Turton et al: On the complexities of trauma, loss and the intergenerational transmission of disorganized relationships". *Attachment & Human Development*, 6(3), pp. 255-261; Diamond, D. & Blatt, S. (2017). *Attachment Research and Psychoanalysis: Psychoanalytic Inquiry, 19.4.* Routledge, p. 518.

218 Fearon, P. (2004). "Comments on Turton et al: On the complexities of trauma, loss and the intergenerational transmission of disorganized relationships". *Attachment & Human Development*, 6(3), pp. 255–261.

219 Wyrzykowska, E., Głogowska, K. & Mickiewicz, K. (2014). "Attachment relationships among alcohol dependent persons". *Alcoholism and Drug Addiction*. 27(2), pp. 145–161.

220 Cassidy, J., Jones, J. & Shaver, P. (2013). "Contributions of attachment theory and research: A framework for future research, translation, and policy". *Development and Psychopathology*, 25(4pt2), pp. 1415–1434.

221 Griffin, E., (2020). *Bread Winner: An Intimate History of The Victorian Economy*. New Haven and London: Yale University Press, p. 257.

222 Fairbairn, C., Briley, D., Kang, D., Fraley, R., Hankin, B. & Ariss, T. (2018). "A meta-analysis of longitudinal associations between substance use and interpersonal attachment security". *Psychological Bulletin*, 144(5), pp. 532–555. https://www.ncbi.nlm.nih.gov/pmc/articles/PMC5912983/ [Accessed February 2021].

223 Fraley, R. & Shaver, P. (2000). "Adult Romantic Attachment: Theoretical Developments, Emerging Controversies, and Unanswered Questions". *Review of General Psychology*, 4(2), pp. 132–154.

224 Mineo, L. (2017). *Good genes are nice, but joy is better* Harvard Gazette https://news.harvard.edu/ [Accessed August 2020]; Diener, E., Seligman, M., Choi, H. & Oishi, S. (2018). "Happiest People Revisited". *Perspectives on Psychological Science*, 13(2), pp. 176–184.

225 Klein, M. (1959). "Our Adult World and its Roots in Infancy". *Human*

Relations, 12(4), pp. 291–303.

226 Nicolson, P. (2017). *Genealogy, Psychology and Identity: Tales from a Family Tree*. London and New York: Routledge, p. 59.

227 Dick, D. & Agrawal, A. (2008). "The genetics of alcohol and other drug dependence" *Alcohol Research & Health*, 31(2) pp. 111–118; Weissman, M. M., Berry, O. O., Warner, V. et al. (2016). "A 30-year study of 3 generations at high risk and low risk for depression". *JAMA Psychiatry*, 73(9), pp. 970–77.; Kircanski, K., LeMoult, J., Ordaz, S. & Gotlib, I. (2017). "Investigating the nature of co-occurring depression and anxiety: comparing diagnostic and dimensional research approaches". *Journal of Affective Disorders*, 216, pp. 123–35.

228 Gutierrez-Galve, L., Stein, A., Hanington et al. (2018). 'Association of maternal and paternal depression in the postnatal period with offspring depression at age 18 years'. *JAMA Psychiatry*, pp. 290–296.

229 Gutierrez-Galve, L., Stein, A., Hanington, L., Heron, J., Lewis, G., O'Farrelly, C. & Ramchandani, P. (2019). "Association of Maternal and Paternal Depression in the Postnatal Period with Offspring Depression at Age 18 Years". *JAMA Psychiatry*, 76(3), p. 290-296.

230 Schutzenberger, A. (2014). *The Ancestor Syndrome: Transgenerational Psychotherapy and the Hidden Links in the Family Tree*. Hoboken: Taylor & Francis, p. 18.

231 Ibid.

232 *Admissions Register, Boys*, C/ES155A/11; Record 218, *Thorney Girls Admissions Register*, C/ES155/15.

233 'Annie Crabb' [Annie Wilhelmina Mary Crabb] (1891) *Census return for Church Street, Thorney, Cambridgeshire.* Public Record Office: PRO, 1891 Class: *RG12*; Piece: *1233*; Folio: *44*; Page: *19*; GSU roll: *6096343*. Available at: http://www.ancestry.co.uk [Accessed February 2021].

234 'Laura Crabb' [Laura Blehynden Peters Crabb] (1891) *Census return for Church Street, Thorney, Cambridgeshire.* Public Record Office: PRO, 1891 Class: *RG12*; Piece: *1233*; Folio: *44*; Page: *19*; GSU roll: *6096343*. Available at: http://www.ancestry.co.uk (Accessed February 2021).

235 *Thorney Abbey Girls Logbook 1863–1895*, C/ES155AS, p. 454.

236 Ibid., pp. 452, 473.

237 Gillard, D. (2018). *The History of Education in England – Introduction, Contents, Preface*. Educationengland.org.uk. http://www.educationengland.org.uk/ [Accessed February 2021]

238 Thorney Board Girls' School, 1895-1919, Front cover, 'Extract from the New Code of 1892'.

239 *Thorney Abbey Girls School Log Book 1863–1895*, C/ES155A5; *Thorney Boys 1910-1940, C/ES155A/4.*

240 Gillard, D., 2013. *Elementary Education Act 1870 - Full Text.* Educationengland.org.uk. http://www.educationengland.org.uk/documents/acts/1870-elementary-education-act.html [Accessed February 2021].

241 Bedford, H. A. R., 11th Duke of (1897). *A Great Agricultural Estate, Being the Story of the Origin and Administration of Woburn and Thorney*. London: Murray, p. 103–104.

242 Thorney School Board Cash Book, 1875–1899, 1892, p. 103.

243 Horn, P., (2012). *The Real Lark Rise to Candleford*. Stroud, Gloucestershire: Amberley, p. 50.

244 *Thorney Abbey Girls Logbook 1863–1895*, C/ES155A/5, 20 March 1894, p. 495.

245 Gillard, D. (2018). *The History of Education in England – Introduction, Contents, Preface*. Educationengland.org.uk. http://www.educationengland.org.uk/ [Accessed February 2021]

246 Simon, B. (1965). *Education and the Labour Movement 1870–1920*. London: Lawrence & Wishart, p. 116.

247 Ibid.

248 Lawson, J. and Silver, H. (1973). *A Social History of Education in England*. London: Methuen & Co Ltd, p. 291.

249 Gillard, D. (2018). *The History of Education in England – Introduction, Contents, Preface*. Educationengland.org.uk. http://www.educationengland.org.uk/ [Accessed February 2021].

250 Consultative Committee (1933). Infant and Nursery Schools Report. London: HMSO, Hadow.

251 Ibid., p. 27.

252 Ibid., p. 26.

253 Blackie & Son Archive in the Library Research Annexe, Unit 8, The Point, 29 Saracen Street, Glasgow G22 5HT.

254 Thorney Abbey Girls Logbook 1863–1895, C/ES155AS, Recitations for 1891, p. 423.

255 Ibid.

256 A drawing master from Wisbech visited to give advice. *Thorney Infant School Log Book*, 1 December 1913.

257 Thorney Board Girl's School, 1895–1919, 1st December 1913, p. 199.

258 Thorney Boys 1910–1940, C/ES155A4, 8 April 1910, p. 2.

259 Consultative Committee (1933). Infant and Nursery Schools Report. London: HMSO, Hadow, pp. 13–14.

260 Thorney Board Girl's School, 1895–1919, 4 July 1913, p. 193.

261 Thorney Girls' and infants' 25 January 1907–19 December 1919, *C/ES155A/6*, 9 February 1912, p. 172.

262 Thorney Boys 1910-1940, C/ES155A/4 Report, 28 July 1910, p. 5.

263 Horn, P. (2012). *The Real Lark Rise to Candleford*. Stroud, Gloucestershire: Amberley, p. 44.

264 *Blackie's Comprehensive Arithmetics. Standard III.* (1893). London: Blackie & Son Limited, 49 Old Bailey. E.C., p. 26. (Housed at the Blackie & Son Archive, University of Glasgow Library, Research Annexe.)

265 *The Girls Log Book*, 2 July 1895 – 18 January 1907.

266 Ibid.

267   Ibid.
268   Thorney Abbey Girls Logbook 1863–1895, C/ES155AS, 15 February 1894, p. 494.
269   Thorney School Board Cash Book, 1875–1899, 1892, p. 103.
270   *Thorney Abbey Girls School Log Book* 1863–1895, C/ES155A5, p. 491.
271   Bedford, H. A. R., 11th Duke of (1897). *A Great Agricultural Estate, Being the Story of the Origin and Administration of Woburn and Thorney*. London: Murray, p. 104.
272   *Thorney Abbey Girls Logbook 1863–1895*, C/ES155A, front of book under page titled 'Dimensions of Thorney Girls' & Infant Schools'.
273   Told to the author 2015 by Phyllis Mary Skells *née* Woods, known as Mary and referred to in this work as the author's Cousin Mary and as Walter's niece.
274   Weald and Downland Open Air Museum (2018). 'Other information – education 1870 to 1902'.
275   Boonarkart, C., Suptawiwat, O., Sakorn, K., Puthavathana, P. & Auewarakul, P. (2017). "Exposure to cold impairs interferon-induced antiviral defense". *Archives of Virology*, 162(8), pp. 2231–7.
276   *Thorney Board Girls' School 1863–1895*, 9 October 1891, p. 445.
277   *Thorney Board Girls' School 1863–1895*, 8 July 1892, p. 459.
278   Openairclassroom.org.uk. (n.d.) *Weald and Downland Open Air Museum* (2018). 'Other information – education 1870 to 1902'. http://www.openairclassroom.org.uk/Further%20information/information-education%20 1870%20to%201902.htm [Accessed February 2021].
279   Gardner, P. (2018). The Lost Elementary Schools of Victorian England: The People's Education. New York and London: Routledge, p. 271; *Thorney Abbey Girls Logbook 1863–1895*, C/ES155AS, p. 495, 29 March 1894, '5 girls examined at boy's school for labour certificate'.
280   *Thorney Boys 1910–1940*, C/ES155A4, 31 March 1913, p. 19.
281   Ibid., 2 & 28 June 1910, p. 5.
282   Nationalarchives.gov.uk. (n.d.). The National Archives | Exhibitions | 1901 Census | Living at the time of the census | Men's Work. http://www.nationalarchives.gov.uk/pathways/census/living/making/men.htm [Accessed February 2021]; Mills, D. (1973). *English Rural Communities*. London: Macmillan Education, Limited, pp. 195–219.
283   Springall, L. M. (1936). *Labouring Life in Norfolk Villages 1834–1914*. 1st edition. London: George Allen & Unwin Ltd, p. 126.
284   Smiles, S. (1866). *Self-help: with Illustrations of Character, Conduct and Perseverance*. Revised edition. John Murray.
285   'The application of the principle of thrift', from a speech by the mayor of Peterborough, *Peterborough Advertiser*, Saturday 8 January 1898, p. 6, column 1.
286   Smiles, S. (1866). *Self-help: with Illustrations of Character, Conduct and Perseverance*. Revised edition. London: John Murray.
287   Smith, M. K. (2008). "Octavia Hill: housing, space and social reform". *The Encyclopaedia of Informal Education*. www.infed.org/thinkers/octavia_hill.htm [Accessed February 2021].

288 Hill, O and Ouvry, Elinor S. (1933). *Extracts from Octavia Hill's 'Letters to Fellow-Workers', 1864 to 1911. (Letters on Housing).* London: Adelphi Books Infed.org.   http://infed.org/mobi/octavia-hill-housing-and-social-reform/ [Accessed February 2021]

289 Kelly's Directories (1883). *Kelly's Directory of Cambridgeshire.* 8th edition. London: London: Kelly & Co.

290 Strange, J. (2012). "Fatherhood, Providing, and Attachment in Late Victorian and Edwardian Working-Class Families". *The Historical Journal*, 55(4), pp. 1007–1027.

291 Davies, S., Rev. (1838). *Young Men; or an Appeal to the Several Classes of Society in their Behalf.* London: Hatchard & Son and L. and G. Seeley, p. 180.

292 Ibid., p. 173.

293 Himmelfarb, G., (1988). "Manners into Morals: What the Victorians Knew". *The American Scholar*, 57(2), pp. 223-232.

294 Adams, W.H.A., (1867). *The Boy Makes the Man: A Book of Anecdotes and Examples for the Use of Youth.* Edinburgh: T. Nelson and Sons p. 13.

295 St George, A., (1993). *The Descent of Manners: Etiquette, Rules & The Victorians.* 1st ed. London: Chatto & Windus, p. 33.

296 First appeared in 1858.

297 Colton, R. (2013). *From Gutters to Greensward: Constructing Healthy Childhood in the Late-Victorian and Edwardian Public Park.* Unpublished PhD Thesis. The University of Manchester. https://www.research.manchester.ac.uk/portal/files/54583799/FULL_TEXT.PDF [Accessed February 2021].

298 According to the *Kelly's Directory* of 1896, the chief crops were wheat and oats. According to R. Melbourne's *Isle of Ely (Land of Britain)*, the predominant crops in Thorney in Walter's time were wheat, barley, potatoes and sugar beet; pp. 279, 297 (1843 description of the harvest).

299 Nefa.net (2018). 'Archive – the land'. http://www.nefa.net/archive/peopleandlife/land/wilson.htm [Accessed February 2021].

300 We often think of the word 'vacation' as an American import, but like 'chores' and 'recess' it is an old English word. Etymonline.com. *(2019)*. Online Etymology Dictionary | Origin, history and meaning of English words. https://www.etymonline.com [Accessed August 2020].

301 Cousin Susan Oldroyd née Parker, born 1947.

302 *Peterborough Advertiser* on Saturday, 23 July 1898.

303 Anonymous (2019). *The Rules of Cribbage. Instructions for 5, 6 and 7 card Crib.* https://www.mastersofgames.com/rules/cribbage-rules.htm. [Accessed February 2021].

304 Anonymous   (2015).   http://www.museumofgaming.org.uk/documents/Newsletter2.pdf [Accessed February 2021].

305 *Sheffield Independent*, Monday 28 November 1892; front cover; Tucker, R. (1996). *Origins and Early History of Tiddlywinks.* North American Tiddlywinks Association http://tiddlywinks.org/history/origins-and-early-history-of-tiddlywinks/ [Accessed February 2021].

306 Tucker, R. (1996). *Origins and Early History of Tiddlywinks.* North American Tiddlywinks Association http://tiddlywinks.org/history/origins-and-earlyhistory-of-tiddlywinks/[Accessed February 2021].

307 Gas light was introduced to the village in 1860. Gas was sold to the tenants at 8/4d. per 1000 cubic feet of gas consumed, with quantities recorded on domestic gas meters which were read quarterly. Falco, S. (2016). *The Gradual Simplification of a Scheme: The Phase-by-Phase Documentary and Fabric Analysis of the Duke of Bedford's Model Cottage Provision at Thorney 1849–65.* Unpublished PhD Thesis. University of Cambridge. p. 85; p. 93.

308 Taylor, J. (2000). *Lighting in the Victorian Home.* buildingconservation. com. https://www.buildingconservation.com/articles/lighting/lighting.htm [Accessed February 2021].

309 *Peterborough Advertiser*, Wednesday 05 April 1899, p. 4, column 7.

310 Agathocleous, T., (2006). *Illustrated Word.* [online] Brbl-archive.library. yale.edu. http://brbl-archive.library.yale.edu/exhibitions/illustratedword/ comics/09comics.html [Accessed February 2021]; Wonderfullyvulgar.de. n.d. *Wonderfully Vulgar.* http://www.wonderfullyvulgar.de/a/a_23.html [Accessed February 2021].

311 *Peterborough Advertiser*, Wednesday 10 September 1902, p. 3, column 4.

312 Ibid.

313 Ibid.

314 A game similar to pinball in which small balls are hit and then allowed to roll down a sloping board on which there are holes, each numbered with the score achieved if the ball goes into it, with pins acting as obstructions.; Kelly's Directories (1904). *Kelly's Directory of Cambridgeshire.* London: Kelly's Directories Ltd.

315 Anon. (2019). *Historical Thesaurus of English.* The University of Glasgow. https://ht.ac.uk/category/#id=46961 [Accessed August 2020].

316 Advertised as a 'pictorial series' for children as a Christmas gift, *Peterborough Advertiser*, Saturday 19 November 1898, column 2, p. 3.

317 The public opening of the reading room was on the 29 September 1892 followed by the lending and reference libraries on 10 April 1893. Hillier, R. (2000). "Libraries and Reading Rooms in Peterborough and the Early History (1892–1952) of the Public Library Service". *The Peterborough Museum Society Proceedings 1991–2000*, p. 22.

318 The eels were once used as currency. Page, W., Proby, G. & Ladds, S.I. (eds.) (1936) "The Middle Level of the Fens and its reclamation", in *A History of the County of Huntingdon*, Volume 3, London: Victoria County History London, pp. 249–290. https://www.british-history.ac.uk/vch/ hunts/vol3/pp249-290 [Accessed February 2021]. The last catcher retired in 2016. The Telegraph. (2016). *Eel fisherman quits amid plunging eel numbers.* https://www.telegraph.co.uk/science/2016/03/15/eel-fisherman-quits-amid-plunging-eel-numbers [Accessed February 2021].

319 Friends of Thorney (2014). *Thorney in Focus – An Historic Village in the Fens.* Great Britain: Friends of Thorney, p. 82.

320 Masters, J. (2018). "The Rules of Fivestones and Jacks". Master Games Ltd,.https://www.mastersofgames.com/rules/jacks-rules.htm   [Accessed February 2021].

321 The British Library. (2019). *Marbles.* https://www.bl.uk/collection-items/marbles [Accessed February 2021].

322 Tucker, E. (2008).   *Children's Folklore: A Handbook.* Westport, CT: Greenwood Publishing Group, p. 59.

323 Slater, J. and Bunch, A., (2000).   *Fen Speed Skating.* [Place of publication not identified]: Cambridgeshire Libraries Publications, p. 11.

324 Ibid., p. 12.

325 In 1928 Horn represented Great Britain at the Olympics: Prabook.com. (2019). *Cyril Horn.* https://www.olympic.org/cyril-horn [Accessed August 2020].

326 Birmingham Daily Post, 26 December 1890.

327 G. Willcocks and the Boydells.

328 Birmingham Daily Post, 26 December 1890.

329 Heathcote, J. M. (1876). *Reminiscences of Fens Mere,* London: Longmans, Green and Co. p. 54.

330 *Thorney Abbey Girls Logbook 1863–1895*, C/ES155AS, 1 February 1894, p. 494.

331 *Peterborough Advertiser*, Saturday 01 January 1898, p. 6, column 1.

332 *The Peterborough Standard*, Saturday 22 February 1902.

333 *Nottingham Journal*, Friday 30 December 1859, p. 8, column 4.

334 Slater, J. and Bunch, A., (2000).   *Fen Speed Skating.* [Place of publication not identified]: Cambridgeshire Libraries Publications, p. 12.

335 Collection.sciencemuseumgroup.org.uk. (2020). *Whippet Spring Frame Safety Bicycle, 1885* | Science Museum Group Collection. https://collection.sciencemuseumgroup.org.uk/objects/co25423/whippet-bicycle   [Accessed February 2021]; Gracesguide.co.uk. (n.d). *Whippet Bicycle - Graces Guide.* Available at: https://www.gracesguide.co.uk/Whippet_Bicycle [Accessed February 2021].

336 *Cambridge Daily News*, Friday 28 December 1901.

337 *Worcester Journal*, Saturday 22 August 1896, p. 5, column 4.

338 *Wigton Advertiser*, Saturday 20 February 1897.

339 *Clarion*, Saturday 27 February 1897, p. 71, column 1.

340 *Whitstable Times and Herne Bay Herald*, Saturday 20 February 1897, p. 7, column 2.

341 *Peterborough Advertiser*, Wednesday 06 September 1899, p. 3, column 7.

342 *Peterborough Advertiser*, Wednesday 04 July 1900, p. 2, column 5.

343 *The Peterborough Standard*, Saturday 1 September 1900.

344 Masters, J. (2018). *The Online Guide to Traditional Games.* http://www.tradgames.org.uk/ [Accessed February 2021].

345 *Lincolnshire Free Press*, Tuesday 30 November 1897; Lincolnshire Free Press - Tuesday 26 May 1896, 1896. Thorney Quoit Match. p. 8, column 5.

346   *Peterborough Advertiser*, Wednesday 29 August 1900.

347   Herbert, T. (ed.) (2000). The British Brass Band: A Musical and Social History. Oxford: Oxford University Press, p. 32.

348   Anon. (2019). *Social Cohesion* | Healthy People 2020. https://www. healthypeople.gov/2020/topics-objectives/topic/social-determinants-health/ interventions-resources/social-cohesion. Office of Disease Prevention and Health Promotion [Accessed August 2020]; Cramm, J., van Dijk, H. & Nieboer, A. (2012). "The Importance of Neighborhood Social Cohesion and Social Capital for the Well Being of Older Adults in the Community". The Gerontologist, 53(1), pp. 142–152.

349   Phyllis Mary Skells (née Woods), 2015.

350   *Peterborough Advertiser*, 1899. Personal Notes [About the movements of prominent people.]. p. 2, column 3.

351   *The Peterborough Standard*, Saturday 26 May 1900, p. 1-3.

352   Ibid.

353   Ibid.

354   *Lincolnshire Free Press*, Tuesday 29 June 1897, p. 3, column 6.

355   *The Peterborough Standard*, Saturday 26 May 1900.

356   See the complete letter in Appendix D.

357   *The Peterborough Standard*, Saturday 5 May 1900.

358   *The Peterborough Standard*, Saturday 17 January 1903.

359   *Stamford Mercury*, Friday 7 June 1895.

360   *Peterborough Advertiser*, Saturday 30 July 1898, p. 6, column 8.

361   Herbert, T. (ed.) (2000). *The British Brass Band: A Musical and Social History*. Oxford: Oxford University Press, p. 32.

362   Artisan: a worker in a skilled trade, especially one that involves making things by hand.

363   *Census Returns of England and Wales, 1881*. Kew, Surrey, England: The National Archives of the UK (TNA): Public Record Office (PRO), 1881.

364   'The object of Forestry is to unite the virtuous and good in all sects and denominations of man in the sacred bonds of brotherhood so that while wandering through the Forest of this World they may render mutual aid and assistance to each other'. Appears under heading 'Court No.3095 Banner – Reverse' The Foresters Heritage Trust (2018). 'The Foresters Heritage Trust: the history of the Foresters Friendly Society'. http://www. aoforestersheritage.com/Banners.html [Accessed February 2021].

365   *The Peterborough Standard*, 16 June 1894.

366   'Two half-days given this week – one on Tuesday for Forester's Fete.' Thorney Board Girls' School 1863 – 1895, 13th June 1890, p. 416; *Peterborough Standard*, 16 June 1894.

367   Appears under heading 'Court No.3095 Banner – Reverse' The Foresters Heritage Trust (2018). 'The Foresters Heritage Trust: the history of the Foresters Friendly Society'. http://www.aoforestersheritage.com/Banners. html [Accessed February 2021].

368   *The Peterborough Standard*, 16 June 1894.

369   Cooper, W. & Anthony, K. (1984). *The Ancient Order of Foresters Friendly Society, 150 years, 1834–1984*. Southampton, England: The Executive Council of the Society.

370   *Peterborough Advertiser*, Saturday 18 June 1898, p. 8, columns 5–6.

371   On 23 June 1893, a half day was given for a Chapel School treat.

372   *The Peterborough Standard*, 23 July 1903 p. 5.

373   Canè, C. (2014). "The royal tradition of afternoon tea: from Queen Victoria to Elizabeth II". http://royalcentral.co.uk/blogs/the-royal-tradition-of-afternoon-tea-from-queen-victoria-to-elizabethii-28820 [Accessed February 2021].

374   *The Peterborough Standard*, 23 July 1903.

375   Ibid.

376   Hales, S. (2019). *A history of afternoon tea: why we love it and how to host your own*. Lovefood.com. https://www.lovefood.com/guides/87666/a-history-of-afternoon-tea-why-we-love-it-and-how-to-host-your-own [Accessed February 2021].

377   *Peterborough Stamford Mercury*, Friday 31 May 1895. Complimentary benefit at the theatre in Peterborough for A. D. Vernon.

378   *The Peterborough Standard*, 25 January 1902.

379   Ibid., 20th January 1894.

380   Hood, T. & Scatcherd, N. (1875). *The trial of Eugene Aram for the murder of Daniel Clark of Knaresborough who was convicted at York Assizes, Aug. 5, 1759 .... Also, The dream of Eugene Aram: a poem*. Knaresborough: J. D. Hannam.

381   Phyfe, W. (1901). 5000 Facts and Fancies. New York: G. P. Putnam, p. 225.

382   23 February; reported in *The Peterborough Standard* on 24 February 1894.

383   *The Peterborough Standard*, 18 January 1900.

384   It shocks me that minstrel shows were aired by BBC Television in Britain until 1978.

385   Bunyan was an English writer and Puritan preacher best remembered as the author of the Christian allegory *The Pilgrim's Progress*.

386   *Lincolnshire Free Press*, Tuesday 26 March 1889.

387   *Peterborough Advertiser*, Saturday 16 April 1898, p. 8, columns 6-7.

388   *Peterborough Advertiser*, Wednesday 21 March 1900, p. 2, column 4.

389   *The Peterborough Standard*, 4 January 1902; M. Skells (2013).

390   Schuller, T. (2017). "What Are the Wider Benefits of Learning Across the Life Course?" *Foresight*. UK: Government Office for Science. https://assets.publishing.service.gov.uk/government/uploads/system/uploads/attachment_data/file/635837/Skills_and_lifelong_learning_-_the_benefits_of_adult_learning_-_schuller_-_final.pdf [Accessed February 2021].

391   *The Peterborough Standard*, 20 January 1894.

392   *Peterborough Advertiser*, Saturday 12 February 1898, p. 8, column 4; *The Peterborough Standard*, 3 February 1900.

393 Garwood, E., Bonney, P., Marr, M., Ommanney, E., Gregory, J. & Howorth, H. (1898). "An Exploration in 1897 of Some of the Glaciers of Spitsbergen: Discussion". *The Geographical Journal*, 12(2), p. 151.

394 Anon. (2019). *The Peckovers*. Wisbech: The Wisbech Society and Preservation Trust Limited. https://www.wisbech-society.co.uk/the-peckovers. [Accessed February 2021].

395 *Lincolnshire Free Press*, Tuesday 22 October 1889, p. 8, column 4.

396 *The Peterborough Standard*, 3 February 1900.

397 Miss Evelyn Egar of East Wryde Farm went on to have a career in nursing. She trained at Taunton and Somerset hospital 1904–1908. She qualified as a midwife in 1909. Evelyn served in WW1 as a nursing sister from Oct 1914 – Jan 1917 and was awarded the British War Medal and Victory Medal. She returned from Egypt in 1921, registered as a nurse in 1922 and returned from Aden, Yemen in 1926.

398 *Stamford Mercury*, Friday 2 February 1894, p. 6, column 2. According to the 1891 census, the Foreman sisters were students of a milliner where they lived with their brother, a farmer, and widowed mother.

399 'Observations of curious insects and common crop pests by Miss Omerod, Simpkin, Marshall and Co. London', *Peterborough Advertiser*, Saturday 19 March 1898, p. 3, column 4.

400 *Peterborough Advertiser*, Saturday 3 December 1898, p. 8, column 6.

401 For example, *The Peterborough Standard*, Saturday 21 April 1894.

402 *Peterborough Advertiser*, Saturday 30 July 1898, p. 7, column 5.

403 *The Peterborough Standard* of Tuesday 30 July 1895.

404 Ibid.

405 *The Peterborough Standard*, Saturday 7 July 1900.

406 In M. Skell's private collection of papers.

407 *Thorney Magazine*, July 1984.

408 *The Peterborough Standard*, Saturday 5 August 1905.

409 *Thorney Boy's School Log book 1910 – 1940*, 20th October 1911, p. 11. .

410 *The Hospital with extra nursing supplement*, 1894. The Early History of the Hospital Sunday and Saturday Funds. 16 (414) (XVI), p.4 51. https://www.ncbi.nlm.nih.gov/pmc/articles/PMC5263633/pdf/hosplond70245-0013.pdf [Accessed February 2021]. Originally part of church's 'Periodical Collections for Local Charities' donating money for one's local hospital became known as the annual 'Hospital Sunday'. As in Thorney in many areas fundraising extended from the service in church to activities in the local community.

411 Cherry, S. (2000). "Hospital Saturday, workplace collections and issues in late nineteenth-century hospital funding". *Medical History*, 44(4), pp. 461–488.

412 Our Journey. (n.d.). *Alfred Caleb Taylor and the First X Ray Machine Outside London*. https://ourjourneypeterborough.org/story/alfred-caleb-taylor-and-the-first-x-ray-machine-outside-london [Accessed February 2021].

413 22 May, reported by *The Peterborough Standard*, Saturday 25 May 1895.

414 *Peterborough and Huntingdonshire Standard* (1894). Proposed Local Government Changes – Separation from Peterborough. p. 3.

415 Walton, J. (1983). *The English Seaside Resort*. Leicester: Leicester University Press.

416 *Peterborough Advertiser*, Wednesday 19 September 1900.

417 Davies, G. (2017). *Forgotten Yarmouth Entertainments*. Lowestoft: Poppyland Publishing, p. 34.

418 "Yarmouth Seaside Holidays – Historical Introduction". Norfolk Museums. https://www.museums.norfolk.gov.uk/-/media/museums/downloads/learning/great-yarmouth/seaside-holidays-information-for-teachers.pdf. [Accessed February 2021]

419 Walton, J. (1983). *The English Seaside Resort*. Leicester: Leicester University Press.

420 Barnes, A. (2006). "The First Christmas Tree". *History Today* 56 (12). https://www.historytoday.com/archive/history-matters/first-christmas-tree. [Accessed February 2021]

421 Anonymous. (1848) "Christmas Tree at Windsor Castle". From the *Christmas supplement to the Illustrated London News*, 23 December. The British Library, Shelfmark: p. 7611.

422 *The Times* (London, England), 28 December 1858, p. 8.

423 Munger, M. (2017). *Ten Years of Winter: The Cold Decade and Environmental Consciousness in the Early 19th Century*. Unpublished Ph.D. Thesis. University of Oregon.

424 Allen, S. (2013). *Charles Dickens' "A Christmas Carol" Told Uncomfortable Truths About Victorian Society, But Does it Have Anything to Teach Us Today?* Oxford Royale Academy. https://www.oxford-royale.com/articles/dickens-christmas-carol-lessons/ [Accessed February 2021].

425 *Peterborough Advertiser*, Wednesday 21 December 1898, p. 4, column 4.

426 *Cambridge Independent Press*, Friday 27 December 1895. pp. 8, column 7.

427 *Peterborough Advertiser*, Wednesday 28 December 1898.

428 *Peterborough Advertiser*, Saturday 01 January 1898, p. 6, column 2.

429 *Peterborough Advertiser*, Wednesday 21 December 1898, p. 4, column 3.

430 Robinson, B. (2017). "The Human Reformation" //www. bbc.co.uk/history/british/tudors/human_reformation_01.shtml [Accessed February 2021].

431 *Peterborough Advertiser*, Saturday 01 January 1898, p. 6, column 2.

432 *Accounts and papers of the House of Commons: Volume 41*, (1845), p. 18.

433 Kelly's Directories (1904). *Kelly's Directory of Cambridgeshire*, London: Kelly's Directories Ltd., p. 215.

434 Clergy Visitation Records for the Peterborough Diocese for the year 1875, at the Northampton Record Office.

435 As told to the author by Cousin Mary (Phyllis Mary Skells née Woods); *Peterborough Advertiser*, Saturday 5 March 1898.

436 Johnson, M. (2016). *The National Politics and Politicians of Primitive Methodism: 1886–1922.* Unpublished PhD thesis. University of Hull.

437 *Peterborough Advertiser*, Saturday 5 February 1898.

438 Brown, R., (2011). *Why Was the State of Working-Class Religion A Problem In The Mid-Nineteenth Century?* Available at: http://richardjohnbr.blogspot.com/2011/11/why-was-state-of-working-class-religion.html   [Accessed February 2021].

439 Ellison, R. (1999). "Preaching and sermon publishing" in *The Victorian pulpit: Spoken and Written sermons in Nineteenth Century Britain.* Selinsgrove: Susquehanna University Press, p. 52; H. H. M. Herbert believed to have been Henry Howard Molyneux Herbert, 4th Earl of Carnarvon.

440 *Thorney Abbey Girls Logbook 1863–1895*, C/ES155AS, 18 March 1892, p. 454.

441 *Tanner, J. ed., (1917).* The Historical Register of The University of Cambridge, Being A Supplement to The Calendar with a Record of University Offices, Honours and Distinctions To The Year 1910. *Cambridge: Cambridge University Press*, p. 744.

442 Kelly, E. R. (ed.), (1883). *Kelly's Directory of Cambridgeshire, Norfolk and Suffolk.* 8th ed. London: London: Kelly & Co p. 117.

443 The Duke was patron of the Streatham Antiquarian and Natural History Society. *Norwood News*, 1934. Loss on Exhibition. p. 17, column 5; *Lincolnshire Chronicle*, 1838. MUNICIPAL MUNIFICENCE. To the Editor of the Lincolnshire Chronicle. The EDITOR of the MERCURY and IMPROPRIATORS; *Bedfordshire Mercury*, 1879. Bedford Wool Fair. p. 5, column 5.

444 The Duke and Duchess of Bedford also visited Queen Victoria at Windsor Castle. For example, RA VIC/MAIN/QVJ (W) 14th March 1893, Princess Beatrice's copies.

445 Douglas, L. (1991). *Health and Hygiene in the Nineteenth Century.* http://www.victorianweb.org/science/health/health10.html [Accessed February 2021]

446 *Peterborough Advertiser*, Saturday 5 March 1898.

447 This Parker family branch died out with Isaac's generation: all four children born to Stephen Parker and Mary Jane Desborough née Bennett died before 1911.

448 The National Institute of Neurological Disorders and Stroke. *Friedreich's Ataxia Factsheet.* www.ninds.nih.gov. [Accessed February 2021].

449 *Thorney Abbey Girls Logbook 1863–1895*, C/ES155AS, 4 October 1895, p. 398.

450 Marsh, J. (2019). *Health & Medicine in the 19th Century.* London: Victoria and Albert Museum.

451 Hatton, T., (2011). "Infant Mortality and The Health of Survivors: Britain 1910-1950. *Economic History Review*, 64 (3), pp.951-972, p. 3.

452 Ibid.

453 *The Peterborough Standard*, 'Intemperance and its effect', Saturday 26 April 1902.

454   *Peterborough Advertiser*, Wednesday 26 October 1898. Arthur Newsholme, the medical officer of health for Brighton finally related it to the contamination of fresh, powdered, or condensed cow's milk in the infants' homes. Morabia, A., Rubenstein, B. and Victora, C., (2013). "Epidemiology and Public Health in 1906 England: Arthur Newsholme's Methodological Innovation to Study Breastfeeding and Fatal Diarrhea". *American Journal of Public Health*, 103(7), pp. e17-e22.

455   *Wisbech Standard*, Friday 22 March 1889.

456   *Peterborough Advertiser*, Saturday 23 July 1898.

457   *Peterborough Advertiser*, Saturday 23 July 1898.

458   'Excluded Francis Cobb on account of his sister's illness.' *Thorney Board Girl's School, 1895 – 1919*, 13th October 1913, p. 196; 'The attendance for the past month has been exceedingly poor. This is partly due to illness + partly to field work.' *Thorney Board Girl's School 1863 – 1895*, 3rd May 1889, p. 392; *Thorney Board Girls' School 1863 – 1895*, 1st July 1892, p. 459.

459   Anderson, I. (1993). *The decline of mortality in the nineteenth century: with special reference to three English towns*. Unpublished MA Thesis. University of Durham, p. 69.

460   Horn, P. (2012). *The Real Lark Rise to Candleford*, Stroud, Gloucestershire: Amberley Publishing, p. 171.

461   *Thorney Infant School Log Book*, 25 October – 6 December 1912, p. 181.

462   *Thorney Infant School Log Book*, 9–19 January 1913, p. 183.

463   Marriott, W. (1920). "Some Phases of the Pathology of Nutrition in Infancy". *Archives of Pediatrics and Adolescent Medicine*, 20(6), pp. 461–485.

464   Hollinshead, S. (2015). *Transformatory Landscapes: Spaces of Health, Reform and Education on the Lincolnshire Coast*, Unpublished Ph.D. Thesis. *University of Nottingham. p 165.*

465   Ibid.

466   *Western Times*, 1901. Oakhampton Convalescent Home. p. 3, column 3.

467   Anders, E. (2014). *Locating Convalescence in Victorian England*. REMEDIA. https://remedianetwork.net/2014/11/07/locating-convalescence-in-victorian-england/ [Accessed February 2021].

468   *Thorney Abbey Girls School Log Book 1863–1895*, C/ES155A5, 10 March 1893.

469   *Thorney Abbey Girls School Log Book 1863–1895*, C/ES155A5.

470   Conversation with Cousin Mary, Phyllis Mary Skells née Woods, 2013.

471   *Thorney Infant School Log Book, 6 December 1912, p. 181.*

472   Hatton, T., (2011). "Infant Mortality and The Health of Survivors: Britain 1910-1950. *Economic History Review*, 64 (3), pp.951-972.

473   Koch, R. (1882). *The Etiology of Tuberculosis*. Berlin: The Physiological Society of Berlin. p. 109–115. https://pdfs.semanticscholar.org/oad7/9c002654f48546e0fb181788661d165a9301.pdf [Accessed August 2020]; The World Health Organisation recognises Mycobacterium tuberculosis as the world's top infectious disease killer. About a quarter

of the world's population is infected with Mycobacterium tuberculosis and thus at risk of developing TB disease. Global tuberculosis report 2019. Geneva: World Health Organization; 2019. License: CC BY-NC-SA 3.0 IGO, p. vi; 1.

474 Atkins, P. J. (1999). "Milk consumption and tuberculosis in Britain, 1850–1950". In A. Fenton (ed.) *Order and Disorder: The Health Implications of Eating and Drinking in the Nineteenth and Twentieth Centuries,* pp. 83–95. https://dro.dur.ac.uk/10386/1/10386.pdf [Accessed February 2021].

475 Anon. (2019). *Bovine tuberculosis: OIE - World Organisation for Animal Health.* [Accessed August 2020].

476 Atkins, P. J. (1999). "Milk consumption and tuberculosis in Britain, 1850–1950". In A. Fenton (ed.) *Order and Disorder: The Health Implications of Eating and Drinking in the Nineteenth and Twentieth Centuries,* pp. 83–95. https://dro.dur.ac.uk/10386/1/10386.pdf [Accessed February 2021].

477 Ibid., p. 1.

478 Foot, S. (2011). The Alexandra Hospital for Children with Hip Disease, Unpublished MA Thesis. London: Institute of Historical Research p. 24; Anderson, I. (1993). *The decline of mortality in the nineteenth century: with special reference to three English towns.* Unpublished MA Thesis. University of Durham, p. 34.

479 *Morning Post,* 1898. 'Tuberculosis in Milk' (Letters to the editor of the Morning Post), p. 6.

480 *Dundee Courier,* (1898). 'The Tuberculosis Scare. The Insurance Scheme. Objections by Perth Butchers', p. 3.

481 Atkins, P. J. (1999). "Milk consumption and tuberculosis in Britain, 1850–1950". In A. Fenton (ed.) *Order and Disorder: The Health Implications of Eating and Drinking in the Nineteenth and Twentieth Centuries,* pp. 83–95. https://dro.dur.ac.uk/10386/1/10386.pdf [Accessed February 2021].

482 Ibid., p. 6.

483 Foot, S. (2011). *The Alexandra Hospital for Children with Hip Disease.* Unpublished MA Thesis. London: Institute of Historical Research.

484 Borsay, A., (2005). *Disability and Social Policy in Britain Since 1750.* Basingstoke: Palgrave Macmillan, p. 51.

485 Mruk, C. (2013). "Defining self-esteem as a relationship between competence and worthiness: how a two-factor approach integrates the cognitive and affective dimensions of self-esteem". *Polish Psychological Bulletin,* 44(2), pp. 157–64.

486 Harris, M. & Orth, U. (2019). "The link between self-esteem and social relationships: A meta-analysis of longitudinal studies". *Journal of Personality and Social Psychology* 119(6):1459–1477.

487 While the work of psychologist Justin Sokol, Dr Oliver Robinson and others, build on Erikson's work, bringing it into the 21st century, they studied young adults who live in a very different social milieu to the one which Walter and his siblings inhabited. I therefore chose the Erikson

model for deepening my understanding of Walter. Sokol, Justin T. (2009) "Identity Development Throughout the Lifetime: An Examination of Eriksonian Theory," *Graduate Journal of Counseling Psychology*: 1(2), Article 14. pp 1-11; Robinson, O.C. (2015). "Emerging adulthood, early adulthood and quarter-life crisis: Updating Erikson for the twenty-first century". In: R. Žukauskiene (ed.) *Emerging adulthood in a European context*. New York: Routledge, pp. 17–30.

488 Horn, P. (2012). *The Real Lark Rise to Candleford*. Stroud, Gloucestershire: Amberley Publishing, p. 57.

489 Mitch, D. (2004) "Can Economic Decline lead to more secure employment in the absence of internal labor markets? The case of Norfolk farm workers in late nineteenth and early twentieth century England." In David Mitch et. al (eds.) *The Origins of the Modern Career, 1850 to 1950*. Aldershot: Ashgate Publishing. pp. 281-304. p. 281.

490 Armstrong, A. (1972). "The use of information about occupation", In: E. Wrigley, (ed). *Nineteenth-Century Society: Essays in the Use of Quantitative Methods for the Study of Social Data*. Cambridge: Cambridge University Press. pp. 191–310.

491 Waller, I. H. (2008). *My Ancestor Was an Agricultural Labourer*. London: Society of Genealogists Enterprises Ltd p. 17.

492 *Biggleswade Chronicle*, 1951. Fit for a Princess. p. 3, column 4.

493 Evans, G. (1977). *Where Beards Wag All*. London: Faber, p. 124.

494 Kebbel, T.E. (1887). *The Agricultural Labourer. A short summary of his position.* London: W.H. Allen & Co, p. 61.

495 Bedford, H. A. R., 11th Duke of (1897). *A Great Agricultural Estate, Being the Story of the Origin and Administration of Woburn and Thorney*. London: Murray, p. 163.

496 Bedfordshire Archives and Records Service. "Woburn experimental farm Husborne Crawley". http://bedsarchives.bedford.gov.uk/CommunityArchives/. HusborneCrawley/WoburnExperimentalFarmHusborneCrawley.aspx [Accessed February 2021].

497 Experiment: Intensive cereals Experiment Code: W/RN/13 'One of the first experiments to demonstrate the problem associated with soil acidification on cereal production following long-term use of ammonium fertilisers. Winter wheat and spring barley, Stackyard. Also known as the Woburn Continuous Wheat and Barley experiments. 1876-1990.' Era.rothamsted. ac.uk. (n.d.) *E-RA: Woburn Farm*. Available at: http://www.era.rothamsted. ac.uk [Accessed February 2021]; Johnston, A. E. (1975). "Woburn Experimental Farm: a hundred years of agricultural research". *Journal of the Royal Agricultural Society of England*. 138, pp. 18–26.

498 Bedford, H. A. R., 11th Duke of (1897). *A Great Agricultural Estate, Being the Story of the Origin and Administration of Woburn and Thorney*. London: Murray, p. 165.

499 Ibid., p. 172-173.

500 Bracey, H. (1998). *English Rural Life: Village Activities, Organizations and Institutions.* London: Routledge, p. 220.

501 Bedford, H. A. R., 11th Duke of (1897). *A Great Agricultural Estate, Being the Story of the Origin and Administration of Woburn and Thorney.* London: Murray, p. 164.

502 Ibid., p. 170.

503 *The Peterborough Standard,* Saturday 17 November 1900.

504 *The Peterborough Standard,* Saturday 7 July 1900.

505 Assistant Commissioner's Reports on the Agricultural Labourer. The Royal Commission on Labour. Vol. V. - Pt. I General Report. Parliamentary Papers 1893-94. Vol 37, pt. 11.-1 [C.6894-XXV.], p. 38.

506 As remembered by his son-in-law Harry Drabble.

507 Sites.rootsweb.com. 2014. Cambridgeshire, Englandgenweb Project - Cambridgeshire Agriculture & the Labourer. Available at: https://sites. rootsweb. com/~engcam/history/agricultureandlabor.html [Accessed February 2021].

508 Burnett, J. (2018). "Country diet". In: G. Mingay, (ed.), *The Victorian Countryside* Vol.2, 1st edition. London: Routledge & Kegan Paul, pp. 554-65; Denton, J.B. (1868). *The Agricultural Labourer.* London: [E.] Stanford; Fox, W. (1900). *Earnings of Agricultural Labourers: Report by Mr. Wilson Fox on the wages and earnings of agricultural labourers in the United Kingdom, with statistical tables and charts.* London: Eyre and Spottiswoode for H.M.S.O Cd.346 (Board of Trade, Labour Department.).

509 Upwell-born Alec Goodman, a Grand National Winning jockey, was the first farmer to introduce steam ploughing onto the Thorney Estate in 1865. En.wikipedia.org. 2020. *Thorney, Cambridgeshire.* https://en.wikipedia. org/wiki/Thorney,_Cambridgeshire#Notable_people [Accessed February 2021].

510 Waller, I. H. (2008). *My Ancestor Was an Agricultural Labourer.* London: Society of Genealogists Enterprises Ltd., p. 27.

511 Ibid., p. 29.

512 Ibid., p. 5.

513 *Peterborough Advertiser,* Saturday 29 January 1898. 'A Co-operative tea and concert was [sic] given by the Thorney branch of the Peterborough Co-operative Society. A very large number of visitors sat down for tea and the evening was packed.'

514 Horn, P. (2012). *The Real Lark Rise to Candleford.* Stroud, Gloucestershire: Amberley Publishing, p 34.

515 *The Thorney Society Newsletter,* 2016. Money, money, money - or is it? (139), p. 1.

516 Horn, P. (2012). *The Real Lark Rise to Candleford.* Stroud, Gloucestershire: Amberley Publishing, p. 228.

517   *The Peterborough Standard*, Saturday 8 September 1900.

518   Waller, I. H. (2008). *My Ancestor Was an Agricultural Labourer*. London: Society of Genealogists Enterprises Ltd, p. 25.

519   Roser, M. (2018). "Life expectancy". https://ourworldindata.org/life-expectancy [Accessed February 2021]

520   Mitch, D. (2004) "Can Economic Decline lead to more secure employment in the absence of internal labor markets? The case of Norfolk farm workers in late nineteenth and early twentieth century England." In David Mitch et al (eds.) *The Origins of the Modern Career, 1850 to 1950*. Aldershot: Ashgate Publishing. pp. 281-304. p. 295.

521   *The Peterborough Standard*, Saturday 31 March 1900.

522   Interview with Walter's niece Phyllis Mary Skells née Woods by the author, 2013; 1901 England Census, Class: RG13; Piece: 1469; Folio: 42; p. 13.

523   Bedford, H. A. R., 11th Duke of (1897). *A Great Agricultural Estate, Being the Story of the Origin and Administration of Woburn and Thorney.* London: Murray, p. 91.

524   Clause 52 of the Malicious Damage Act 1861 states: 'Whosoever shall wilfully or maliciously commit any Damage, Injury, or Spoil to or upon any Real or Personal Property whatsoever...shall, on Conviction thereof before a Justice of the Peace, at the Discretion of the Justice, either be committed to the Common Gaol or House of Correction, there to be imprisoned only, or to be imprisoned and kept to Hard Labour, for any Term not exceeding Two Months, or else shall forfeit and pay such Sum of Money not exceeding Five Pounds as to the Justice shall seem meet, and also such further Sum of Money as shall appear to the Justice to be a reasonable Compensation for the Damage, Injury, or Spoil so committed, not exceeding the Sum of Five Pounds.' https://www.legislation.gov.uk/ukpga/Vict/24-25/97/enacted/data.pdf.   [Accessed February 2021].

525   Lang, M. (1980). *Scenes from Small Worlds, the Family, the Child and Society in Selected Children's Periodicals of the 1870s.* Unpublished PhD Thesis, University of Leicester. p. 28.

526   Bedford H. A. R., 11th Duke of (1897). *A Great Agricultural Estate, Being the Story of the Origin and Administration of Woburn and Thorney.* London, Murray, p. 85.

527   Roberts, J. L. (1997). *The Ruin of Rural England: An Interpretation of Late Nineteenth Century Agricultural Depression, 1879-1914.* Unpublished Ph.D. Thesis. Loughborough University.

528   Horn, P. (2012). *The Real Lark Rise to Candleford.* Stroud, Gloucestershire: Amberley Publishing, p. 10.

529   Supplement from the *Wisbech Advertiser*, 16 May 1896.

530   According to a reference for Walter by Clerk of Works - Hugh Williams, 1907.

531   *The Peterborough Standard*, Saturday 21 April 1900.

532 Walter Parker's apprenticeship document, 1902.

533 *Building News and Engineering Journal* (1907).

534 As told to the author by Walter's niece Mary (Phyllis Mary Skells née Woods, 1918–2016).

535 With an annual rent of £7.15s according to The Inland Revenue 1910 Valuation Survey. This would be £906.84 according to the 'Historic inflation calculator: how the value of money has changed since 1900'. https://www.thisismoney.co.uk/money/bills/article-1633409/Historic-inflation-calculator-value-money-changed-1900.html [Accessed February 2021].

536 Falco, S. (2016). *The Gradual Simplification of a Scheme: The Phase-by-Phase Documentary and Fabric Analysis of the Duke of Bedford's Model Cottage Provision at Thorney 1849–65.* Unpublished PhD Thesis. University of Cambridge. p. 49.

537 According to the *Cambridgeshire Archives Service Historical Research Service Report* of 9 August 2018, the Land Values Duty map (V.16) and schedule book (470/O117), 1910, Thorney, dated 29 November 1910, state that Stephen was the occupier of 28 Wisbech Road. His landlord was R. T. Smith, presumably the same man who had helped Stephen at many events, had apprenticed Walter and had traded as Smith Brothers, contractor to the Duke. Stephen also rented an allotment from R. & L. Buckworth, and the address is given as 'Cobblers Fen'.

538 Valuation record created under the 1910 Finance (Land Values Duties) Act, c. 1911, held by the Cambridgeshire Archive, UK 2nd edition 1903 Taxation Survey, Upwell XIII.I5.13.

539 Working conditions in the building trade could be appalling, so much so that Robert Tressell wrote about them in his 1914 novel illuminating Edwardian inequality: Tressel, R. (1914). *The Ragged-Trousered Philanthropists.* London: Grant Richards Ltd., p. 55. The original title page, drawn by Tressell, carried the subtitle: "Being the story of twelve months in Hell, told by one of the damned, and written down by Robert Tressell." Tressell, R. (1983) [1955]. "Publisher's Foreword". *The Ragged Trousered Philanthropists.* London: Lawrence and Wishart.

540 Springall, L. M. (1936). *Labouring Life in Norfolk Villages 1834–1914.* 1st edition. London: George Allen & Unwin Ltd., p. 103.

541 Schutzenberger, A. (2014). *The Ancestor Syndrome: Transgenerational Psychotherapy and the Hidden Links in the Family Tree.* Hoboken: Taylor and Francis.

542 *Grc.nasa.gov. (n.d.)* History of Flight: How Did We Learn to Fly Like the Birds? *https://www.grc.nasa.gov/www/k-12/UEET/StudentSite/historyofflight. html.* [Accessed February 2021]; Thehenryford.org. (n.d.) 1903 Ford Model A Runabout - The Henry Ford. https://www.thehenryford.org. [Accessed February2021]; Cass, T., (2007). *Museum of Technology, The History of Gadgets and Gizmos: A Short History of The Gramophone.*

Museumoftechnology.org.uk. http:// www.museumoftechnology.org.uk/ stories/grams.php [Accessed February 2021]. Fineman, M., (2004). *Kodak and the Rise of Amateur Photography.* Metmuseum.org. https://www. metmuseum.org/toah/hd/kodk/hd_kodk. htm [Accessed February 2021]; Encyclopedia Britannica. (n.d.). *Zeppelin* | Definition, History, Hindenburg, *&* Facts. *https://www.britannica.*com/technology/zeppelin [Accessed February 2021]; Encyclopedia.com. (2020). *Radio Broadcasting, History Of* | Encyclopedia.Com. https://www. encyclopedia.com/media/encyclopedias-almanacs-transcripts-and-maps/adio-broadcasting-history [Accessed February 2021].

543   *Stock and Stores Account, Thorney Boys School 1878–1898* C/EB, p. 140.

544   Jefferies, R. (1947). *Life of the Fields.* London: Lutterworth Press, p. 234.

545   Lloyd, A. (2019). *Strangers in a Land of Promise: English Emigration to Canada 1900–1914.* The University of Edinburgh.

546   'Letters from Canada', *The Isle of Ely & Wisbech Advertiser*, 31 January 1906, and 28 February 1906.

547   Anon. (1974). *Hardship and happiness.* Steep Rock, Man: Interlake Pioneers, p. 5. https://digitalcollections.lib.umanitoba.ca. [Accessed February 2021].

548   Anon. (1903). *Canada, the Granary of the World.* Toronto: Eastern & Western Land Corporation, Ltd., p. 20. https://archive.org/details/ canadagranaryofwooeast [Accessed February 2021].

549   Laut, A. (1917). *The Canadian Commonwealth.* Chautauqua, N.Y.: Chautauqua Press, p. 95-96.

550   Inflationcalculator.ca. (n.d.). *Inflation Calculator | Keep Track of Canadian CPI and Inflation.* https://inflationcalculator.ca/ [Accessed February 2021].

551   Laut, A. (1917). *The Canadian Commonwealth.* Chautauqua, N.Y.: Chautauqua Press, p. 96.

552   Historymuseum.ca. *The Last Best West: Advertising for Immigrants to Western Canada, 1870–1930.* https://www.historymuseum.ca/cmc/ exhibitions/hist/advertis/adindexe.shtml [Accessed February 2021].

553   Example, *Dundee Courier*, Monday 26 February 1906.

554   *Wisbech Advertiser*, Friday 1 March 1907.

555   Internet Archive. (1900). *Concise School Atlas of the Dominion of Canada [microform]: Historical and Physical Features of Provinces, Districts and Territories of the Dominion.* https://archive.org/details/cihm_54896 [Accessed February 2021].

556   Ibid.

557   Fischer, A., Camacho, M., Ho, T., Whitfield-Gabrieli, S. & Gotlib, I. (2018). "Neural markers of resilience in adolescent females at familial risk for major depressive disorder". *JAMA Psychiatry*, 75(5), p. 493-502, p. 493; Fischer, A., Camacho, M., Ho, T., Whitfield-Gabrieli, S. & Gotlib, I. (2017). "Looking at the brighter side: functional connectivity biomarkers of resilience to adolescent depression in emotion regulation networks".

Neuropsychopharmacology, 42: S501 https://www.nature.com/articles/npp2017266 [Accessed February 2021].

558 My Year of Living Mindfully. (2020) [film] Shannon & Julian Harvey. Australia: Elemental Media https://www.myyearoflivingmindfully.com/onlinepremiere [Accessed February 2021].

559 Schutzenberger, A. (2014). *The Ancestor Syndrome: Transgenerational Psychotherapy and the Hidden Links in the Family Tree*. Hoboken: Taylor & Francis, p. 14.

560 McCullough, J. (2018). *The Canada Guide: In-depth Reference Website for All Things Canadian*. https://thecanadaguide.com/history/the-20th-century/ [Accessed February 2021].

561 Rollero, C. & De Piccoli, N. (2010). "Place attachment, identification and environment perception: an empirical study". *Journal of Environmental Psychology*, 30(2), pp. 198–205; Altman, I. & Low, S.M. (1992). *Place Attachment*. Boston, MA: Springer US.

562 Bibbings, L. (2018). "Section 5 (1) Criminal Law Amendment Act 1885". in E. Rackley & R.Auchmuty (eds), *Women's Legal Landmarks: Celebrating the history of women and law in the UK and Ireland*. Oxford: Hart Publishing; Parliament.uk (2019). 'Regulating sexual behaviour: the 19th century'. https://www.parliament.uk [Accessed September 2020]. English common law had traditionally set the age of consent within the range of ten to twelve years of age, but the Offences Against the Person Act 1875 raised this to thirteen in Great Britain and Ireland.; Me Too Movement. (2019). https://metoomvmt.org/ [Accessed August 2020]. Waites, M. (2005). *The Age of Consent: Young People, Sexuality, and Citizenship*. Basingstoke: Palgrave Macmillan.

563 Freud delivered a lecture entitled 'The aetiology of hysteria' before the Society for Psychiatry and Neurology in Vienna. Freud, S. (1896). *The aetiology of hysteria*, pp. 207–214. https://freud2lacan.b-cdn.net/The_Aetiology_of_Hysteria.pdf [Accessed February 2021]. See also, Freud, S. (1896; 1962), "Heredity and the aetiology of the neuroses". *Standard Edition*, 3:141–156. London: Hogarth Press, p. 376, &. 378. Smith, I. (ed.) (2010). *Freud: Complete works*. Valas.fr. https://www.valas.fr/IMG/pdf/Freud_Complete_Works.pdf [Accessed February 2021]. He retracted his understanding in a letter to Fliess dated 21 September 1897, his primary reason: 'surely such widespread perversions against children are not very probable'. In Masson, M. (1986). *The Complete Letters to Wilhelm Fliess, 1887–1904*. Cambridge, MA: Harvard University Press; Schaffner, A. (2012). *Modernism and Perversion Sexual Deviance in Sexology and Literature, 1850–1930*. Basingstoke: Palgrave Macmillan, p. 161.

564 Phillips, S. (2013). "Genealogy as Therapy". *HuffPost Contributor platform*. https://www.huffingtonpost.co.uk/scott-phillips/ genealogy-as-therapy-gene_b_4448250.html [Accessed February 2021].

565   Moore, D. (2017). *The Developing Genome: An Introduction to Behavioral Epigenetics*. Oxford: Oxford University Press, p. 222.

566   Kierkegaard, S. (1843). *Journalen JJ:167 SørenKierkegaardsSkrifter*: vol. 18 Copenhagen: Søren Kierkegaard Research Center. http://homepage.math. uiowa.edu/~jorgen/kierkegaardquotesource.html [Accessed February 2021]

567   Hollis, J. (2013). *Hauntings – Dispelling the Ghosts Who Run Our Lives*. Asheville, NC: Chiron Publications, p. 94.

568   Ibid., p. 89.

Bibliography

Books and journals

Adams, W.H.A., (1867). *The Boy Makes the Man: A Book of Anecdotes and Examples for the Use of Youth. Edinburgh*: T. Nelson and Sons.

Aftab, A., (2016). "Late Victorian Psychiatry as Depicted in Stonehearst Asylum". *American Journal of Psychiatry Residents' Journal*, 11(5), p. 16.

Agathocleous, T., (2006). *Illustrated Word*. [online] Brbl-archive.library.yale.edu. http://brbl-archive.library.yale.edu/exhibitions/illustratedword/comics/09comics. html [Accessed August 2020].

Allen, S. (2013). *Charles Dickens' "A Christmas Carol" Told Uncomfortable Truths About Victorian Society, But Does it Have Anything to Teach Us Today?* Oxford Royale Academy. https://www.oxford-royale.com/articles/dickens-christmas-carol-lessons/ [Accessed February 2021].

Altman, I. & Low, S.M. (1992). *Place Attachment*. Boston, MA: Springer US

Anders, E. (2014). *Locating Convalescence in Victorian England*. https://remedianetwork.net/2014/11/07/locating-convalescence-in-victorian-england. [Accessed February 2021].

Anderson, I. (1993). *The decline of mortality in the nineteenth century: with special reference to three English towns*. Unpublished MA Thesis. University of Durham.

Anonymous. (1848) "Christmas Tree at Windsor Castle". From the *Christmas supplement to the Illustrated London News*, 23 December. The British Library, Shelfmark: p. 7611.

Anonymous. (2019). *Social Cohesion | Healthy People 2020*. https://www. healthypeople.gov/2020/topics-objectives/topic/social-determinants-health/ interventions-resources/social-cohesion. Office of Disease Prevention and Health Promotion [Accessed February 2021].

Anonymous. (2019). *Historical Thesaurus of English*. The University of Glasgow. https://ht.ac.uk/category/#id=46961.

Anonymous. (1903). *Canada, the Granary of the World. Toronto*. Eastern & Western Land Corporation, Ltd., p. 20. https://archive.org/details/ canadagranaryofwo0east.

Anonymous. (1903). "Inebriate reformatories". *The British Medical Journal*, 2(2243), pp. 1653—4.

Anonymous. (1894) *Assistant Commissioner's Reports on the Agricultural Labourer*. The Royal Commission on Labour. Vol. V. — Pt. I General Report. Parliamentary Papers 1893—94. Vol 37, pt. 11.-1 [C.6894-XXV.]

Anonymous. (1867). "A Question for Dr Hawkins" *The British Medical Journal*, 1(338), p. 759.

Armstrong, A. (1972). "The use of information about occupation", In: E. Wrigley, (ed). *Nineteenth-Century Society: Essays in the Use of Quantitative Methods for the Study of Social Data*. Cambridge: Cambridge University Press. pp. 191—310.

Arnold-Forster, A. (2014). *Clitoridectomies: Female Genital Mutilation c. 1860—2014*. Notches Blog. http://notchesblog.com.

Atkins, P. J., (2003). "Mother's milk and infant death in Britain, circa 1900—1940". *Anthropology of food*. Vol:2. https://doi.org/10.4000/aof.310 [Accessed February 2021].

Atkins, P. J. (1999). "Milk consumption and tuberculosis in Britain, 1850—1950". In A. Fenton (ed.) *Order and Disorder: The Health Implications of Eating and Drinking in the Nineteenth and Twentieth Centuries*, pp. 83—95. https://dro.dur.ac.uk/10386/1/10386.pdf [Accessed February 2021].

Atkinson, P., Francis, B., Gregory, I. & Porter, C. (2017). "Spatial modelling of rural infant mortality and occupation in nineteenth-century Britain". *Demographic Research*, 36, pp. 1337—1360.

Atkinson, P., Francis, B., Gregory, I. and Porter, C., (2017). "Patterns of infant mortality in rural England and Wales, 1850—1910". *The Economic History Review*, 70(4), pp.1268—1290.

Barnes, A. (2006). "The First Christmas Tree". *History Today* 56 (12). https://www.historytoday.com/archive/history-matters/first-christmas-tree.

Barret, L., (2020). *How Emotions are made: The Secret Life of the Brain*. [S.l.]: Picador.

Beach, B. & Hanlon, W. (2016). "Coal smoke and mortality in an early industrial economy". *The Economic Journal*, 128(615), pp. 2652—75.

Beckingham, D. (2010). "An historical geography of liberty: Lancashire and the Inebriates Acts". *Journal of Historical Geography*, 36(4), pp. 388—401.

Bedford, H. A. R., 11th Duke of (1897). *A Great Agricultural Estate, Being the Story of the Origin and Administration of Woburn and Thorney*. London: Murray.

Berridge, B. (2011). "House on the hill: Victorian style". *Druglink*, 26(2), p. 14.

Berridge, V. & Edwards, G. (1982). 'Opium and the people: opiate use in nineteenth-century'. *Medical Journey*, 26(4), pp. 458—62.

Berridge, V. (2004). "Punishment or treatment? Inebriety, drink, and drugs, 1860—2004". *The Lancet*, 364, pp. 4—5.

Beveridge, A. and Renvoize, E., (1988). "Electricity: A History of its use in the Treatment of Mental Illness in Britain During the Second Half of the 19th Century". *British Journal of Psychiatry*, 153(2), pp. 157—162.

Bevis, T. (2005). *Walking around Thorney: A Synopsis of a Unique Social Experiment*. March: T. Bevis.

Bibbings, L. (2018). "Section 5 (1) Criminal Law Amendment Act 1885". in E. Rackley & R. Auchmuty (eds), *Women's Legal Landmarks: Celebrating the history of women and law in the UK and Ireland*. Oxford: Hart Publishing.

Biglan, A., Flay, B., Embry, D. & Sandler, I. (2012). 'The critical role of nurturing environments for promoting human well-being'. American Psychologist, 67(4), pp. 257—271.

Boonarkart, C., Suptawiwat, O., Sakorn, K., Puthavathana, P. & Auewarakul, P. (2017). "Exposure to cold impairs interferon-induced antiviral defense". *Archives of Virology*, 162(8), pp. 2231—2237.

Borsay, A., (2005). *Disability and Social Policy in Britain Since 1750*. Basingstoke: Palgrave Macmillan

Bowlby, J. (2006). *Attachment and loss*. 2nd ed. New York: Basic Books.

Bracey, H. (1998). *English Rural Life: Village Activities, Organizations and Institutions*. London: Routledge.

Bradley, K. (2013). *The Town of Well: Some Glimpses of the Early History of Upwell and the Surrounding Countryside*. Upwell: Published by Keith Bradley.

Braun, S. R., Gregor, B. & Tran, U. S. (2013). "Comparing bona fide psychotherapies of depression in adults with two meta-analytical approaches". *PLoS ONE*, 8(6): e68135. doi:10.1371/journal.pone.0068135.

Brennan, J. and Houde, K. (2017). *History and systems of psychology*. 7th ed. Cambridge University Press.

Bretherton, I. (1992). "The origins of attachment theory: John Bowlby and Mary Ainsworth". *Developmental Psychology*, 28(5), pp. 759—775.

Brown I. (1866). *On the Curability of Certain Forms of Insanity, Epilepsy, Catalepsy, and Hysteria in Females*. London: Robert Hardwicke.

Brown, R., (2011). *Why Was the State of Working-Class Religion A Problem In The Mid-Nineteenth Century?* Available at: http://richardjohnbr.blogspot.com/2011/11/why-was-state-of-working-class-religion.html [Accessed February 2021].

Burnett, J. (2018). "Country diet". In: G. Mingay, (ed.), *The Victorian Countryside* Vol.2, 1st edition. London: Routledge & Kegan Paul, pp. 554—65.

Burns, R. (2010) "The effects of parental alcoholism on child development" *Graduate Research Papers*. 151. https://scholarworks.uni.edu/grp/151 [Accessed August 2020].

Bushel, C., (2013). *The Hysteria Surrounding Hysteria: Moral Management and The Treatment of fe-male insanity in Bristol Lunatic Asylum.* Unpublished Undergraduate thesis. University of Bristol.

Buzzing, P. (1989). *Estate management at Goodwood in the mid-nineteenth century: A study in changing roles and relationships.* Unpublished PhD thesis. The Open University.

Canè, C. (2014). "The royal tradition of afternoon tea: from Queen Victoria to Elizabeth II". http://royalcentral.co.uk/blogs/ the-royal-tradition-of-afternoon-tea-from-queen-victoria-to-elizabethii-28820 [Accessed February 2021].

Carey, N. (2013). *The Epigenetics Revolution: How Modern Biology Is Rewriting Our Understanding of Genetics, Disease and Inheritance.* New York: Columbia University Press.

Carpenter, D., (2017). *Rag Rugging.* Heritage Crafts Association. https://heritagecrafts.org.uk/rag-rugging/

Cass, T., (2007). *Museum of Technology, The History of Gadgets and Gizmos: A Short History of The Gramophone.* Museumoftechnology.org.uk. http://www.museumoftechnology.org.uk/stories/grams.php.

Cassidy, J., Jones, J. & Shaver, P. (2013). "Contributions of attachment theory and research: A framework for future research, translation, and policy". Development and Psychopathology, 25(4pt2), pp. 1415—1434 *Census Returns of England and Wales* (1881). Kew, Surrey, England: The National Archives of the UK (TNA): Public Record Office (PRO), 1881.

Chamberlain, G. (2006). "British maternal mortality in the nineteenth and early twentieth centuries". *Journal of the Royal Society of Medicine*, 99(11), pp. 559—63.

Cherry, S. (2000). "Hospital Saturday, workplace collections and issues in late nineteenth-century hospital funding". *Medical History*, 44(4), pp. 461—488.

Clayton, J. (n.d.) *A Study of Some Aspects of the Power and Influence of the Duke of Bedford in the Village of Thorney 1851—1919.*

Clayton, P. & Rowbotham, J. (2009). "How the mid-Victorians worked, ate and died". *International Journal of Environmental Research and Public Health*, 6(3), pp. 1235—53.

Cobbe, F. P. (1878). "Wife torture in England [wife beating]". *The Contemporary Review*, vol. 32, 1st edition, pp. 55—87.

Colich, N., Ho, T., Ellwood-Lowe, M. et al. (2017). "Like mother like daughter: putamen activation as a mechanism underlying intergenerational risk for depression". *Social Cognitive and Affective Neuroscience*, 12(9), pp. 1480—9.

Colton, R. (2013). *From Gutters to Greensward: Constructing Healthy Childhood in the Late-Victorian and Edwardian Public Park.* Unpublished PhD thesis. The University of Manchester. https://www.research.manchester.ac.uk/portal/.

Cooley, C. (1902). *Human Nature and the Social Order.* New York: Charles Scribner's Sons.

Cooper, W. & Anthony, K. (1984). *The Ancient Order of Foresters Friendly Society, 150 years, 1834—1984.* Southampton, England: The Executive Council of the Society.

Costa, D., Yetter, N. & DeSomer, H. (2018). "Intergenerational transmission of paternal trauma among US Civil War ex-POWs". *Proceedings of the National Academy of Sciences*, 115(44), pp. 11215—11220.

Costello, V. (2012). *A Lethal Inheritance.* New York: Prometheus Books.

Cramm, J., van Dijk, H. & Nieboer, A. (2012). "The Importance of Neighborhood Social Cohesion and Social Capital for the Well Being of Older Adults in the Community". *The Gerontologist*, 53(1), pp. 142—152.

Dana, C. (1909). *Alcoholism as a cause of insanity. Philadelphia*: American Academy of Political and Social Science.

Davies, G. (2017). *Forgotten Yarmouth Entertainments.* Lowestoft: Poppyland Publishing.

Davies, S., Rev. (1838). *Young Men; or an Appeal to the Several Classes of Society in their Behalf.* London: Hatchard & Son and L. and G. Seeley.

de Pennington, J. (2017). *British History in depth: Beneath the Surface: A Country of Two Nations.* bbc.co.uk. http://www.bbc.co.uk/history/british/victorians/bsurface_01.shtml [Accessed February 2021].

Denton, J.B. (1868). *The Agricultural Labourer*. London: [E.] Stanford.

Diamond, D. & Blatt, S. (2017). Attachment Research and Psychoanalysis: Psychoanalytic Inquiry, 19.(4). New York and London: Routledge.

Dick, D. & Agrawal, A. (2008). "The genetics of alcohol and other drug dependence" *Alcohol Research & Health*, 31(2) pp. 111—118.

Diener, E., Seligman, M., Choi, H. & Oishi, S. (2018). "Happiest People Revisited". *Perspectives on Psychological Science*, 13(2), pp. 176—184. doi: 10.1037/pspp0000265.

Douglas, L. (1991). *Health and Hygiene in the Nineteenth Century.* http://www.victorianweb.org/science/health/health10.html. [Accessed February 2021].

Dwork, D., (1987). "The milk option. An aspect of the history of the infant welfare movement in England 1898—1908". *Medical History*, 31(1), pp. 51—69.

Dyhouse, C., (1978). "Working-Class Mothers and Infant Mortality in England, 1895—1914". *Journal of Social History*, 12(2), p. 255.

Elbossaty, W. (2018). "Pharmaceutical influences of Epsom salts". *American Journal of Pharmacology and Pharmacotherapeutics,* 5(1:2), pp. 1—3 doi:10.21767/2393—8862.100011.

El-Guebaly, N., West, M., Maticka-Tyndale, E. & Pool, M. (1993). "Attachment among adult children of alcoholics". *Addiction*, 88(10), pp. 1405—1411.

Ellison, R. (1999). "Preaching and sermon publishing" in *The Victorian pulpit: Spoken and Written sermons in Nineteenth Century Britain.* Selinsgrove: Susquehanna University Press.

Evans, G. (1977). *Where Beards Wag All.* London: Faber.

Fairbairn, C., Briley, D., Kang, D., Fraley, R., Hankin, B. & Ariss, T. (2018). "A meta-analysis of longitudinal associations between substance use and interpersonal attachment security". *Psychological Bulletin*, 144(5), pp. 532—555. https://www.ncbi.nlm.nih.gov/pmc/articles/PMC5912983/.

Falco, S. (2016). *The Gradual Simplification of a Scheme: The Phase-by-Phase Documentary and Fabric Analysis of the Duke of Bedford's Model Cottage Provision at Thorney 1849—65.* Unpublished PhD Thesis. University of Cambridge.

Fearon, P. (2004). "Comments on Turton et al: On the complexities of trauma, loss and the intergenerational transmission of disorganized relationships". *Attachment & Human Development*, 6(3), pp. 255—261.

Feldman, R., (2017). The Neurobiology of Human Attachments. *Trends in Cognitive Sciences*, 21(2), pp.80–99.

Fineman, M., (2004). *Kodak and the Rise of Amateur Photography*. Metmuseum. org. https://www.metmuseum.org/toah/hd/kodk/hd_kodk.Htm.

Fischer, A., Camacho, M., Ho, T., Whitfield-Gabrieli, S. & Gotlib, I. (2018). "Neural markers of resilience in adolescent females at familial risk for major depressive disorder". *JAMA Psychiatry*, 75(5), p. 493–502

Fischer, A., Camacho, M., Ho, T., Whitfield-Gabrieli, S. & Gotlib, I. (2017). "Looking at the brighter side: functional connectivity biomarkers of resilience to adolescent depression in emotion regulation networks". *Neuropsychopharmacology*, 42: S501 https://www.nature.com/articles/npp2017266 [Accessed February 2021].

Flanders, J. (2003). *The Victorian House*. London: Harper Perennial.

Flatman, C., (2020). *The Origins of The Riots in Littleport And Ely In May 1816 and The Reaction of The Establishment to the Disturbances*. Unpublished MA Thesis. The Open University.

Foot, S. (2011). *The Alexandra Hospital for Children with Hip Disease*. Unpublished MA Thesis. London: Institute of Historical Research.

Forbes, T. (1971). "The Regulation of English Midwives in The Eighteenth and Nineteenth Centuries". *Medical History*, 15(4), pp. 352–362.

Fowler, S. (2008). *The people, the places, the life behind doors*. Barnsley, UK: Pen & Sword Books Ltd.

Fox, W. (1900). *Earnings of Agricultural Labourers: Report by Mr. Wilson Fox on the wages and earnings of agricultural labourers in the United Kingdom, with statistical tables and charts*. London: Eyre and Spottiswoode for H.M.S.O Cd.346.

Fraley, R. & Shaver, P. (2000). "Adult Romantic Attachment: Theoretical Developments, Emerging Controversies, and Unanswered Questions". *Review of General Psychology*, 4(2), pp. 132–154.

Freud, S. (1917). "Mourning and melancholia". In *The Standard Edition of the Complete Psychological Works of Sigmund Freud, Volume XIV (1914–1916): On the History of the Psycho-Analytic Movement, Papers on Metapsychology and Other Works*, pp. 237–58.

Freud, S. (1896). *The aetiology of hysteria*, pp. 207–214. https://freud2lacan.b-cdn.net/The_Aetiology_of_Hysteria.pdf [Accessed February 2021].

Freud, S. (1896; 1962), "Heredity and the aetiology of the neuroses". *Standard Edition*, 3:141–156. London: Hogarth Press.

Gardner, P. (2018). *The Lost Elementary Schools of Victorian England: The People's Education*. New York and London: Routledge.

Garwood, E., Bonney, P., Marr, M., Ommanney, E., Gregory, J. & Howorth, H. (1898). "An Exploration in 1897 of Some of the Glaciers of Spitsbergen: Discussion". *The Geographical Journal*, 12(2), pp. 151–158

George, R. (1843). *An Enquiry into the Principles of Human Happiness and Human Duty*. London: William Pickering.

Gerritsen, J. W. (2000). *The Control of Fuddle and Flash: A Sociological History of the Regulation of Alcohol and Opiates* (International Studies in Sociology and Social Anthropology). Brill Academic Publishers.

Gillard, D. (2018). *The History of Education in England – Introduction, Contents, Preface*. Educationengland.org.uk. http://www.educationengland.org.uk/history/.

Goodman, R. (2013). *How to be a Victorian: A Dawn-to-Dusk Guide to Victorian Life*. New York: Liveright Publishing Corporation.

Goose, N. (2006). "Farm service, seasonal unemployment and casual labour in mid nineteenth-century England". *Agricultural History Review*, 54(2), pp. 274–303.

Gottschalk, S. (2003). "Reli(e)ving the Past: Emotion Work in the Holocaust's Second Generation". *Symbolic Interaction*, 26(3), pp.355–380.

Griffin, E. (2014). *Liberty's Dawn: A People's History of the Industrial Revolution*. 1st edition. New Haven and London: Yale University Press.

Griffin, E., (2020). *Bread Winner: An Intimate History of The Victorian Economy*. New Haven and London: Yale University Press.

Groneman, C., (1994). "Nymphomania: The Historical Construction of Female Sexuality". *Signs: Journal of Women in Culture and Society*, 19(2), pp. 337–367.

Gutierrez-Galve, L., Stein, A., Hanington, L., Heron, J., Lewis, G., O'Farrelly, C. & Ramchandani, P. (2019). "Association of Maternal and Paternal Depression in the Postnatal Period with Offspring Depression at Age 18 Years". *JAMA Psychiatry*, 76(3), p. 290–296 doi: 10.1001/jamapsychiatry.2018.3667.

Hales, S. (2019). *A history of afternoon tea: why we love it and how to host your own*. Lovefood.com. https://www.lovefood.com/guides/87666/ahistory-of-afternoon-tea-why-we-love-it-and-how-to-host-your-own [Accessed February 2021].

Haley, B. (1978). *The Healthy Body and Victorian Culture*. Cambridge, Mass.: Harvard University Press.

Hamlin, C. (1995). "Could you starve to death in England in 1839? The ChadwickFarr controversy and the loss of the "social" in public health". *American Journal of Public Health*, 85(6), pp. 856—866.

Hands, T. (2019). *Drinking in Victorian and Edwardian Britain*. [S.l.]: Palgrave Macmillan.

Harris, M. & Orth, U. (2019). "The link between self-esteem and social relationships: A meta-analysis of longitudinal studies". *Journal of Personality and Social Psychology* 119(6):1459—1477.

Hatton, T., (2011). "Infant Mortality and The Health of Survivors: Britain 1910—1950. *Economic History Review*, 64 (3), pp.951—972.

Heathcote, J. M. (1876). *Reminiscences of Fens Mere*. London: Longmans, Green and Co.

Heijmans, B., Tobi, E., Stein, A., Putter, H., Blauw, G., Susser, E., Slagboom, P. & Lumey, L. (2008). "Persistent epigenetic differences associated with prenatal exposure to famine in humans". *Proceedings of the National Academy of Sciences*, 105(44), pp. 17046—17049.

Herbert, T. (ed.) (2000). *The British Brass Band: A Musical and Social History*. Oxford: Oxford University Press.

Hickmott, A. (1899) *Houses for the people: a summary of the powers of local authorities under the Housing of the Working Classes Act, 1890, and the use which has been and can be made of them* (Revised 2nd ed). London: Fabian Society.

Higginbotham, P. (2019). *Poor Law and Workhouse Administration and Staff*. Workhouses.org.uk.

Hill, O and Ouvry, Elinor S. (1933). *Extracts from Octavia Hill's 'Letters to Fellow-Workers', 1864 to 1911. (Letters on Housing)*. London: Adelphi Books Infed. org. http://infed.org/mobi/octavia-hill-housing-and-social-reform/.

Hillier, R. (2000). "Libraries and Reading Rooms in Peterborough and the Early History (1892—1952) of the Public Library Service". *The Peterborough Museum Society Proceedings 1991—2000*. Peterborough: Peterborough Museum Society.

Himmelfarb, G., (1988). "Manners into Morals: What the Victorians Knew". *The American Scholar*, 57(2), pp. 223—232.

Holdsworth, W. A. (1872). *The Licensing Act, 1872, with Explanatory Introduction and Notes; An Appendix containing the Unrepealed Clauses of Previous Licensing Acts and An Index.*, London: George Routledge and Sons.

Hollinshead, S. (2015). *Transformatory Landscapes: Spaces of Health, Reform and Education on the Lincolnshire Coast*, Unpublished Ph.D. Thesis. University of Nottingham.

Hollis, J. (2013). *Hauntings – Dispelling the Ghosts Who Run Our Lives*, Asheville, NC: Chiron Publications

Hollon, S., DeRubeis, R., Shelton, R. et al. (2005). 'Prevention of relapse following cognitive therapy vs medications in moderate to severe depression'. Archives of General Psychiatry, 62(4), pp. 417–422.

Holmes, V. (2017). In Bed with the Victorians: The Life-Cycle of Working Class Marriage. London: Palgrave Macmillan.

Holmes, E. (1911) *What Is and What Might Be: A Study of Education in General And Elementary Education in Particular* (1911). London: Constable & Co. Ltd.

Hood, T. & Scatcherd, N. (1875). *The trial of Eugene Aram for the murder of Daniel Clark of Knaresborough who was convicted at York Assizes, Aug. 5, 1759 .... Also, The dream of Eugene Aram: a poem.* Knaresborough: J. D. Hannam.

Hopkins, E. (1974). "Working Conditions in Victorian Stourbridge". *International Review of Social History*, 19(3), pp.401–425.

Horn, P. (2012). *The Real Lark Rise to Candleford*, Stroud, Gloucestershire: Amberley Publishing.

Hunt G., Mellor J., Turner J. (1990) "Women and the Inebriate Reformatories". In Jamieson L., Corr H. (eds) *State, Private Life and Political Change. Explorations in Sociology*. Palgrave Macmillan, London. pp. 163–185 https://doi.org/10.1007/978–1–349–20707–7_9.

Iyengar, U., Rajhans, P., Fonagy, P., Strathearn, L. & Kim, S. (2019). "Unresolved Trauma and Reorganization in Mothers: Attachment and Neuroscience Perspectives". Frontiers in Psychology, 10. https://doi.org/10.3389/fpsyg.2019.00110.

Jaadla, H. & Reid, A. (2017). "The geography of early childhood mortality in England and Wales, 1881–1911". *Demographic Research*, 37, pp. 1861–1890.

Jefferies, R. (1947). *Life of the Fields*. London: Lutterworth Press.

Johnson, M. (2016). *The National Politics and Politicians of Primitive Methodism: 1886–1922*. Unpublished PhD thesis. University of Hull.

Johnston, A. E. (1975) "Woburn Experimental Farm: a hundred years of agricultural research". *Journal of the Royal Agricultural Society of England*. 138, pp. 18—26.

Johnston, C. & Gaas, C. (2006). "Vinegar: medicinal uses and antiglycemic effect". *Medscape General Medicine*, 8(2).

Kebbel, T.E. (1887). *The Agricultural Labourer: A short summary of his position*. London: W.H. Allen & Co.

Kelly, E. R. (ed.), (1883). *Kelly's Directory of Cambridgeshire, Norfolk and Suffolk*. 8th ed. London: Kelly's Directories Ltd.

Kendler, K. S., Kessler, R. C., Walters, E. E. et al. (1995). "Stressful life events, genetic liability, and onset of an episode of major depression in women". *American Journal of Psychiatry*, 152(6), pp. 833—42.

Kerr, N. (1886). "Society for the study and cure of inebriety". *Inaugural address delivered in the Medical Society London Rooms*, 25 April 1884, London: H. K. Lewis and Co., Ltd.

Kertz, S., Koran, J., Stevens, K. & Björgvinsson, T. (2015). "Repetitive negative thinking predicts depression and anxiety symptom improvement during brief cognitive behavioral therapy". *Behaviour Research and Therapy*, 68, pp. 54—63.

Kessler, R., Chiu, W., Demler, O. & Walters, E. (2005). "Prevalence, severity, and comorbidity of 12-month DSM-IV disorders in the National Comorbidity Survey replication". *Archives of General Psychiatry*, 62(6), p. 617—627.

Kessler, R., Crum, R. & Warner, L. (1997). "Lifetime co-occurrence of DSM-III-R alcohol abuse and dependence with other psychiatric disorders in the National Comorbidity Survey". *Archives of General Psychiatry*, 54(4), pp. 313—321.

Kierkegaard, S. (1843). *Journalen JJ:167 SørenKierkegaardsSkrifter*: vol. 18 Copenhagen: Søren Kierkegaard Research Center. http://homepage.math.uiowa.edu/~jorgen/kierkegaardquotesource.html [Accessed February 2021].

Kim, S., Fonagy, P., Allen, J. & Strathearn, L. (2014). "'Mothers' unresolved trauma blunts amygdala response to infant distress'". *Social Neuroscience*, 9(4), pp. 352—363.

Kircanski, K., LeMoult, J., Ordaz, S. & Gotlib, I. (2017). "Investigating the nature of cooccurring depression and anxiety: comparing diagnostic and dimensional research approaches". *Journal of Affective Disorders*, 216, pp. 123—35.

Kirmayer, L., Brass, G. & Tait, C. (2000). "The Mental Health of Aboriginal Peoples: Transformations of Identity and Community". *The Canadian Journal of Psychiatry*, 45(7), pp. 607–616.

Kleeman, J., 2019. "Why parents are addicted to Calpol". *The Guardian*, https://www.theguardian.com/lifeandstyle/2019/jun/04/why-parents-are-addicted-to-calpol [Accessed February 2021].

Klein, M. (1959). "Our Adult World and its Roots in Infancy". *Human Relations*, 12(4), pp. 291–303.

Koch, R. (1882). *The Etiology of Tuberculosis*. Berlin: The Phsyiological Society of Berlin. p. 109–115.

Lang, M. (1980). *Scenes from Small Worlds, the Family, the Child and Society in Selected Children's Periodicals of the 1870s*. Unpublished PhD Thesis, University of Leicester.

Laut, A. (1917). *The Canadian Commonwealth*. Chautauqua, N.Y.: Chautauqua Press.

Lavebratt, C., Almgren, M. & Ekström, T. (2011). "Epigenetic regulation in obesity". *International Journal of Obesity*, 36(6), pp. 757–765.

Lawson, J. and Silver, H. (1973). *A Social History of Education in England*. London: Methuen & Co Ltd.

Lester, B., Conradt, E., LaGasse, L., Tronick, E., Padbury, J. & Marsit, C. (2018). "Epigenetic Programming by Maternal Behavior in the Human Infant". *Pediatrics*, 42(4), p.e20171890

Levinson, D. (2006). "The genetics of depression: a review". *Biological Psychiatry*, 60(2), pp. 84–92.

Lloyd, A. (2019). *Strangers in a Land of Promise: English Emigration to Canada 1900–1914*. The University of Edinburgh.

Long, J. (2013). "The surprising social mobility of Victorian Britain". *European Review of Economic History*, 17(1), pp. 1–23.

Loudon, I. (1988). "Puerperal insanity in the nineteenth century". *Journal of the Royal Society of Medicine*, 81(2), pp. 76–79.

Loudon, I. (1992). *Death in childbirth: An International Study of Maternal Care and Maternal Mortality 1800–1950*. Oxford: Clarendon Press.

Luddy, M. (2009). *Women and Philanthropy in Nineteenth-Century Ireland*. Cambridge, UK: Cambridge University Press.

Mann, K., Hermann, D. & Heinz, A. (2000). "One hundred years of alcoholism: the twentieth century". *Alcohol and Alcoholism*, 35(1), pp. 10—15. https://academic.oup.com/alcalc/article/35/1/10/142396.

Marchiano, L. (2017). *Our Children's Psychological Inheritance.* blogs.psychcentral.com.

Marriott, W. (1920). "Some Phases of the Pathology of Nutrition in Infancy". *Archives of Paediatrics and Adolescent Medicine*, 20(6), pp. 461—485.

Marsh, J. (2019). *Health & Medicine in the 19th Century.* London: Victoria and Albert Museum.

Mason, N. (2001). "The Sovereign People are in a Beastly State": The Beer Act of 1830 and Victorian Discourse on Working-class Drunkenness. *Victorian Literature and Culture*, 29(1), pp. 109—127.

Masson, M. (1986). *The Complete Letters to Wilhelm Fliess, 1887—1904.* Cambridge, MA: Harvard University Press.

Masters, J. (2018). *The Online Guide to Traditional Games.* http://www. tradgames. org.uk/ [Accessed August 2020].

Masters, J. (2018). "The Rules of Fivestones and Jacks". *Master Games Ltd.* www. mastersofgames.com [Accessed February 2021].

McCullough, J. (2018). *The Canada Guide: In-depth Reference Website for All Things Canadian.* https://thecanadaguide.com/history/the-20th-century/. [Accessed February 2021].

McEwen, B. and Akil, H., (2020). "Revisiting the Stress Concept: Implications for Affective Disorders". *The Journal of Neuroscience*, 40(1), pp. 12—21. https:// www.jneurosci.org/content/40/1/12#T2. [Accessed February 2021].

McEwen, B., Gray, J. and Nasca, C., (2015). "Recognizing resilience: Learning from the effects of stress on the brain". *Neurobiology of Stress*, 1, pp. 1—11.

Mealing, B. (2013). *Life in a Victorian School.* Cheltenham: The History Press.

Mearns, G. (2011). "'Long Trudges Through Whitechapel': The East End of Beatrice Webb's and Clara Collet's Social Investigations", *Interdisciplinary Studies in the Long Nineteenth Century*, 19(13). https://doi.org/10.16995/ntn.634.

Miller, S. & Skertchly, S. (1878). *The Fenland, Past and Present.* London: Longmans, Green, and Co.

Mills, D. (1973). *English Rural Communities: The Impact of Specialised Economy.* London: Macmillan Education.

Millward, R. & Bell, F. (2001). "Infant Mortality in Victorian Britain: The Mother as Medium". *The Economic History Review*, 54(4), p. 727.

Mineo, L. (2017). "Over nearly 80 years, Harvard study has been showing how to live a healthy and happy life". *Harvard Gazette*. https://news.harvard. edu/ gazette/story/2017/04/over-nearly-80-years-harvard-study-has-beenshowing-how-to-live-a-healthy-and-happy-life/.

Mitch, D. (2004) "Can Economic Decline lead to more secure employment in the absence of internal labor markets? The case of Norfolk farm workers in late nineteenth and early twentieth century England." In David Mitch et al (eds.) *The Origins of the Modern Career, 1850 to 1950*. Aldershot: Ashgate Publishing. pp. 281—304.

Moalem, S. (2014). *Inheritance: How Our Genes Change Our Lives and Our Lives Change Our Genes*. London: Sceptre Books.

Moore, D. (2017). *The Developing Genome: An Introduction to Behavioural Epigenetics*. Oxford: Oxford University Press.

Morabia, A., Rubenstein, B. and Victora, C., (2013). "Epidemiology and Public Health in 1906 England: Arthur Newsholme's Methodological Innovation to Study Breastfeeding and Fatal Diarrhea". *American Journal of Public Health*, 103(7), pp. e17-e22.

Mruk, C. (2013). "Defining self-esteem as a relationship between competence and worthiness: how a two-factor approach integrates the cognitive and affective dimensions of self-esteem". *Polish Psychological Bulletin*, 44(2), pp. 157—64.

Munger, M. (2017). *Ten Years of Winter: The Cold Decade and Environmental Consciousness in the Early 19th Century*. Unpublished Ph.D. thesis. University of Oregon.

Newsholme, A., (1899). *The Elements of Vital Statistics*. London: S. Sonnenschein & Co.

Nicholls, J. (2009). *The Politics of Alcohol: A History of the Drink Question in England*. Oxford: Oxford University Press.

Nicolson, P. (2017). *Genealogy, Psychology and Identity: Tales from a Family Tree*. London and New York: Routledge.

Oldroyd, R. (2015). *Growing Up in Upwell*. Personal Archive.

Page, W., Proby, G. & Ladds, S.I. (eds.) (1936) "The Middle Level of the Fens and its reclamation", in *A History of the County of Huntingdon*, Volume 3, London: Victoria County History London, pp. 249—290.

Paine, W. (1899). "The Law of Inebriate Reformatories and Retreats, comprising the Inebriates Acts, 1879 to 1898." *Journal of Mental Science*, 46(195), pp. xxxvii.

Pappas, S. (2020). *Opioid Crisis Has Frightening Parallels to Drug Epidemic of Late 1800s*. www.livescience.com [Accessed February 2021].

Perez, E. (2015). *Family Roles: Towards a systematic application of the role method*. Unpublished Graduate Paper, Concordia university.

Phillips, S. (2013). "Genealogy as Therapy". *HuffPost Contributor platform*. https://www.huffingtonpost.co.uk/scott-phillips/ genealogy-as-therapy-gene_b_4448250.html. [Accessed February 2021]

Philp, R.K. (1875). *The Lady's Every-Day Book; A Practical Guide in The Elegant Arts and Daily Difficulties of Domestic Life*. London: Bemrose & Sons.

Phyfe, W. (1901). *5000 Facts and Fancies*. New York: G. P. Putnam.

Pratt, M., Zeev-Wolf, M., Goldstein, A. & Feldman, R. (2019). "Exposure to early and persistent maternal depression impairs the neural basis of attachment in preadolescence". *Progress in Neuro-Psychopharmacology and Biological Psychiatry*, 93, pp. 21—30.

Prescott, C. A., Aggen, S. H. & Kendler, K. S. (2000). "Sex-specific genetic influences on the comorbidity of alcoholism and major depression in a population-based sample of US twins". *Archives of General Psychiatry*, 57(8), pp. 803—11.

Reader, W. J. (1967). *Life in Victorian England. London*: B. T. Batsford Ltd.

Remely, M., de la Garza, A., Magnet, U., Aumueller, E. & Haslberger, A. (2015). "Obesity: epigenetic regulation — recent observations". *Biomolecular Concepts*, 6(3), pp.163—75.

Renvoize, E. and Beveridge, A., (1989). "Mental illness and the late Victorians: A study of patients admitted to three asylums in York, 1880—1884". *Psychological Medicine*, 19(1), pp. 21—22.

Riemer, A. R., Gervais, S,J., Skorinko, J. L. M. et al. (2018). "She looks like she'd be an animal in bed: dehumanization of drinking women in social contexts". *Sex Roles*, 80(9—10), pp.617—629.

Roberts, J. L. (1997). *The Ruin of Rural England: An Interpretation of Late Nineteenth Century Agricultural Depression, 1879—1914*. Unpublished Ph.D. Thesis. Loughborough University.

Robinson, B. (2017). "The Human Reformation" //www. bbc.co.uk/history/british/tudors/human_reformation_01.shtml [Accessed February 2021].

Robinson, O.C. (2015). Emerging adulthood, early adulthood and quarter-life crisis: Updating Erikson for the twenty-first century. In. R. Žukauskiene (Ed.) *Emerging adulthood in a European context*. New York: Routledge, pp. 17—30.

Rollero, C. & De Piccoli, N. (2010). "Place attachment, identification and environment perception: an empirical study". *Journal of Environmental Psychology*, 30(2), pp. 198—205.

Roser, M. (2018). "Life expectancy". https://ourworldindata.org/life-expectancy [Accessed February 2021].

Ryckman, R. (2012). *Theories of Personality*. 10th ed. Belomont, CA: Wadsworth Publishing Co. Inc.

Sacchet, M., Levy, B., Hamilton, J. et al. (2016). "Cognitive and neural consequences of memory suppression in major depressive disorder". *Cognitive, Affective, & Behavioral Neuroscience*, 17(1), pp. 77—93.

Saleem, S., Asghar, A., Subhan, S. & Mahmood, Z. (2014). "Parental Rejection and Mental Health Problems in College Students: Mediating Role of Interpersonal Difficulties". *Pakistan Journal of Psychological Research*, 34(3), pp.639—653.

Sanu, A. & Eccles, R. (2008). "The effects of a hot drink on nasal airflow and symptoms of common cold and flu". *Rhinology*, 46 (4), pp. 271—5.

Saphire-Bernstein, S., Way, B., Kim, H., Sherman, D. & Taylor, S. (2011). "Oxytocin receptor gene (OXTR) is related to psychological resources". *Proceedings of the National Academy of Sciences*, 108(37), pp. 15118—15122.

Saunders, N. J. (2014). *The Poppy: A History of Conflict, Loss, Remembrance, and Redemption*. London: Oneworld Publications.

Schaffner, A. (2012). *Modernism and Perversion Sexual Deviance in Sexology and Literature, 1850—1930*. Basingstoke: Palgrave Macmillan.

Schuller, T. (2017). "What Are the Wider Benefits of Learning Across the Life Course?" *Foresight*. UK: Government Office for Science. https://assets.publishing.service.gov.uk/government/uploads/system/uploads/attachment_data/file/635837/Skills_and_lifelong_learning_-_the_benefits_of_adult_learning_-_schuller_-_final.pdf

Schutzenberger, A. (2014). *The Ancestor Syndrome: Transgenerational Psychotherapy and the Hidden Links in the Family Tree*. Hoboken: Taylor & Francis.

Scull, A. & Favreau, D. (1986). "The Clitoridectomy Craze". *Social Research*, 53(2), p. 75.

Seymour S.C. (2013) "'It Takes a Village to Raise a Child': Attachment Theory and Multiple Child Care in Alor, Indonesia, and in North India". In: Quinn N., Mageo J.M. (eds) *Attachment Reconsidered. Culture, Mind, and Society.* New York: Palgrave Macmillan.

Shelton, D. (2012). "Man-midwifery history: 1730- 1930". *Journal of Obstetrics and Gynaecology*, 32(8), pp. 718—723. https://www.thisismoney.co.uk/money/bills/article-1633409/Historic-inflation-calculator-value-money-changed-1900.html

Shih, R., Belmonte, P. & Zandi, P. (2004). "A review of the evidence from family, twin and adoption studies for a genetic contribution to adult psychiatric disorders". *International Review of Psychiatry*, 16(4), pp. 260—83.

Showalter, E. (1987). *The Female Malady: Women, Madness and English Culture, 1830—1980.* London: Virago.

Simon, B. (1965). *Education and the Labour Movement 1870—1920.* London: Lawrence & Wishart.

Skelly, J. (2008). "When seeing is believing: women, alcohol, and photography in Victorian England". *Queen's Journal of Visual & Material Culture*, no1, pp. 1—17.

Skelly, J. (2014). *Addiction and British visual culture, 1751—1919.* Farnham: Ashgate Publishing Limited.

Slater, J. and Bunch, A., (2000). *Fen Speed Skating.* [Place of publication not identified]: Cambridgeshire Libraries Publications.

Smiles, S. (1866). *Self-help: with Illustrations of Character, Conduct and Perseverance.* Revised edition. John Murray.

Smith, I. (ed.) (2010). *Freud: Complete works.* Valas.fr. https:// ScienceDaily www.valas.fr/IMG/pdf/Freud_Complete_Works.pdf.

Smith, M. K. (2008). "Octavia Hill: housing, space and social reform". *The Encyclopaedia of Informal Education.* www.infed.org/thinkers/octavia_hill. htm.

Smith, W. P. (2012). *Discovering Upwell. Illustrated edition.* England: Carrillson Publications

Sokol, Justin T. (2009) "Identity Development Throughout the Lifetime: An Examination of Eriksonian Theory," *Graduate Journal of Counseling Psychology*: 1(2), Article 14. pp 1—11.

Solomon, A. (2001). *The Noonday Demon: An Anatomy of Depression*. New York: Scribner.

Sotero, M. (2006). "A Conceptual Model of Historical Trauma: Implications for Public Health Practice and Research", *Journal of Health Disparities Research and Practice*, 1(1), pp. 93—108.

Springall, L. M. (1936). *Labouring Life in Norfolk Villages 1834—1914*. 1st edition. London: George Allen & Unwin Ltd.

St George, A., (1993). *The Descent of Manners: Etiquette, Rules & The Victorians*. 1st ed. London: Chatto & Windus.

Stevens, E., Patrick, T. & Pickler, R. (2009). "A History of Infant Feeding". *Journal of Perinatal Education*, 18(2), pp. 32—39.

Strange, J. (2006) "Dangerous Motherhood: Insanity and Childbirth in Victorian Britain by Hilary Marland". [Review article]. *History*, 91(303), p. 471.

Strange, J. (2010). *Death, grief and poverty in Britain, 1870—1914*. Cambridge: Cambridge University Press

Strange, J. (2012). "Fatherhood, Providing, and Attachment in Late Victorian and Edwardian Working-Class Families". *The Historical Journal*, 55(4), pp. 1007—1027.

Strathearn, L., Mertens, C., Mayes, L., Rutherford, H., Rajhans, P., Xu, G., Potenza, M. & Kim, S. (2019). "Pathways Relating the Neurobiology of Attachment to Drug Addiction". *Frontiers in Psychiatry*, 10: 737 https://www.frontiersin.org/articles/10.3389/fpsyt.2019.00737/full [Accessed February 2021].

Sullivan, P., Neale, M. & Kendler, K. (2000). "Genetic epidemiology of major depression: review and meta-analysis". *American Journal of Psychiatry*, 157(10), pp. 1552—62.

Tanner, J. ed., (1917). *The Historical Register of The University of Cambridge, Being A Supplement to The Calendar with a Record of University Offices, Honours and Distinctions To The Year 1910*. Cambridge: Cambridge University Press.

Taylor, J. (2000). *Lighting in the Victorian Home*. www.buildingconservation.com. [Accessed February 2021].

Thompson, F. (1981). "Social Control in Victorian Britain". *The Economic History Review*, 34(2), pp. 189—208.

Thompson, R., Mata, M., Gershon, A. & Gotlib, I. (2017). "Adaptive coping mediates the relation between mothers' and daughters' depressive symptoms:

A moderated mediation study". *Journal of Social and Clinical Psychology*, 36(3), pp. 171–195.

Tressel, R. (1914). *The Ragged-Trousered Philanthropists*. London: Grant Richards Ltd.

Tucker, E. (2008). *Children's Folklore: A Handbook*. Westport, CT: Greenwood Publishing Group.

Tucker, R. (1996). *Origins and Early History of Tiddlywinks*. North American Tiddlywinks Association http://tiddlywinks.org [Accessed February 2021].

Tunaru, S., Althoff, T. F., Nüsing, R. M., Diener, M. & Offermanns, S. (2012). "Castor oil induces laxation and uterus contraction via ricinoleic acid activating prostaglandin EP3 receptors". *Proceedings of the National Academy of Sciences of the United States of America*, 109(23), pp. 9179–9184.

Turner, S., Mota, N., Bolton, J. & Sareen, J. (2018). "Self-medication with alcohol or drugs for mood and anxiety disorders: A narrative review of the epidemiological literature". *Depression and Anxiety*, 35(9), pp. 851–860.

Vaillant, G. (2009). *Natural History of Alcoholism Revisited*. Cambridge: Harvard University Press.

Veale, L. and Endfield, G., (2016). "Situating 1816, the 'year without summer', in the UK". *The Geographical Journal*, 182(4), pp. 318–330.

Veenendaal, M., Painter, R., de Rooij, S., Bossuyt, P., van der Post, J., Gluckman, P., Hanson, M.& Roseboom, T. (2013). "Transgenerational effects of prenatal exposure to the 1944–45 Dutch famine". *BJOG: An International Journal of Obstetrics & Gynaecology*, 120(5), pp. 548–554.

Waites, M. (2005). *The Age of Consent: Young People, Sexuality, and Citizenship*. Basingstoke: Palgrave Macmillan.

Waller, I. H. (2008). *My Ancestor Was an Agricultural Labourer*. London: Society of Genealogists Enterprises Ltd.

Wallis, J. (2018). "A Home or a Gaol? Scandal, Secrecy, and the St James's Inebriate Home for Women" *Social History of Medicine*, 31(4), pp.774–795 https://doi.org/10.1093/shm/hky020.

Walton, J. (1983). *The English Seaside Resort*. Leicester: Leicester University Press.

Webb, S. & Webb, B. (1903) *History of Liquor Licensing in England Principally from 1700 to 1830*. London: Longman, Green, & Co.

Weiner, B. & White, W. (2007). "The Journal of Inebriety (1876—1914): history, topical analysis, and photographic images". *Addiction*, 102(1), pp. 15—23.

Weissman, M. M., Berry, O. O., Warner, V. et al. (2016). "A 30-year study of 3 generations at high risk and low risk for depression". *JAMA Psychiatry*, 73(9), pp. 970—77.

Weissman, M. (2009). "Translating intergenerational research on depression into clinical practice". *JAMA Psychiatry*, 302(24), pp. 2695—2696.

West, C. (1848). *Lectures on the Diseases of Infancy and Childhood*. London: Longman, Brown, Green, & Longmans.

Winskill, P.T. (1892). *The Temperance Movement and Its Workers, Volume 1; A Record of Social, Moral, Religious, and Political Progress*. London: Blackie and Son Limited.

Wise, S., (2013). *Inconvenient People: Lunacy, Liberty and The Mad-Doctors in Victorian England*. Berkeley, CA: Counterpoint.

Worden, J. & Silverman, P. (1996). "Parental death and the adjustment of school-age children". *OMEGA — Journal of Death and Dying*, 33(2), pp. 91—102.

Wyrzykowska, E., Głogowska, K. & Mickiewicz, K. (2014). "Attachment relationships among alcohol dependent persons". *Alcoholism and Drug Addiction*. 27(2), pp. 145—61.

Yeazell, R. B. (2013). "Marriage". *Victorian Review*, 39(2), pp. 208—215.

Žukauskiene, R. (2015). (ed.) *Emerging adulthood in a European context*. New York and London: Routledge.

Newspapers

Accounts and papers of the House of Commons. 1845, Volume 41, p. 18.

Biggleswade Chronicle, 1951. p. 3, column 4.

Building News and Engineering Journal (1907) v.92—93. London: Office for Publication and Advertisements.

Cambridge Chronicle and Journal, Friday, 27 December 1816.

Cambridge Daily News, Friday 28 December 1901.

Cambridge Independent Press, Friday 27 December 1895. p. 8, column 7.

Cambridge Independent Press, Saturday 02 April 1887, p. 7, column 4.

Clarion, Saturday 27 February 1897, p. 71, column 1.

Dundee Courier, 1898. 'The Tuberculosis Scare. The Insurance Scheme. Objections by Perth Butchers.

Dundee Courier, Monday 26 February 1906.

Kelly's Directory of Cambridgeshire. London: Kelly's Directories, p. 215.

Lincolnshire Free Press, Tuesday 26 March 1889.

Lincolnshire Free Press, Tuesday 29 June 1897, p. 3, column 6.

Lincolnshire Free Press, Tuesday 30 November 1897.

Lincolnshire Free Press, Tuesday 26 May 1896.

Morning Post, 1898. 'Tuberculosis in Milk' (Letters to the editor of the Morning Post), p. 6.

Norfolk Chronicle and Norwich Gazette, Saturday 07 September 1816. p. 2, column 4.

Norfolk Chronicle and Norwich Gazette, Saturday 6 December 1845, Supplement, column 8.

Nottingham Journal, Friday 30 December 1859, p. 8, column 4.

Peterborough Advertiser, 19 March 1898, p. 3, column 4.

Peterborough Advertiser, Saturday 01 January 1898, p.6, column 2.

Peterborough Advertiser, Saturday 08 January 1898, p. 6, column 1.

Peterborough Advertiser, Saturday 19 March 1898, p. 3, column 4.

Peterborough Advertiser, Saturday 16 April 1898, p. 8, columns 6—7.

Peterborough Advertiser, Saturday 23 July 1898.

Peterborough Advertiser, Saturday 3 December 1898, p. 8, column 6.

Peterborough Advertiser, Saturday 5 February 1898.

Peterborough Advertiser, Saturday, 23 July 1898.

Peterborough Advertiser, Saturday 30 July 1898, p. 6, column 8.

Peterborough Advertiser, Saturday 30 July 1898, p. 7, column 5.

Peterborough Advertiser, Wednesday 21 December 1898, p. 4, column 4.

Peterborough Advertiser, Wednesday 26 October 1898.

Peterborough Advertiser, Wednesday 21 December 1898, p. 4, column 3.

Peterborough Advertiser, Wednesday 28 December 1898.

Peterborough Advertiser, 1899. Personal Notes [About the movements of prominent people.]. p. 2, column 3.

Peterborough Advertiser, 18 January 1899, p. 4, column 3.

Peterborough Advertiser, Wednesday 06 September 1899, p. 3, column 7.

Peterborough Advertiser, Wednesday 21 March 1900, p. 2, column 4.

Peterborough Advertiser, Wednesday 04 July 1900, p. 2, column 5.

Peterborough Advertiser, Wednesday 29 August 1900.

Sheffield Independent, Monday 28 November 1892, front cover.

The Peterborough Standard, Saturday 21 April 1894.

The Peterborough Standard, Saturday 16 June 1894.

The Peterborough Standard, Saturday 25 May 1895.

The Peterborough Standard, Tuesday 30 July 1895.

The Peterborough Standard, Saturday 21 April 1900.

The Peterborough Standard, Saturday 26 May 1900, p. 1—3.

The Peterborough Standard, Saturday 7 July 1900.

The Peterborough Standard, Saturday 17 November 1900.

The Peterborough Standard, Saturday 26 May 1900.

The Peterborough Standard, Saturday 31 March 1900.

The Peterborough Standard, Saturday 1 September 1900.

The Peterborough Standard, Saturday 8 September 1900.

The Peterborough Standard, Saturday 5 May 1900.

The Peterborough Standard, Saturday 4 January 1902.

The Peterborough Standard, Saturday 25 January 1902.

The Peterborough Standard, Saturday 22 February 1902.

The Peterborough Standard, Saturday 26 April 1902.

The Peterborough Standard, Saturday 17 January 1903.

The Peterborough Standard, Saturday 5 August 1905.

The Stamford Mercury, Friday 31 May 1895.

The Stamford Mercury, Friday 2 February 1894, p. 6, column 2.

The Stamford Mercury, Friday 7 June 1895.

The Isle of Ely & Wisbech Advertiser, Wednesday 31 January 1906, and Sunday 28 February 1906.

The Times (London, England), 28 December 1858, p. 8.

Thetford & Watton Times and People's Weekly Journal, Saturday 26 February 1881, p. 5, column 3.

Thetford & Watton Times and People's Weekly Journal, Saturday 3 December 1887.

Thorney Magazine, July 1984.

Thorney Quoit Match. p. 8, column 5.

Western Times, 1901. Oakhampton Convalescent Home. p. 3, column 3.

Whitstable Times and Herne Bay Herald, Saturday 20 February 1897, p. 7, column 2.

Wigton Advertiser, Saturday 20 February 1897.

Wisbech Advertiser, Friday 1 March 1907.

Wisbech Standard, Friday 22 March 1889.

Worcester Journal, Saturday 22 August 1896, p. 5, column 4.

Websites

'Court No.3095 Banner — Reverse' The Foresters Heritage Trust (2018). 'The Foresters Heritage Trust: the history of the Foresters Friendly Society'. http://www.aoforestersheritage.com/Banners.html [Accessed February 2021].

'Yarmouth Seaside Holidays — Historical Introduction'. Norfolk Museums. https://www.museums.norfolk.gov.uk/-/media/museums/downloads/learning/great-yarmouth/seaside-holidays-information-for-teachers.pdf [Accessed February 2021].

Anon. (2019). Bovine tuberculosis: OIE — World Organisation for Animal Health. [Accessed August 2020]

Anonymous. (1974). Hardship and happiness. Steep Rock, Man: Interlake Pioneers, p. 5. https://digitalcollections.lib.umanitoba.ca [Accessed February 2021].

Anonymous. (2000). *England 12 | IDEA: International Dialects of English Archive.* https://www.dialectsarchive.com/england-12 [Accessed February 2021].

Bedfordshire Archives and Records Service. 'Woburn experimental farm Husborne Crawley'. http://bedsarchives.bedford.gov.uk/CommunityArchives/. HusborneCrawley/WoburnExperimentalFarmHusborneCrawley.aspx [Accessed February 2021].

Collection.sciencemuseumgroup.org.uk. (2020). *Whippet Spring Frame Safety Bicycle, 1885* | Science Museum Group Collection. https://collection. sciencemuseumgroup.org.uk/objects/co25423/whippet-bicycle [Accessed February 2021].

Encyclopedia Britannica. n.d. Zeppelin | Definition, History, Hindenburg, & Facts. Davies, G https://www.britannica.com/technology/zeppelin [Accessed February 2021].

Encyclopedia.com. 2020. Radio Broadcasting, History Of | Encyclopedia.Com. https://www.encyclopedia.com/media/encyclopedias-almanacs-transcripts-and-maps/radio-broadcasting-history [Accessed February 2021].

Era.rothamsted. ac.uk. n.d. E-RA: Woburn Farm. Available at: http://www.era. rothamsted. ac.uk [Accessed February 2021].

Gracesguide.co.uk. n.d. Whippet Bicycle — Graces Guide. Available at: https:// www.gracesguide.co.uk/Whippet_Bicycle [Accessed February 2021].

Grc.nasa.gov. n.d. History of Flight: How Did We Learn to Fly Like the Birds? https://www.grc.nasa.gov/www/k-12/UEET/StudentSite/historyofflight.html [Accessed February 2021]

Historymuseum.ca. The Last Best West: Advertising for Immigrants to Western Canada, 1870—1930. https://www.historymuseum.ca/cmc/exhibitions/hist/advertis/adindexe.shtml [Accessed February 2021]

Inflationcalculator.ca. (n.d.). Inflation Calculator | Keep Track of Canadian CPI and Inflation. https://inflationcalculator.ca/ [Accessed August 2020].

Internet Archive. (1900). Concise School Atlas of the Dominion of Canada [microform]: Historical and Physical Features of Provinces, Districts and Territories of the Dominion. https://archive.org/details/cihm_54896 [Accessed February 2021].

Legislation.gov.uk. (2020). Vagrancy Act 1824. http://www.legislation.gov.uk/ukpga/Geo4/5/83 [February 2021]

Me Too Movement. (2019). https://metoomvmt.org/ [Accessed August 2020].

My Year of Living Mindfully. (2020) [film] Shannon & Julian Harvey. Australia: Elemental Media https://www.myyearoflivingmindfully.com/onlinepremiere [Accessed February 2021].

Our Journey. (n.d.). Alfred Caleb Taylor and the First X Ray Machine Outside London. https://ourjourneypeterborough.org [Accessed August 2020].

Parliament.uk (2019). 'Regulating sexual behaviour: the 19th century'. https://www.parliament.uk [Accessed September 2020].

Sites.rootsweb.com. 2014. Cambridgeshire, Englandgenweb Project — Cambridgeshire Agriculture & the Labourer. Available at: https://sites.rootsweb.com/~engcam/history/agricultureandlabor.html [Accessed February 2021].

The Hospital with extra nursing supplement, 1894. The Early History of the Hospital Sunday and Saturday Funds. 16 (414) (XVI), p.4 51. https://www.ncbi.nlm.nih.gov/pmc/articles/PMC5263633/pdf/hosplond70245—0013.pdf [Accessed February 2021].

The National Institute of Neurological Disorders and Stroke. Friedreich's Ataxia Factsheet. https://www.ninds.nih.gov. [Accessed February 2021].

The Peckovers. Wisbech: The Wisbech Society and Preservation Trust Limited. https://www.wisbech-society.co.uk/the-peckovers. [Accessed February 2021].

Thehenryford.org. (n.d.) 1903 Ford Model A Runabout — The Henry Ford. https://www.thehenryford.org. [Accessed February 2021].

Why Was the State of Working-Class Religion A Problem In The Mid-Nineteenth Century? [online] Richardjohnbr.blogspot.com. [Accessed February 2021].

Index

THE
BOOK
OF
WITCHES

ALSO EDITED BY JONATHAN STRAHAN

THE
BOOK
OF
WITCHES

EDITED BY

JONATHAN STRAHAN

ILLUSTRATED BY

ALYSSA WINANS

HARPER Voyager
An Imprint of HarperCollins *Publishers*

THE BOOK OF WITCHES. Copyright © 2023 by Jonathan Strahan. All rights reserved. Printed in the United States of America. No part of this book may be used or reproduced in any manner whatsoever without written permission except in the case of brief quotations embodied in critical articles and reviews. For information, address HarperCollins Publishers, 195 Broadway, New York, NY 10007.

HarperCollins books may be purchased for educational, business, or sales promotional use. For information, please email the Special Markets Department at SPsales@harpercollins.com.

Harper Voyager and design are trademarks of HarperCollins Publishers LLC.

FIRST EDITION

Designed by Paula Russell Szafranski

Illustrations © Alyssa Winans

Library of Congress Cataloging-in-Publication Data has been applied for.

ISBN 978-0-06-311322-0

23 24 25 26 27 LBC 5 4 3 2 1